COLLABORATIVE
LITERACY

We would like to dedicate this book to all children and youth who have a love of reading and desire to develop that love, but need a little support to do so.

We would like to also dedicate this book to students who have been identified as gifted or advanced readers. Because of your love for literacy and desire to perform in the regular classroom, you have challenged educators and researchers to develop more efficient classroom teaching strategies that can be used with all students regardless. We are grateful that you see the world as a collaboration of literacy engagements with the goal of building connections beyond individual desires or goals, but as unified engagements, which motivate and stimulate accomplishing minds.

We would also like to dedicate this book to parents and teachers who work attentively and effortlessly to help children develop a love of reading, while at the same time achieve their personal best at high levels.

COLLABORATIVE LITERACY

USING GIFTED STRATEGIES TO ENRICH LEARNING FOR EVERY STUDENT

SUSAN E. ISRAEL • DOROTHY A. SISK • CATHY COLLINS BLOCK

CORWIN PRESS
A SAGE Publications Company
Thousand Oaks, California

For information:

Corwin Press
A Sage Publications Company
2455 Teller Road
Thousand Oaks, California 91320
www.corwinpress.com

Sage Publications Ltd.
1 Oliver's Yard
55 City Road
London EC1Y 1SP
United Kingdom

Sage Publications India Pvt. Ltd.
B-42, Panchsheel Enclave
Post Box 4109
New Delhi 110 017 India

Printed in the United States of America

Library of Congress Cataloging-in-Publication Data

Israel, Susan E.
Collaborative literacy: Using gifted strategies to enrich learning for every student/Susan E. Israel, Dorothy A. Sisk, Cathy Collins Block.
    p. cm.
Includes bibliographical references and index.
ISBN 1–4129–1697–6 (cloth)—ISBN 1–4129–1698–4 (pbk.)
    1. Gifted children—Education—United States. 2. Language arts—United States.
3. Gifted children—Education—United States—Curricula. I. Sisk, Dorothy A.
II. Block, Cathy Collins. III. Title.
LC3993.9.i85 2007
371.95′34—dc22   2006001809

This book is printed on acid-free paper.

06 07 08 09 10 10 9 8 7 6 5 4 3 2 1

Acquisitions Editor:	Kylee Liegl
Editorial Assistant:	Nadia Kashper
Copy Editor:	Barbara Ray
Typesetter:	C&M Digitals (P) Ltd.
Proofreader:	Dennis Webb
Indexer:	Sylvia Coates
Cover Designer:	Audrey Snodgrass

Contents

Acknowledgments

We would like to acknowledge the parents and teachers at St. Luke Catholic School in Indianapolis, Indiana, and all the schools that have worked with us over the years to provide support and leadership with implementing teaching approaches with the expectation that all children achieve. For ultimately, appreciating the need to create a resource for teachers to help realize that goal while supporting the needs of gifted students, as well as all students in the regular classroom.

We would like to acknowledge Elizabeth S. Israel, who helped us recognize that gifted students or advanced readers who are in the regular classroom, regardless of the grade or ability level, have a strong desire to use their talents to grow and learn and should be allowed to do so.

Corwin Press gratefully acknowledges the contributions of the following reviewers:

Linda Baker
Professor of Psychology
University of Maryland,
Baltimore, MD

Kathryn L. Bauserman, PhD
Assistant Professor
Indiana State University
Terre Haute, IN

Natalie Bernasconi
Teacher
La Paz Middle School
Salinas, CA

Nancy Marie Borie Betler
Full-time Mentor, NBCT
Charlotte, NC

Deborah Hersh Carter
MEd, NBCT
AIG Teacher
Moore County Schools, NC

Karen L. Fernandez
Literacy Instructor
Denver Public Schools
Denver, CO

Donna Babb Frinks
Teacher of Gifted Education
Leon County Schools
Tallahassee, FL

Patti Hendricks
NBCT, English Language Arts
Sunset Ridge Middle School
West Jordan, UT

Jamie L. Jahnig
English Teacher
Cheyenne Central High School
Cheyenne, WY

Sharon K. MacKenzie
Literacy Facilitator
Charlotte Mecklenburg Schools
Charlotte, NC

About the Authors

 **Susan E. Israel, PhD,** is an assistant professor at the University of Dayton, where she teaches graduate- and undergraduate-level reading courses. She has published in the area of gifted literacy for the International Reading Association and has been involved with teaching gifted students for more than 17 years. She enjoys reading, teaching overseas, writing, walking, quilting, and making doll clothes. Her most recent research investigates the developmental aspect of cognitive and affective domains of comprehension, as related to neuroscience and literacy theories. Her most recent publications include a comprehensive volume on *Metacognition in Literacy Learning* (2005, co-editor); *Reading First and Beyond* (2005, co-author), *Early Reading Pioneers* (2006, co-editor), *An Anthology of Poetry* (2006, co-author), and *Quotes to Inspire Great Reading Teachers* (2006, co-author).

 **Dorothy A. Sisk, EdD,** is a professor at Lamar University, where she serves as the Conn Chair for Gifted Education. She has won numerous awards for distinguished excellence and service in the field of literacy and gifted education. She is the former director of the U.S. Office of Gifted and Talented and President of the World Council for Gifted and Talented. She serves as a delegation leader for the Citizens Ambassadors Program in Russia, China, Cuba, and Hungary. She is the author of *Creative Teaching of the Gifted* (1987) and co-author of *Teaching Gifted in the Regular Classroom* and *Spiritual Intelligence: Developing Higher Consciousness*, with E. Paul Torrance.

 **Cathy Collins Block, PhD,** is a professor of Education at Texas Christian University, where she has served on the graduate faculty since 1977. She is a leading expert in the field of reading and literacy. Her recent publications in reading comprehension have become best-selling books in the field of education. She is a member of the International Reading Association's Board of Education and Gifted Special Interest Group.

Contributors

Nicole Caylor
Texas Christian University
Fort Worth, TX

Jennifer Gilmore
Texas Christian University
Arlington, TX

Sheri R. Parris
Texas Christian University
Fort Worth, TX

Whitney Wheeler
Texas Christian University
Fort Worth, TX

Introduction: Setting the Purpose for Building Collaborative Literacy

Susan E. Israel

What does building collaborative literacy mean? When the authors of this book collaborated on the idea of using gifted and higher level thinking strategies to increase literacy engagements, they were guided by a collaboration framework to generate the key ideas used in this book. The book begins with one author generating one idea. Eventually the ideas are discussed with further development of new ideas, with each author adding more knowledge to construct the product. The value of how collaboration helps develop and enrich reading, writing, speaking, and thinking experiences was realized by the end product, a book on building collaborative literacy for all students in the regular classroom.

According to *The Literacy Dictionary: The Vocabulary of Reading and Writing* by Harris and Hodges (1995), the term "collaborative learning" means learning by working together in small groups, as to understand new information or to create a common product (p. 35). Harris and Hodges follow that definition with a note that reads, "There are many variations of collaborative learning, from exploration of a topic to its mastery and from the beginning to final stages of product development. This term does not specify roles or responsibilities of members and groups, and the practices it describes include little to intensive group interaction" (p. 35). The same resource defines literacy in five different ways. The authors of *The Literacy Dictionary* believe all the definitions of literacy are employed at different times and are further defined on the basis of the expectations and goals of the engagement or learning tasks. That said, we follow the definition presented by Richard L. Venezky on page 142 (Harris & Hoges, 1995) to construct a definition of literacy to mean the ability and knowledge necessary to read, write, speak, and think in order to develop and refine understanding. The expression "building collaborative literacy for teachers" means the capacity to provide opportunities for engaged learners such as gifted students to increase, extend, modify, and evaluate their own literacy development. The first chapter of this book provides the theoretical framework for the guiding principles of building a collaborative literacy framework that supports all learners in the regular classroom who want to benefit from gifted and higher level thinking strategies to improve and enhance literacy.

Collaborative Literacy: Using Gifted Strategies to Enrich Learning for Every Student is a book to help teachers who want to build collaborative literacy and provide engaging research-based learning experiences for all students, including advanced readers, gifted students, gifted students with special needs, and high-achieving students in the regular classroom. It also provides ways educators and parents can work together to extend the learning process from the school environment to the home environment related to literacy instruction. This user-friendly volume is divided into four main parts. Part one summarizes the most recent research in gifted education, as well as the concept of building collaborative literacy. Part two summarizes how to build learning communities with gifted students and all students in the regular classroom. Part three summarizes how specific gifted and higher level thinking strategies can be used when building collaborative literacy environments. Part four summarizes key aspects on how to begin implementing the ideas and strategies in the book, as well as synthesize resources for all educators. The key elements in each part are discussed below.

PART ONE

- Current research on gifted education and literacy
- Understanding how to build collaborative literacy
- Identifying and engaging advanced readers and gifted students in collaborative literacy
- Making connections with how to build collaborative literacy with all students

PART TWO

- Creating enriched collaborative literacy environments
- Meeting the needs of advanced readers and gifted students in a multicultural classroom
- Building collaborative literacy during reading and writing instruction
- Constructing collaborative literacy with parents

PART THREE

- Developing comprehension and higher level thinking
- Increasing natural curiosities and creative thinking and speaking
- Learning through inquiry and technology
- Evaluating collaborative literacy

PART FOUR

- Increasing teacher self-efficacy about building collaborative literacy
- Responding to questions
- Reflecting in the mind of a busy teacher
- Building rich collaborative literacy environments with effective resources

The rationale for the book stems from the need to provide regular-classroom teachers with a research-based resource that synthesizes literacy strategies used in gifted education and higher level thinking strategies from the field of reading education to build collaborative literacy. There are many other benefits to using gifted and higher level thinking strategies to improve literacy development. First, the field of literacy can benefit from learning how to incorporate gifted education literacy strategies into the regular literacy classroom. This approach not only benefits advanced readers, gifted students, and gifted students with special needs, but more important helps all achieving students benefit and learn. Second, special-area teachers receive much training in the area of gifted education, and unless this training is shared with others, it never reaches the regular-classroom teachers. Teachers in the regular classroom will learn about specific literacy strategies that can readily be incorporated into their classrooms. Third, this book makes a distinct contribution in that it focuses on strategies used in gifted education and literacy strategies to build collaborative literacy. Fourth, throughout the United States, most gifted students spend a significant part of their week in classrooms with regular education teachers who may or may not have received training in developing higher order thinking and questioning and education strategies for the gifted.

HOW DOES BUILDING COLLABORATIVE LITERACY RELATE TO ALL TEACHERS IN K–12 EDUCATION?

- *Teachers of reading and writing:* The focus in all classrooms, regardless of the content area or grade level, is reading and writing instruction. Current research in the areas of gifted and literacy is presented in a friendly manner, and it follows the research by providing practical applications.

- *Reading specialists and literacy coaches:* The trend in education and literacy is to provide professional development for all teachers including reading specialists and literacy coaches. These teachers play a significant role in the literacy development of their students. Each chapter provides details on the role of the teacher and the student in building collaborative literacy; therefore, training in how to build collaborative literacy for reading specialists and literacy coaches can be easily integrated in the curriculum.
- *Teachers of the gifted:* The material presented in the book can be used by teachers of the gifted in any setting because the material is presented in a unique and well-researched yet practical manner. This is the first comprehensive book on how to help gifted students and all students develop in the area of literacy by using approaches that work with gifted students and advanced readers.
- *Parents:* This book can benefit all parents who want to help their child develop in the area of literacy regardless of their ability level. Parents of the gifted can benefit because the book provides details on how to integrate the strategies. Parents can use the strategies and modify them at home and follow the building collaborative literacy ideas to help their child.
- *Individuals teaching undergraduate and graduate education courses:* This book is a valuable research-based resource to aid educators in higher education who desire to help classroom teachers understand the current research in gifted education and literacy and how this research can be integrated in classroom settings.
- *Small study groups:* Small study groups will find studying particular chapters helpful. Those who have no knowledge or training in the area of gifted education or literacy might want to read chapters specifically related to those areas. Parents of gifted children can use this book in small study groups with other parents to help them understand the current research and how to use the research in home and school settings.
- *Accomplished teachers:* Many accomplished teachers who have been teaching students over the years who want to continue to provide meaningful learning experiences to all their students, including gifted students, will find this book to support that need with the goal of reaching all learners. Ideas presented in the book can be easily incorporated. Accomplished teachers will find the book extremely useful because the ideas are backed by proven research.

WHAT ARE THE UNIQUE FEATURES OF THIS BOOK?

In every chapter, you will find the following unique features:

- *Personal Reflection:* Summarizes personal thoughts from a perspective of individuals involved in gifted education, including teachers of gifted students, gifted students, and parents who are familiar with issues in gifted education. These reflections exemplify the contents of the chapter to follow.

- *Graphic Organizer:* Provides an overview of the goals of the chapter. Each chapter opens with a graphic organizer designed to enhance and synthesize the connections within the chapter and the goals included for each chapter.
- *Collaborative Literacy at Work:* Summarizes the key ideas found in the chapter, as well as defines key terms that will assist the reader in building prior knowledge regarding the strategies being discussed.
- *Rich Research Base:* Describes the research base for the ideas in each chapter and reflects the contents of the chapter.
- *Ideas Into Action:* Provides examples of how collaborative literacy looks in action and how to adapt the benefits and results of the program's ideas and literacy strategies.
- *Teachers Putting Ideas Into Action:* Provides activities or asks questions that teachers and professors can use to extend the contents of the chapter.
- *Summary*: Presents the key points presented in the chapter in a way that will allow the reader to reflect on the ideas and create practical steps for implementation prior to going on to the next chapter.

HOW TO USE THE MAJOR STRENGTHS OF THE BOOK TO ENHANCE YOUR READING EXPERIENCE

Are you interested in learning about rich research-based strategies?

- Pay attention to the research base guiding each of the strategies.
- Use the references as a way to extend your personal and professional repertoire of research and readings on the topics being discussed.
- Each chapter outlines strategies that will keep the reader's interest and are relevant to regular classroom teaching experiences.
- Credence to the viewpoints is given by providing research from learning experts in the field of gifted education and literacy education.

Are you interested in learning about personal reflections of other teachers on similar topics and how you can use the reflections to guide your thinking?

- First investigate each area by reading the personal reflections located at the beginning of each chapter, which have been included to make the ideas presented seem more real and more doable.
- Locate specific research-based strategies that apply to your personal area of interest.
- The lessons are easy to adopt. Identify the ways you can adopt the ideas immediately following the chapter being read. This can be done using the Teacher Idea Organizer at the end of the book.

Are you interested in reading a book that is user-friendly and understandable regardless of whether you are a first-year teacher, literacy coach, parent, or accomplished teacher?

- The purpose and goals have been clearly stated and will help the reader transition from simply reading the book to becoming engaged in the book.
- The unique features in each chapter have been written to help the reader create a mental pathway that is consistent from beginning to end. The chapters are logically ordered and flow from learning about the gifted to understanding how to develop collaborative literacy communities and to understanding specific research-based strategies on how to realize the goals of the book.
- The overarching purpose and ideas emphasize demonstrating how to build collaborative literacy to help gifted students, as well as other students.

Are you interested in using the ideas presented in this book to enhance the workshop methods of reading and writing instruction?

- The main emphasis of the book and chapter contents is on enhancing literacy experiences by building collaborative literacy environments.
- The wealth of literacy ideas is presented in a way that can be easily implemented in reading and writing workshops.
- The reader will experience the breadth and depth of many of the strategies during the experience of reading this book and will learn how to integrate them in literacy engagements. At the same time, the reader will also simply be introduced to strategies, with more detail provided in the references discussing each strategy. This model allows the reader to develop a more robust repertoire of strategies and select specific ones they want to learn about in-depth.

ESTABLISHING READER GOALS

This book provides the reader with a unique window into understanding how to build collaborative literacy by responding to the statement, Why not use gifted and higher level thinking strategies for all students in the regular classroom? With that in mind, you can establish several personal goals for reading this book and use this list as a reflection tool while reading each chapter. When you are finished, you can return to your list of goals and evaluate what you have learned and how you can apply this new information in the classroom. The goal of this book is to help you learn about the following:

- How to create collaborative literacy classrooms where all students have access to new and enriching knowledge.
- How to integrate gifted education and higher level thinking strategies in the regular classroom in literacy instruction and content areas.
- How to use collaborative literacy tools to enrich the learning environment for all students.

PART I

Gaining Wisdom About Gifted Students to Build Collaborative Literacy

1

What Does Building Collaborative Literacy Mean in the Classroom?

Dorothy A. Sisk

Melanie was an early reader, first mimicking commercials on television at the age of three to the amusement of her parents, then pointing to items in the grocery store that she recognized, including milk, cookies, and strawberries, telling her mother in which aisle the items were located. When she began kindergarten, the teacher focused on colors, numbers, and the alphabet. At home, she stopped reading, and openly voiced her opinion that the other students didn't like her. Her very wise mother took Melanie on her lap and explained that she was like an explorer who went places others didn't, like Columbus, and that sometimes people don't understand explorers. Melanie sat quietly reflecting on that statement, then tearfully asked her mother why she hadn't told her sooner, because she thought something was wrong with her.

Melanie's mother shared this incident with the teacher, who suggested that she talk with the Gifted Child Coordinator. Melanie was assessed and identified as a highly gifted student. The coordinator arranged for Melanie to work with a group of first- and second-grade students in a pull-out session for reading. In collaborative literacy lessons, in which the children read stories and used higher level thinking questions and activities, with an emphasis on making connections to self and others, Melanie began to be "her old self." She eagerly looked forward to her reading session and once again began reading her favorite fairy tales at home.

This chapter explores the concept of collaborative literacy, its relationship to the transactional theory of reading, and implications of Vygotsky's theory to collaborative literacy. We introduce characteristics of advanced readers and gifted students like Melanie and examine the research base for collaborative literacy. We discuss Collaborative Strategic Reading (CSR), a strategy that fosters collaborative literacy, and the role of the teacher in building collaborative literacy. We also discuss collaborative literacy with parents, with suggested activities for parents to use at home to support literacy. A section on Ideas in Action includes the Schoolwide Enrichment Model Reading (SEM-R) framework, the parallel curriculum, and novel study through drama. We discuss collaborative literacy programs in cooperation with universities and colleges as an example of collaborative literacy efforts in the community. To further explore the use of collaborative literacy, we share ideas for teachers in a section called "Teachers Putting Ideas into Action."

The chapter goals are to

- Build an understanding of the concept of collaborative literacy
- Develop awareness of the importance of the transactional theory and its relationship to collaborative literacy
- Develop an awareness of Vygotsky's contribution to collaborative literacy
- Develop awareness and knowledge of learning characteristics of advanced readers and gifted students
- Develop knowledge of research-based strategies that complement collaborative literacy
- Develop an awareness that collaborative literacy involves students, teachers, parents, and communities
- Develop awareness and knowledge of three strategies and program adaptations that illustrate collaborative literacy in action

COLLABORATIVE LITERACY

Collaborative literacy as used in this text builds on the ideas of Rosenblatt (1978), who described the process of reading as a carefully orchestrated relationship between the reader and the text in a social situation. Collaborative literacy can be simply defined as the use of multiple strategies to engage the readers in a group setting. For gifted students, who are quite social by nature (Frasier, Garcia, & Passow, 1995), this approach builds on their needs and characteristics in the reading process. Situational conditions to be considered for engaging students in collaborative literacy include time, location, mood, pressures, reasons, intents, and purposes, all of which interact to influence a reader's selection of reading strategies. Rosenblatt identified two purposes for reading, efferent and aesthetic. She defined efferent as readers focusing attention on information that they gather, retrieve, or remember while reading a text. An example of efferent reading focusing on remembering is when students read to prepare a report on a novel or to write a book critique.

Aesthetic reading, the second purpose for reading, is when the reader builds on past experiences, connects these experiences to the text, enjoys the beauty of the text, and becomes enthralled in the text as an active participant. A wonderful example of an aesthetic experience is middle-school students reading *Hope for the Flowers* by Trina Paulus (1972), in which two caterpillars named Stripe and Yellow experience following the crowd, in this case a crowd of caterpillars. They begin to ascend a climbing pillar of caterpillars, only to find after a horrific struggle that there is nothing at the top. When middle-school students read the last page, they often sit quietly reflecting on the story, thinking about the significance of the story as it relates to their interactions with others, particularly when Stripe says to Yellow, "Did you ever notice how difficult it is to step on someone's face when they are looking at you?"

RELATIONSHIP OF COLLABORATIVE LITERACY TO THE TRANSACTIONAL THEORY OF READING

Collaborative literacy is based on the transactional theory of reading, which stresses that the social and situational context for reading influences the types of reading tasks to be introduced. There is a dynamic interaction among context, the reasons for reading, the types of text included in the reading, the purposes for reading, and the strategies that the reader uses. Transactional theories of the reading process, introduced with the work of Dewey and Bentley (1949), stress that the reader, the text, and the social or situational setting all interact during the reading process. These theories suggest that students learn to actively construct meaning from positive encounters with texts, building on their own experiences along with the information on the printed page. For gifted students and advanced readers, this is a dynamic interaction that can be maximized in collaborative literacy.

IMPLICATIONS OF THE VYGOTSKY THEORY FOR COLLABORATIVE LITERACY

Lev Vygotsky (1896–1934), a Russian psychologist and educator, stressed that cognitive development is greatly affected by language learning and its use with others in society. He maintained that thought and language in the mind of a child grow out of interactions with others, and then when children are in social situations, they use language as a tool to explore their world. Vygotsky describes cognitive development in terms of how well a child could perform a specific task in collaboration with others; he called this the "zone of proximal development." The zone of proximal development can also be defined as "that which students can do in collaboration, they can later do alone." Gifted students and advanced readers can work together, and with other students, and become engrossed in challenging tasks that engage them in higher levels of understanding and performance. According to Vygotsky, they can then accomplish this performance independently.

Vygotsky (1978) stressed that students as learners internalize language activities, including reading and writing, in a three-stage process. Internalization begins with the student observing others, in some cases watching his or her teacher or parent or other students, as they perform a language task. In the second stage of internalization, the student mimics the language task, such as when a young child holds his or her favorite book, reads the text as the parent did, and sometimes pretends to be reading. The third stage of internalization is when the student can perform the task independently. Internalization stresses the importance of the teacher or parent modeling the process, and students in collaborative literacy modeling the process for one another. Vygotsky's theory calls for a child-centered and activity-centered approach to literacy, which enables the reader to use language as an exploratory tool.

CHARACTERISTICS OF ADVANCED READERS AND GIFTED STUDENTS

Advanced readers can be defined as students who enjoy reading, make time to read, identify themselves as readers, define reading as a way of life, view the purpose of reading as entertainment, have aesthetic transactions with reading, and have positive feelings about other readers. Beers (1998) called these students avid readers. Leu and Kinzer (2003) reported that students who are gifted demonstrate exceptional performance with most cognitive and linguistic tasks, and that teachers first recognize gifted students by their precocious language use.

Gifted students have a broad fund of information and often talk about topics well in advance of their age-mates, and the manner in which they speak is often quite mature. Many, but not all, gifted students are early readers. Silverman (2003) listed a number of learning characteristics of giftedness that affect collaborative literacy: early or avid reading ability, long attention span, excellent memory, extensive vocabulary, rapid learning ability, compassion for others, and good problem-solving/reasoning abilities. Silverman conducted

Figure 1.1   Silverman's List of Characteristics of Giftedness

Good problem-solving/reasoning abilities	Preference for older companions
Rapid learning ability	Wide range of interests
Extensive vocabulary	Great sense of humor
Excellent memory	Early or avid reading ability
Long attention span	Concerned with justice, fairness
Personal sensitivity	At times, judgment seems mature for age
Compassion for others	Keen powers of observation
Perfection	Vivid imagination
Intensity	High degree of creativity
Moral sensitivity	Tends to question authority
Unusual curiosity	Shows ability with numbers
Perseverant when interested	Good at jigsaw puzzles
High degree of energy	

several studies between 1981 and 1986 (reported in Silverman 2003) to determine the validity of a set of characteristics of giftedness, and the original list has been refined to incorporate these research findings.

Silverman (2003) said that if a child demonstrates more than three-fourths of these traits, it is likely that he or she is gifted. Rogers (1986) found the following characteristics to clearly differentiate the development of 38 gifted and 42 average third- and fourth-grade students at the .01 level of significance: rapid learning ability, extensive vocabulary, good memory, long attention span, perfectionism, preference for older companions, sophisticated sense of humor, early interest in books, ability in puzzles and mazes, maturity, curiosity, perseverance, and keen powers of observation.

RESEARCH BASE FOR COLLABORATIVE LITERACY

The research base for collaborative literacy is evident in the Schoolwide Enrichment Model Reading (SEM-R) project implemented by Reis (2004). SEM-R uses the Type III strategies of the Renzulli (1978a) Triad model for enrichment in reading to provide opportunities for students to work collaboratively and independently to improve their reading. The research project, sponsored by the U.S. Department of Education Javits program, found significant differences on pretest and posttest measures in fluency of students in second, third, fourth, and fifth grade, and significant differences in attitude toward reading and comprehension. The SEM-R is an extension of the original Renzulli (1978b) Triad model, a well-known and successful enrichment program for gifted students.

Several pretest and posttest instruments were administered to the students, including the Iowa Test of Basic Skills (ITBS), the Reading Comprehension Subtest, and the Elementary Reading Attitude Survey (McKenna & Kear,

1990). In addition, pretest and posttest reading fluency was assessed by asking the students to read three brief passages for a period of one minute in a pretest and posttest format. The sample included a total of 240 students in third, fourth, fifth, and sixth grade. Students were randomly assigned to an experimental group to receive the SEM-R framework, and to a control group who continued with the traditional afternoon remedial reading program being implemented in their school, Success for All (Slavin et al. 1992).

The research project was implemented in high-poverty urban schools in which over 90% of the students qualified for free lunch. Reis (2004) found that talented readers, as well as average and below-average readers, benefited from the SEM-R intervention. Significant differences were found on the ITBS at the .02 level of significance; significant differences were found on pretest to posttest scores on the Attitude Toward Reading Scale at the .04 level, and significant differences were found on pretest to posttest measures of reading fluency.

Collaborative literacy calls for the use of multiple strategies that engage the learner in highly motivating group activities such as Readers Theater and Book Club Discussions. The research base for collaborative literacy indicates that the more motivated readers become, the more likely they are to eagerly engage in collaborative literacy strategies and to work harder at building personal meaning and improving their reading achievement. Motivation influences the interest, purpose, emotion, and persistence of the student as they engage with texts (Butcher & Kintsch, 2003; Schallert & Martin, 2003).

A STRATEGY TO FOSTER COLLABORATIVE LITERACY: COLLABORATIVE STRATEGIC READING (CSR)

Collaborative Strategic Reading (CSR) is a structured comprehension strategy that can be used with expository text (Klinger & Vaughn, 1999). It involves four strategies that students experience in small groups. Klinger and Vaughn suggest that the teacher function as a facilitator to monitor the process of the group. Monitoring is necessary to get a group of students oriented to the strategy; however, very quickly small groups of four or five students can work independently, taking on the specific roles suggested by Klinger and Vaughn. These roles include the leader, the "clunk" expert who looks for hard words that the

Figure 1.2   Collaborative Strategic Reading

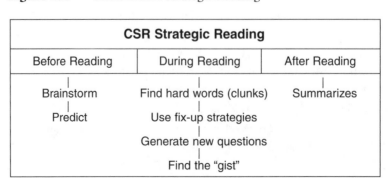

Figure 1.3   Four Strategies of Collaborative Strategic Reading (CSR)

- Use the before-reading strategy of reviewing students prior knowledge and set purposes

- Monitor one's reading by using the "clunk" strategy

- State the main idea or "getting the gist"

- Use the after-reading strategy of summarizing and generating questions

group may not know, and the "gist" expert who is responsible for focusing on the abstract idea or the most important points of the text, such as the most important idea, person, place, or thing.

Klinger and Vaughn suggest that CSR be initiated with a before-reading text activity that would involve the students in brainstorming knowledge that they have about the topic and predicting what they think they will learn, or, with advanced readers and gifted students, what they want to learn. The opportunity to do prereading activities helps ensure that students share their previous knowledge and that all of the students are better able to start CSR with similar information. The after-reading strategy that Klinger and Vaughn suggest calls for the teacher to ask questions to check whether the students understand the text and can answer the questions identified in the prereading activity. However, for the advanced readers and gifted students, the after-reading activity could consist of questions such as: What else do we need to know? And what new questions do we want to explore?

Role of the Teacher in Collaborative Literacy

The teacher's role in collaborative literacy is to provide instruction on essential reading and writing skills; provide a variety of stories and poems for reading; design learning centers in which the students can use their literacy skills in a variety of real-world situations; model reading and writing behaviors; offer caring and useful guidance on when to use specific reading skills and strategies; and, most important, create a learning environment that actively engages the students in collaborative literacy in reading and writing with other students. Figure 1.4 indicates the role of the student.

Figure 1.4   Role of the Student in Collaborative Literacy

- Work cooperatively in small groups

- Using higher order thinking skills to identify key concepts in textual material (efferent)

- Make connections to oneself (aesthetic), enjoy beauty of textual material

- Identify areas of interest for further independent or small group study

- Engage in creative/expository writing

(Continued)

Figure 1.4 (Continued)

- Respond to textual material (books)

- Engage in discussions using higher order thinking

- Infer and connect concepts

- Ponder with depth and from multiple perspectives in discussions

- Anticipate and relate observations in journals

Collaborative literacy makes use of direct and indirect strategies, as illustrated in Figure 1.5.

Figure 1.5   Direct and Indirect Strategies

Direct	**Indirect**
• Lecture	• Synectics
• Practice/Recitation	• Role playing
• Strategy-based instruction	• Cooperative learning
• Coaching	• Simulation
• Concept building	• Inquiry-based learning
• Demonstration	• Problem-based learning
• Socratic questioning	• Mentorship
• Guided visualization	• Independent study
	• Independent investigation

Successful collaborative literacy activities have an essential framework that the classroom teacher can follow. Figure 1.6 shows a teacher checklist suggested by Ryan (2003) that has proved helpful.

Figure 1.6   Teacher Checklist for Successful Collaborative Literacy

---

- Are there specific objectives for the activity?

- Were the objectives designed collaboratively by the students and the teachers?

- Are the instructions for the group activities clear and concise?

- Are the students tolerant of differing points of view, and are differing points of view sought in the activities?

- Do all students have equal access to the materials and text needed for the activities?

- Are all students engaged in interactive activities such as trust building, conflict management, and the use of constructive criticism?

- Is there time for self-reflection in the collaborative activities?

- Is there sufficient time for the students to complete the objectives?

Collaborative Literacy with Parents

Parents can be active participants in collaborative literacy activities, such as planning and implementing reading and writing activities and instruction for their children. In schools that use collaborative literacy with parents, parents supervise classroom centers, tell stories about their families, read books aloud, and model the use of reading and writing.

Parents are a rich source of information concerning their children, particularly about the child's individual perception and attitude toward reading. Many gifted students and advanced readers are frustrated by having grade-level limits imposed on their choice of reading material. Advanced readers or gifted students frequently are capable of reading stories well beyond their grade level. Ideas can be gathered from parents through interviews, questionnaires, home journals on literacy activities, and parent focus groups.

Parents can work with small groups of other parents to plan activities that can be implemented as after-school experiences in which parents and students can co-create memory books and photo albums and engage in creative writing and poetry.

Tracey (2000) suggests a number of activities that parents can use to encourage and support literacy experiences at home:

- Encourage your child to talk about what you are reading to him or her
- Help children understand the story by encouraging them to describe the story in their own words
- Praise your child when he or she asks a good question or makes interesting comments about a book
- Relate the book to your child's life by talking about interesting things the book reminds you of that really happened
- Ask questions that begin with why and how
- Wait for answers, allowing the child time to think of a good answer
- Point to the words as you read with younger children
- Take turns while reading with older children
- Carefully choose books that are not too easy or too difficult
- Have fun and make reading together an enjoyable experience

Collaborative Literacy Schools in Cooperation with Universities and Colleges

Ohio State University has developed a University Literacy Collaborative as a long-term professional development program designed to provide a comprehensive, schoolwide approach to literacy instruction in the primary grades. The goal of the program is to raise the base of instruction for all students. Participation in the program helps schools achieve this goal in three ways:

- Developers provide a dynamic framework for literacy lessons that build connections between reading and writing.

- It develops local capacity by training a building-level literacy coordinator.
- Developers require that the safety net of Reading Recovery be available for children in the first grade who are at risk of reading failure.

The collaborative literacy program at Ohio State University began in 1986 when a group of Reading Recovery teachers from the Columbus Public Schools and staff from the university formed a study group to examine more effective ways to teach children. The first class of literacy coordinators was trained in 1993–1994. Schools that participate in the collaborative literacy program make a five-year commitment that includes supporting and training a Literacy Coordinator to work with the teachers in their schools, and releasing him or her half-time to coach teachers and collect data to monitor the progress of the students during the implementation of the program.

Teachers using the collaborative literacy program use an integrated approach to teaching language arts. They provide authentic opportunities for reading and writing based on a continuum of more to less teacher support. They employ four contexts for reading: reading aloud to children, shared reading, guided reading and reading workshop, and independent reading. In addition, they employ four contexts for writing: language experience and shared writing, interactive writing, guided writing and writing workshops, and independent writing. The teachers use flexible collaborative grouping, sometimes working with homogeneous groups of readers, and at other times with heterogeneous groups, depending on the instructional purpose. The approach emphasizes reflective practice in which teachers are encouraged to continually reflect upon the effectiveness of their teaching through discussions, videotape analysis, and systematic observation of their students' progress.

A modification of the Ohio State University Collaborative Literacy Program could include a focus on advanced readers and gifted students, and use successful strategies that have been used with gifted students with all of the students.

IDEAS INTO ACTION

Schoolwide Enrichment Model Reading (SEM-R)

The Schoolwide Enrichment Model Reading (SEM-R) framework incorporates the Type III component of the Renzulli (1978a) Triad model, in which students move from teacher-directed opportunities to self-choice activities. Reis (2004) identified a number of collaborative literacy activities that include opportunities to explore new technology, use higher level questioning and thinking skills in discussion groups, and engage in creativity training in language arts, learning centers, interest-based projects, free-reading, and book chats. The intent of these activities is for students to learn to read critically and to locate a variety of reading materials, especially high-quality, challenging literature. Options for independent study are available for students during the Type III component. Figure 1.7 illustrates the SEM-R framework.

Figure 1.7   Schoolwide Enrichment Model Reading (SEM-R)

Phase 1: Exposure	Phase 2: Training and Self-Selected Reading	Phase 3: Interest and Choice Components

High-interest books to read aloud
  – Picture books
  – Fiction/novels
  – Nonfiction
  – Poetry
Higher order thinking probing questions
Bookmarks for teachers with questions regarding Bloom's taxonomy, biography, character, illustrations, and other topics relevant to the study of literature
	• Training and discussions
	• Sustained silent reading
	• One-on-one teacher conference on reading strategies and instruction
	• Bookmarks for students posing higher order questions regarding character, plot, setting, considering the story, and other useful topics
		• Introducing creative thinking
		• Exploring the internet
		• Genre studies
		• Library exploration
		• Responding to books
		• Investigation centers
		  – Creative thinking
		  – Exploring the internet
		  – Reading nonfiction
		  – Focus on biographies
		• Buddy reading
		• Books on tape
		• Literature circles
		• Creative or expository writing
		• Type III investigations

SOURCE: Reis, S. M., et al. (2005). Talented readers. Unpublished paper, University of Connecticut, p. 5.

PARALLEL CURRICULUM

The parallel curriculum is a curriculum-planning model based on the composite work of Tomlinson et al. (2002) in an effort to provide guidance to teachers and administrators in planning for curriculum differentiation. The model holds considerable appeal for many educators because they can readily adapt it to any learner, subject domain, or grade level (VanTassel-Baska & Brown, 2005). The parallel curriculum model includes four components: the Core Curriculum, the Curriculum of Connection, the Curriculum of Practice, and the Curriculum of Identity.

The Parallel Curriculum Model			
CORE CURRICULUM	CURRICULUM OF CONNECTIONS	CURRICULUM OF PRACTICE	CURRICULUM OF IDENTITY

The two components of the parallel curriculum model that have particular relevance to collaborative literacy are the Curriculum of Connections and the Curriculum of Identity. The Curriculum of Connections, which expands on the Core Curriculum, is designed to help students understand overarching or key concepts and principles of new content, and to use the thinking skill of analogies to solve problems. The Curriculum of Identity is designed to help students explore a discipline or a field as it relates to their individual interests, goals, and strengths, both now and in the future.

CURRICULUM OF CONNECTIONS

The Curriculum of Connections is designed to help students think about and Apply key concepts, principles, and skills:

- In a range of instances throughout a given discipline, and across disciplines
- Across time and locations
- Across cultures, and as affected by various conditions (economic, technological, political, etc.)
- Through varied perspectives and through the eyes of a variety of people affected by the ideas
- By an examination of the connection between concepts and development of the disciplines

The Curriculum of Connections involves students in making connections to self, other texts, and other people. As students make connections across time, events, topics, disciplines, cultures, and perspectives, they will build their understandings of interdisciplinary themes and intradisciplinary generalizations. Figure 1.8 summarizes the purpose of making connections in the curriculum of connections.

Figure 1.8   Purpose of Making Connections in the Curriculum of Connections

Students will:	
• Improve their depth of understanding	• Improve their problem solving
• Enhance their perspective	• Make the strange familiar
	• Develop their analogical reasoning and metaphoric thinking

CURRICULUM OF CONNECTIONS IN ACTION

The Curriculum of Connections in action and the use of metaphoric thinking can be illustrated in the government class of Mr. James. He and his students identify three organizing key concepts they want to explore—culture, continuity, and diversity—and each student selects a country to compare and contrast with the American culture, using these three concepts. The students study the geography of their selected country, investigate how geography affects the lives of people, and then compare and contrast their country's geography to that of the United States, particularly to the state in which they live. Each student compares and contrasts changes in selected aspects of culture in the United States and in their selected country, including technology, jobs, religion, music, and art over a 20-year period. These examinations of the different aspects of culture address key concepts of continuity and diversity.

Several students develop soundscapes of their countries and explain how changes throughout the two decades have affected the culture. Other students create and maintain diaries of exemplary leaders of the countries and focus on how diversity in the two countries affects culture.

Mr. James uses collaborative literacy strategies with the students by asking them to work together in small groups, to share the information that they locate, to visualize aspects from their reading, and to role play with the entire class. Two students draw a mural, including a timeline and illustrations, that traces changes throughout the two decades in their countries. This mural is then displayed in the town council room, since a town in one of the countries chosen is a sister city of their town.

CURRICULUM OF IDENTITY IN ACTION

The Curriculum of Identity is designed to help students explore a discipline or field as it relates to their individual interests, goals, and strengths, in the present and in the future. The Curriculum of Identity provides specific techniques for learning about individual students' Identities and identifies critical differences among students. It identifies where teachers need to make adjustments in curriculum and instruction to accommodate critical differences and helps to make learning more efficient and effective.

An example shared by Leppien (2003) illustrates the Curriculum of Identity in action with an 11th-grade English class. Students work to meet the prescribed writing standards and take part in writing workshops; each student selects a genre for future exploration. Two students, Amy and Darius, select genres in which they have a personal interest—Amy wants to be a writer of short stories and novels, and Darius wants to be a playwright. The two students study writers relevant to their preferred genres, examining how these people became writers, how their careers evolved over time, the positive aspects in their writing lives, and conversely what was costly to them, what advice they would give aspiring writers, and how their writing affected the authors' cultures, values, and worldviews.

The overarching question that Amy and Darius address is "What does it mean to be a writer?" Students develop a unique way to respond to this question as it relates to their chosen writer, and relate their investigations to themselves as present and future writers. Their reflections are crafted in the genre that they select and the writers they investigate. As the students study their writers, the teacher guides them to develop a fuller sense of what it means to be writers, to investigate how the pursuit of writing can be both a good thing and a bad thing, and to reflect on whether writing is a good match for their own interests, habits, perspectives, and temperaments. The teacher expects that the students will develop insights into ways in which the pursuit of writing can contribute to their individual lives, and ways in which they can contribute to the field of writing. Figure 1.9 illustrates benefits of students spending time involved in the curriculum of identity.

Figure 1.9 Benefits for Students Involved in the Curriculum of Identity

---

- Students master required content

- Students examine and reflect on their individual strengths

- Students clarify, at increasing levels of specificity, the degree of "fit" between their learning profile and targeted field

- Student growth is highlighted, and possible next steps are targeted

- Student creative productivity across the life span is increased

---

COLLABORATIVE LITERACY: A NOVEL STUDY THROUGH DRAMA

Rosenblatt (1994) said that the reader and the text have a spiral reciprocal relationship in which each conditions the other. She introduced the term "transactional" to conceptualize the reader as having a reservoir of linguistic and life experiences that reflect each reader's cultural, social, and personal history, as well as his or her past experiences with language. Rosenblatt said that readers relate to the text, to one another, and to the use of different experiences produced during their transaction. She advocated the use of drama for teachers who want to encourage an aesthetic stance during the reading of a novel. We offer the following account as a case study.

Case Study

Miss Brown, a middle-school teacher of language arts, planned a three-week novel study to establish connections between her students' textual experiences and the social and imaginative world of drama. She used the novel *The Wanderer* by Sharon Creech (2000), the story of a 13-year-old girl named Sophie who sails across the Atlantic toward England, the land of her grandfather. The book focuses on Sophie and her cousin Cody, who are able to survive at sea. The book is an incredible story of courage, which is the theme that Miss Brown has been using with her students.

The teacher reads several paragraphs from the book to establish both knowledge and a feeling for the setting, and then asks the students to create an image of what the boat looks like and what it would it feel like to be on watch for four hours like Sophie as the fog comes in "creeping along on little cat feet." She then asks the students to share the visualizations that they had while she was reading. To encourage full class participation in the discussion, the teacher uses a talking stick, which she passes around for all of the students to use and pass around as they share their visualizations.

One student says, "I saw the gray mist, and I felt the moisture on my face. I saw and heard the huge waves crashing, and the wind roaring."

Another student says, "I saw the fog moving in like a cat, slinking along, then it began to roll in much stronger, like a tiger, sort of loping along in front of the boat. The wind was howling like a live thing."

The students take turns sharing their visualizations, responding with their bodies, in a rolling and shrinking, fearful way, as if they were actually experiencing Sophie's night watch on the tossing sea. Then the teacher asks the students to work in collaborative groups of five to represent the setting of *The Wanderer*. She asks them to create a representation that they all agree upon on large butcher paper. During the activity, they reflect an aesthetic stance while drawing and sketching their visualization of the boat, but also an efferent stance to the text.

The teacher then introduces the strategy of creating a soundscape to encourage the students to describe events and incidents from the novel with sounds and no words. To help the students become comfortable with the use of a soundscape, she asks the entire class to create a soundscape of their school to help ensure that they clearly understand what a soundscape represents. Each student proposes a sound that they believe "belongs" in the school. One student makes a beep, beep noise and then says: "Excuse the interruption, but there will be no recess today." Another makes a buzzing noise to simulate the vacuuming outside the hall, another rustles paper, one moves a chair, one screeches chalk on the board, and another drops a book. When all of the students have made a sound, and they all know what a soundscape is, the teacher asks them to create a soundscape of the boat. Working in groups of five, the students go to various parts of their classroom to discuss the sounds they will use to create a soundscape of *The Wanderer*.

When they are ready to share with one another, one student takes out a flute and begins to play, another student begins to make howling noises, another swishes her hands, and another makes creaking noises. The students share that they are depicting flutelike sounds of birds, the wind howling, the swishing noises of the waves, and the creaking of the boat. Another student makes a plopping noise, which she says is the sound the dolphins make when they surface; another makes a pounding noise, which she says is Sophie's heart because she is afraid. All of the sounds are unique, and the students thoroughly enjoy sharing their soundscape.

The teacher then introduces a strategy called the Interview (Macy, 2004). She randomly chooses a student to play Sophie, and the student quickly pulls out her shirt from her jeans, kicks off her shoes, and rumples her hair. She selects another to play Cody, who kicks off his shoes and rolls up his jeans. The teacher says that there is a welcoming committee when Sophie and Cody arrive home from their journey. In collaborative groups of five, she asks them to identify questions the committee might want to ask them. The students decide which students will role play these individuals represented in the welcoming committee: Sophie and Cody's parents, a local newspaper reporter, a newscast reporter, and several friends. The students ask the following questions of Sophie and Cody:

- Sophie, I saw a picture of you in the bosun's chair. Were you afraid up that high? What could you see?
- Is it hard for a group of people to get along on a boat for a long period of time? Did you fight?
- Did you miss your family?
- What was it like to be on "watch" for four hours?

- Cody, I brought some rope. Can you tie one of those knots for me?
- Did *The Wanderer* have problems? It was an old boat, wasn't it?
- How did you feel when you set sail from Nova Scotia and then finally reached land?
- How has the trip changed you?

The students are relaxed in their role playing; Sophie and Cody answer the questions, and the reporters for the paper and the newscast move off to one side of the classroom to write their stories. All of the class becomes involved in a collaborative writing activity in which they journal as Sophie and Cody did on the trip, selecting one aspect of the trip to share with one another. The teacher is amazed at how empathetic the students are toward Sophie and Cody in their struggle to reclaim who they are. Several students share in their journals that they too had to work hard in being who they want to be, with all the pressure and expectations from friends and family.

Macy (2004) describes a novel study through drama using Gary Paulsen's novel *Hatchet* (1987) in which elementary students create a soundscape of the wilderness where Brian survived following a plane crash in Canada. The 13-year-old boy survived with only his clothing and his hatchet. The teacher asks the students to role play reporters interviewing Brian upon his safe return. She makes the following statement about the important growth of one of the students:

> I think of Dale, who is not a highly motivated student, and it takes a lot of different strategies to get her motivated and working. But I can think of a number of activities where she was loving what she was doing. She was writing; she was reading; she was sharing her material. I think of the news reporter where she came up with fantastic ideas, which she wanted to share with everyone (Macy, 2004, p. 245).

Rosenblatt (1978) said that if a reader takes a predominantly aesthetic stance to the reading, personal feelings, ideas, and attitudes can be stimulated. In this case study, the teacher, through collaborative literacy and the use of a variety of engaging strategies, is able to provide a highly personal transaction, and the reading is shaped by the students' lived-through experiences.

TEACHERS PUTTING IDEAS INTO ACTION

Bringing Heart and Soul into the Classroom

Annemarie Roeper (1995), in her book *Selected Writings and Speeches*, talks about the fact that some people with great intellectual ability do not want to learn for a variety of reasons, and she says we cannot force them to, as much as we might try. She reminds us that motivation is emotional, not cognitive, and that gifted children overflow with emotion, passion, and enthusiasm. She stresses that there is a dichotomy between the needs of the gifted and the goals of education. Find one other teacher to discuss how the "heart and soul" that

Roeper talks about can be brought back into the school. Capture your ideas in your journal and share them with two more teachers in small groups.

SELECTED CHARACTERISTICS OF GIFTED STUDENTS: EMPATHY AND CREATIVITY

Annemarie Roeper (1995) shares the following anecdote:

> A four-year-old gifted child was passionately interested in learning all about animals—she knew all their Latin names. She knew which ones were extinct and why. She knew the importance of the skeleton, etc., she had a beautiful command of language. Her emotions and love for animals could not tolerate the thought that they ate each other. She invented a whole world of animals who were so constructed that they did not need to eat each other. She was filled with sadness about the violence in nature. Her family acknowledged this reaction in her and did not reject it as childish. (p. 45)

In small groups, discuss what a school or teacher would need to understand about this gifted child's needs, and how collaborative literacy experiences could assist her. Examine the parallel curriculum or the SEM-R for ideas and suggestions that could be provided to meet this child's learning needs.

Koan Exploration

John Tarrant (2004) in his book *Bring Me the Rhinoceros*, suggests that a paradox can be used to unwind or disentangle consciousness and language. Zen koans are brief sayings, questions, stories, or a bit of conversation that can stimulate you to examine your thinking. Tarrant says that whenever the mind offers a thought, it is really offering a hypothesis about reality.

Koans originated in China about 1,300 years ago, at about the same period of time as the Arthurian legends in England. Koans will encourage you to notice that things are clear, or to discard the idea that things are not clear.

Use the following koans in small collaborative group discussion, and remember to handle all questions and comments with respect:

- You know what sound two hands make: What is the sound of one hand?
- In old China, someone gave the Governor a rare fan made of rhinoceros horn—an expensive, useless object. The Governor gave it to the local Zen master, and it was forgotten. One day, the Zen master remembered it and said, "Bring me the rhinoceros fan."

> "Umm, it's broken," said the secretary.
> "In that case, bring me the rhinoceros."

Discuss these koans, making sure that everyone in the group has an opportunity to respond and ask questions. Reflect in your journal and/or in the group on any creative breakthroughs that you or the group makes.

Annoying Child Activity

Derrick Jensen, in his book *Walking on Water: Reading, Writing and Revolution* (2004), says that the real point in education is to help students find themselves and their individual passion. He champions the idea of ferreting out and defining one's biases and assumptions. Jensen uses an activity called "The Annoying Child" that can be used in collaborative literacy discussions.

Identify an issue that you feel strongly about, and try to explain it to a group of three or four other teachers. These teachers will play the role of the Annoying Child, and relentlessly ask you questions to ferret out your biases and assumptions. After about 5–10 minutes, reflect in your journal on the experience, and/or discuss any new insights into your own thinking with the group. After hearing one teacher's reflections, another teacher in the group can identify another issue, and the group can again relentlessly ask questions.

Walk on Water

Write in your journal, and/or discuss in a collaborative discussion group of four or five teachers, your response to the phrase "walking on water." Spend about 20–25 minutes on this activity, and make sure everyone has a chance to respond. This activity will stimulate many responses, from literal walks on frozen pools to metaphorical personal "miracles" that the group may have experienced or explored.

Common Ground

In small groups, discuss the following quotation by Mary Parker Follett (1924), and try to make as many connections as you can. Focus on your identity, who you are, and who you want to become.

> The most successful teacher of all is one who sees another picture not yet actualized. See the things which belong in the present picture, and those that are not yet there. Above all, make sure your co-workers see that it is not your purpose which is to be achieved, but a common purpose, born of the desires and activities of the group.

Why Not Use Gifted Literacy Strategies for All Students?

How a teacher can extend the koan exploration strategy: Teachers can extend the koan exploration thinking strategy by having students read a book written by Jon Muth called *Zen Shorts* (2005). This book invites the reader to examine the thinking around a problem-solving situation. The book can also be used to compare cultural aspects of how different groups go about thinking and problem solving.

How a teacher can adapt strategies by grade levels: Younger students can think of hand-clapping games to tell the story of the rhinoceros. Older students can engage in a variety of research topics, such as animals or China. Students can also create synonyms and antonyms for the different vocabulary words used in the koan example.

How a teacher can use strategies across content areas: Math students can learn about how much it costs to repair a variety of objects, such as expensive and useless items discussed. If students are interested in drama or theater, they can research plays written by Chinese authors and compare and contrast the plays with the different koans.

SUMMARY

In this chapter, we explored the concept of collaborative literacy, how it builds on the ideas of Rosenblatt (1978), and its relationship to the transactional theory of reading. We examined the implications of Vygotsky's theory for collaborative literacy, particularly his concept that thought and language in the mind of a child grows out of interactions with others, and when children are in social situations, they use language as a tool to explore the world. We introduced characteristics of advanced readers and gifted students, and shared the research base for collaborative literacy and the concept that it calls for the use of multiple strategies that engage the learner in highly motivating group activities.

We introduced a strategy to foster collaborative literacy, Collaborative Strategic Reading (CSR), suggested by Klinger and Vaughn (1999), as well as the role of the teacher in collaborative literacy and the use of both direct and indirect strategies. We recommended collaborative literacy with parents, since parents can be a rich source of information concerning their children, to plan and implement reading activities for their children. The section on Ideas into Action provided teachers activities to explore the needs and characteristics of gifted children using the work of Annemarie Roeper, to stimulate examination of their own thinking through Zen koans and the work of John Tarrant, and to compare cultural aspects of different groups in John Muth's Zen Shorts. It also discussed the use of both direct program adaptations from the field of gifted education, including the Schoolwide Enrichment Model Reading (SEM-R) program of Renzulli (1978a) and the Parallel Curriculum, a model for planning curriculum based on the work of Tomlinson et al. (2002). This model can be adapted for any learner, subject domain, or grade level. The Parallel Curriculum consists of four components, but the two that have the most to offer to collaborative literacy are the Curriculum of Connections and the Curriculum of Identity.

As an example of collaborative literacy in action, we provided a case study of a teacher using the novel *The Wanderer* by Sharon Creech (2000) with students of all abilities. We discussed collaborative literacy schools as an example of long-term professional development, using Ohio State University as a pioneer in building collaborative literacy programs in schools and universities. To provide greater depth, we included activities for teachers to extend the ideas of the chapter, and opportunities to explore literature to build understanding of the gifted child—particularly, the activity called "The Annoying Child."

Identifying and Engaging Advanced Readers and Gifted Students in Collaborative Literacy

Dorothy A. Sisk

Mario shyly entered his fifth-grade class, followed by his elderly *abuela.* They had just arrived in California from Puebla, Mexico. The grandmother smiled at Mario and said, "Mario es un niño importante." Mario spoke little or no English, and he gazed around the room with his big brown eyes, noting the music center, the easel set up in the back of the room with a student painting a picture, and a small group of laughing students with earphones on, listening to something. He said good-bye to his grandmother, and she said she would meet him after school. The school psychologist tested Mario a week later, and told the teacher, "Just keep him busy and interested, because he is probably borderline developmentally delayed."

Each day Mario's vocabulary increased, and he was always attentive, observing what the other students were doing in class. Barbara, one of the identified gifted students in the class, volunteered to help Mario with assignments, and they were seldom far from one another. Barbara told Mario she wanted to study black holes, and she shared the questions she wanted to investigate. Mario sat and thought, and then asked the teacher, "Could I do a study, too?" The teacher realized she had not asked him to do an independent study, partly because of his limited English, but more so because the psychologist had said he was limited in ability. She smiled, and said, "What do you want to study?" "Music," he replied, "where it comes from, how it makes you feel, and I can play my accordion."

When Mario gave his report, he played a song about the playa in Mexico. The teacher noticed Barbara singing along with him in Spanish, and Mario played another song he called "un canto de mio." He said he wrote it about the class, and how the class made him feel. "The class makes me happy." The teacher asked the principal to have Mario reassessed on the La Prueba, the Spanish version of the Otis Lennon School Ability Test, and he scored high average. She asked that he be retested in the sixth grade, and with his increase in vocabulary and self-concept, and many positive experiences in collaborative literacy, Mario was able to qualify for the district's gifted program on teacher recommendation, grades, achievement, and ability.

COLLABORATIVE LITERACY AT WORK

This chapter provides a brief historical overview of giftedness and gifted education, several significant events preceding current gifted education, and issues and challenges in the education of gifted students, particularly the need to adapt identification procedures to ensure that students like Mario are not overlooked. We will discuss several models of intelligence, including Gardner's (1983) Multiple Intelligences (MI), Sternberg's (2000) Triarchic Theory of Intelligence, and Meeker's (1969) Structure of Intellect (SOI) model. We share the research base for suggested identification procedures for gifted students and advanced readers, followed by a case study that illustrates a psychoeducational identification process and a discussion of the use of the evaluation team approach in screening and identifying giftedness.

A section on "Ideas Into Action" includes Renzulli's (1978) Enrichment Triad model and Kaplan's (2005) Layered Curriculum model, with illustrations of how these models can be used to identify gifted students to differentiate the curriculum and can be used with all students. We discuss recommended assessment practices of gifted students and advanced readers, followed by "Teachers Putting Ideas Into Action" to extend understanding of the identification process and to address the issue of talent loss and talent denied. The chapter goals are to:

- Develop an understanding of the history of giftedness and gifted education
- Develop knowledge and understanding of exemplary models of intelligence that have influenced the field of gifted education
- Develop knowledge of current identification procedures in gifted education that are used by school districts
- Develop knowledge of programs that demonstrate the implementation of prevalent models of education of gifted students (MI, Triarchic, SOI, and the Triad)

RICH RESEARCH BASE: HISTORICAL OVERVIEW OF GIFTEDNESS AND GIFTED EDUCATION

Identifying and educating gifted youths has intrigued societies throughout recorded history. Colangelo and Davis (2003) report:

> In ancient Sparta, military skills were valued so exclusively that giftedness was defined by outstanding skills in combat, warfare, and leadership . . . Renaissance Europe sought out and rewarded its gifted artists, architects, and writers; for example, Michelangelo, da Vinci, Bernini, and Dante . . . Early China brought its child prodigies to the Imperial court where their gifts were nurtured. (p. 5)

In the United States in 1870, the city of St. Louis provided some students opportunities to complete the first eight grades in fewer than 8 years. In 1884, Woburn, Massachusetts, created the Doubled Tillage Plan that permitted bright first-grade children to be accelerated after the first semester to the second semester of second grade. In 1891, Cambridge, Massachusetts, developed a similar program and provided tutors for capable students. In about 1900, Rapid Progress Classes telescoped three years of school into two. In 1902, Worcester, Massachusetts, opened the first special school for gifted children; in 1916, Los Angeles and Cincinnati offered special classes for gifted children, followed in 1919 in Urbana, Illinois, and in 1922 in Manhattan and Cleveland. By 1920, approximately two-thirds of large cities had implemented some type of program for gifted students (Colangelo & Davis, 2003).

Significant Events Preceding Gifted Education Today

The launching of *Sputnik* in 1957 created a great deal of interest in gifted education, and Tannenbaum (1979) described its effects as total talent mobilization. Telescoping was implemented to condense content, similar to what Renzulli (1978) called compacting; high schools offered college courses for bright students.

Elementary classes introduced foreign languages, and schools provided acceleration and ability grouping to assist gifted students to develop their abilities for service to the nation.

The current interest in gifted education began in the 1970s and was influenced by three national reports. The first was *Education of the Gifted and Talented* (U.S. Department of Health, Education, and Welfare, 1972), known as the Marland report, since it was submitted to Congress by the Education Commissioner Sidney Marland. The Marland report indicated that 3 to 5 percent of the nation's students could be considered gifted, that the needs of most gifted students were not being met, that differentiated education for the gifted was a low national priority, and that gifted children without an appropriate education could suffer psychological damage and permanent impairment of their abilities. As a result of this report, a national Office of Gifted and Talented was established in Washington, DC, and a national definition was introduced, including six areas of giftedness based on achievement or potential: general intellectual ability, specific academic aptitude, creative or productive thinking, leadership ability, ability in the visual and performing arts, and psychomotor ability. Currently, most states use this definition of gifted and talented or one quite similar.

The second report, *A Nation at Risk: The Imperative for Education Reform* (U.S. Department of Education, 1983), was submitted by the National Commission on Excellence in Education. This report noted the neglect of academic standards and the abandonment of top academic students. The third report, *National Excellence: A Case for Developing America's Talent* (U.S. Department of Education, 1993), identified a number of issues, including America's ambivalence toward intellect, social and emotional issues, issues of rural and urban schools, and the identification of culturally diverse students.

> A new definition of gifted was introduced by this third report: children and youth with outstanding talent perform or show the potential for performing at remarkably high levels of accomplishment when compared with others of their age, experience, and environment. These children and youth exhibit high performance capability in intellectual, creative, and/or artistic areas, possess unusual leadership capacity, or excel in specific academic fields. They require services or activities not provided by the schools (U.S. Department of Education, 1993, p. 3).

Issues and Challenges in the Education of Gifted Students

Gallagher (2004), the former U.S. Assistant Secretary of Education in the Bureau of Health, Education, and Welfare, and former president of both the World Council for Gifted and Talented and the National Association for Gifted Children, said that one problem that bothers many thoughtful people is the consistent finding that American students, even the best American students, the gifted students, are not competitive with students from other countries in areas such as mathematics and science.

Ross (1993) summarized these concerns in the *National Excellence: A Case Study for Developing America's Talent* report: Only a small percentage of students are prepared for challenging, college-level work, as measured by tests that are not very exacting or difficult.

- The highest achieving U.S. students fare poorly when compared with similar students in other nations.
- Students going on to a university education in other countries are expected to know more than U.S. students, and to be able to think and write analytically about that knowledge on challenging exams.

Gallagher (2000) stressed that there has been a change in the concept of intelligence focusing on its dynamic nature:

- As our knowledge of intelligence increases and expands, a portrait of intelligence as a huge storehouse of information has been replaced by a construct of intelligence as a series of interconnected knowledge structures, a network of interrelationships. (p. 11)

This construct of intelligence is manifested in interconnected knowledge structures and in networks of interrelationships that can be described as the thinking of experts; Chi, Glaser, and Farr (1998) summarize it as follows. Experts

1. Excel mainly in their own domains.

2. Perceive large meaningful patterns in their domains.

3. Work faster than novices at performing the skills of their domains, and they quickly solve problems with little error.

4. Possess superior short-term and long-term memory.

5. See and represent problems in their domains at a deeper level than do novices, who tend to represent problems at a superficial level.

6. Spend a great deal of time analyzing problems qualitatively.

7. Demonstrate strong self-monitoring skills.

In other words, experts are superb problem finders and problem solvers, and they respond to new experiences in a more thoughtful and analytic fashion.

Models of Intelligence

Multiple Intelligence (MI) Model

Gardner's (1983) definition of intelligence is the ability to solve problems or create products that are valued within one or more cultural settings. He proposed seven areas of intelligence in his original work, and added an eighth intelligence in 1995. The intelligences include: (1) verbal/linguistic, (2) logical/mathematical, (3) visual/spatial, (4) musical/rhythmic, (5) bodily/kinesthetic, (6) interpersonal, (7) intrapersonal, and (8) naturalistic. Several studies have documented research based on multiple intelligences translated into practice (Latham, 1997; Smith, Odhiambo, & El Khateeb, 2000; Strahan, Summey, & Banks 1996). Figure 2.1 summarizes the eight intelligences, definitions, behaviors, and teaching strategies that complement the individual intelligence and the use of technology.

The best known project sites for implementation of the MI model are the Key School in Indianapolis, Indiana, and the Atlas project in New York City. The MI model can be used to identify gifts and talents in all students in the eight areas. The suggested teaching strategies can be used in small-group collaborative literacy activities, such as employing an integrated approach to reading with students having opportunities to read, write, and discuss stories to accommodate their linguistic intelligence.

Figure 2.1   Summary of Eight Intelligences

	Definition	**Behaviors**	**Strategies**	**Use of Technology**
Linguistic	Ability to speak or write well (Thinks in words)	Enjoys reading, word games, writing	Integrate reading, writing, discuss, use stories	Word processors, interactive stories, word puzzles/ games
Logical-Mathematical	Ability to reason, calculate, solve problems (Thinks in concepts)	Enjoys experiments, strategy games, organization	Problem solving, patterns, logic puzzles, numbers	Databases, spreadsheets, problem-solving programs, strategy games
Spatial	Ability to draw, paint, sculpt, navigate (Thinks in pictures)	Draws, visualizes, daydreams, doodles	Images, webs, charts, maps, 3D, color, video	Draw/paint programs, graphics, laserdiscs, multimedia
Musical	Ability to sing, play a musical instrument, compose music (Thinks in tones, rhythms)	Sings, whistles, hums, works to music	Integrate music into all subjects, use music for learning	Midi programs, CD-ROMs, multimedia, any programs with music
Bodily-Kinesthetic	Ability to play sports, dance, act, use one's hands (Process through bodily sensations)	Coordinated, uses gestures, good fine/gross motor skills	Hands-on activities, movement, plays	Simulations, keyboarding, programs with manipulatives/ probes, animation
Interpersonal	Ability to relate to others (Processes by sharing with others)	Likes cooperative games, team sports, clubs	Cooperative learning, teaming, pair/share	Telecommunications, programs with 2 or more players, social issues
Intrapersonal	Ability to access one's inner thoughts, feelings (Processes through reflection)	Knows own strengths, weaknesses, reflective	Independent study, time for reflection, journaling	Tutorials, self-improvement programs, self-paced programs
Naturalist	Ability to recognize and classify plants, animals & other parts of natural environment	Likes outdoors, knows plants/ animals, sees/hears patterns in nature	Outdoors as a classroom, plants and animals	Probes, databases/programs about plants, animals, environment

Triarchic Theory of Intelligence

The Triarchic Theory of Intelligence model of Sternberg (2000) is based on an information-processing theory of intelligence. In this model, there are three features of intelligence that represent the mental processes used in thinking: the executive processing component, the performance component, and the knowledge acquisition component. The executive process component is used in planning, decision making, and monitoring performance. The performance component processes are used in executing the executive problem-solving strategies within domains. The knowledge acquisition component is used in acquiring, retaining, and transferring new information. Sternberg said that the interaction and feedback between an individual and the environment within any context allows cognitive development to occur. He has developed the Sternberg Triarchic Abilities Test (STAT), which can be used to identify students who are demonstrating the specific triarchic components.

The Meeker Structure of Intellect (SOI) Model

The Structure of Intellect (SOI) model was based on the Structure of Intelligence (SI) theory of human intelligence developed by Guilford (1967). The SI model of human intelligence described 90 kinds of cognitive functions organized into content, operations, and products. The SOI model, developed by Meeker (1969), applied Guilford's theory to the assessment and training of the abilities; it has been used to identify gifted students and to plan programs for individual students. The SOI has been successfully used for identification with culturally diverse students (Hengen, 1983), for preschool screening for multiethnic disadvantaged gifted students (Bonne, 1985), and as a district-wide effort to identify gifted students (Sisk, 1994).

The SOI model provides a means of understanding individual students by creating profiles of their strengths and weaknesses. Meeker (1976) developed teaching modules that can be used to develop the SOI abilities in students. These modules include mini-lessons for group teaching and self-help modules for individualized student instruction. Meeker stressed that if intelligence can be defined, intelligence can be taught.

RESEARCH BASE FOR SCHOOLWIDE ENRICHMENT MODEL (SEM)

The Schoolwide Enrichment Model (SEM) of Renzulli (1978) has been well supported by research; for example, two SEM longitudinal studies conducted with eighteen and nineteen students, respectively, indicated that students in the sample maintained similar or identical career goals from their early plans in high school. The students remained in their major fields of study in college and were satisfied in their current work. The research also indicated that Type III independent study activities of the Triad Enrichment model appeared to serve as positive training for later productivity.

The state of Washington has used the SEM since 1999, with over 600 high-potential students in first to fifth grades. On reading vocabulary assessments, samples of enrichment school students initially scored 8 points lower than comparison-school students, but they gained 22 points by the end of the school year as compared to a 12-point gain at the comparison schools. The enrichment students' gain was equivalent to an increase of two academic grades of improvement in vocabulary knowledge. The mean number of words used appropriately and spelled correctly in written expression samples also improved at a higher rate for the enrichment students than for the students in the comparison schools (State of Washington, 2005).

Although enrichment-school students initially performed lower than their counterparts at the comparison schools, they gained at a much faster rate than did comparison school students in ability to (1) orally describe enrichment activities and enriched learnings; (2) read from vocabulary lists; (3) read and define selected enrichment-oriented terms; and (4) write longer, complete, and more complex sentences. End-of-year differences were statistically significant in favor of the enrichment-school students on all four variables when adjusted for initial differences.

TALENT SEARCHES

The Talent Searches initiated by Julian Stanley at the Johns Hopkins University under the sponsorship of the Study of Mathematically Precocious Youth (SMPY) have provided evidence that gifted students are underchallenged beginning as early as elementary school and that early identification of giftedness is beneficial to use of their talent. One study (Assouline & Doellinger, 2000) found that academically able students in sixth grade and younger performed as well as or better than average eighth-grade students on the EXPLORE, a test developed by American College Testing (ACT). EXPLORE consists of four multiple-choice tests—English, mathematics, reading, and science reasoning—and provides a composite score representing the average of the four scores.

Two cohorts of intellectually talented students identified by SMPY at Johns Hopkins University in the early and late 1970s were longitudinally tracked, and after 20 years, at age 33, they demonstrated exceptional academic achievements: 90 percent of the students earned bachelor's degrees, and over 25 percent had earned a doctorate (Benbow, Lubinski, Shea, & Eftekhari-Sanjani, 2000).

In a second study, Lubinski, Webb, Morelock, and Benbow (2001) surveyed Talent Search student participants identified in the early 1980s who scored in the top 0.01 percent in ability. They reported:

> Over half of these individuals were pursuing doctorates, and almost without exception they were attending some of the most elite universities in the world. By their mid-twenties, many of them had published scientific articles, written for literary publications, created video games, or secured patents for inventions. One of them had become a full professor before age 25 at a major research university. (p. 214)

Broadened definitions of intelligence and the provision of appropriate education have yielded success in assisting students to develop their talents, to identify areas of interest, and to successfully use their talent. The following case study represents an example of a psychoeducational assessment as described by Assouline (2003).

Case Study

Fred was placed in first grade on the basis of his chronological age, 6 years and 5 months; however, the curriculum was not challenging, and he became frustrated. Fred's parents requested a grade skip from first grade to seventh grade. He was provided a psychoeducational assessment, using the Wechsler Intelligence Scale for Children Revised and the Stanford-Binet, on which he performed at a superior intellectual level. On the Wide Range Achievement Test (WRAT), he performed at the seventh-grade level for reading, math, and spelling. Fred was administered the Raven's Progressive Matrices (RPM), an untimed nonverbal test of figural reasoning, and he earned a score surpassing 98% of eight-year-old students. Fred also was given the Stanford Diagnostic Reading Test, and he scored in the grade equivalent range 3.7–7.3. His lowest performance area was inferential comprehension at the 43% level, and the highest was phonetic analysis at 95%. The Standard Reading Inventory (SRI) was administered; he orally read the fourth- and fifth-grade passages with only a few minor pronunciation errors, and his silent-reading speed was at the instructional level for grade 4.

The psychoeducational assessment results indicated that Fred had demonstrated superior performance on individual intelligence tests and on the RPM, and it was predicted that his academic achievement would be at least two grade levels ahead of his age or grade-mates. Fred demonstrated excellent concentration and attending skills, and placement was recommended in a third/fourth-grade combination class. Prior to the testing, Fred had been home-schooled by his parents. The placement in the combination class proved highly successful.

Fred entered Purdue University at the age of 11, graduated at the age of 17 with a Doctor of Pharmacy, and enrolled in a PhD program at Rockefeller University in New York.

IDEAS INTO ACTION

Recommended Assessment of Gifted Students and Advanced Readers

Richert (2003) suggested a procedure approved by the U.S. Office of Civil Rights that included using available test scores, teacher nomination (grades K–2), parent nomination (grades K–3), and self-nomination (grades 6–11). Data from different sources should be used independently, and a high score on any one source is sufficient to include a student in a gifted program.

Above-Level Testing

Above-level testing can be useful in identifying exceptional talent in a given domain. Students who score at a designated level or higher (usually 95th or 97th percentile) on a grade-level standardized achievement test can be invited to take an above-level test, such as the SAT-1, the ACT Assessment, or the Spatial Test Battery. Over 300,000 students from every state and several countries have participated in above-level testing using the SAT-1 in Talent Searches conducted by Johns Hopkins University and Duke University.

Assessing Advanced Readers

Not all gifted students are talented or advanced readers, and not all advanced readers are gifted (Reis & Small, 2003). Researchers at the National Research Center on Gifted and Talented at the University of Connecticut (Reis & Small, 2003) have studied advanced or talented readers in their research sponsored by the U.S. Department of Education Javits Program for the Gifted and Talented, and they identified four areas that distinguish these students:

1. They enjoy the reading process.

2. They are early readers and may have been self-taught.

3. They are at least two grade levels above their chronological grade placement.

4. They demonstrate advanced processing and advanced language skills.

Advanced readers demonstrated advanced processes with the following seven characteristics:

1. Retain a large quantity of information for retrieval.

2. Automatically integrate prior knowledge and experience in reading.

3. Use higher order thinking skills such as analysis and synthesis.

4. Process information and thoughts at an accelerated pace.

5. Synthesize ideas in a comprehensive way.

6. Perceive unusual relationships and integrate ideas.

7. Grasp complex ideas and nuances.

Many of the above characteristics of advanced readers can be observed when teachers provide collaborative literacy activities. Teachers can create a checklist based on the above advanced processing characteristics and use a Likert scale to assess the students, similar to the checklist constructed from the list of advanced language skills suggested by Reis & Small (2003). Figure 2.2 illustrates this type of checklist.

Figure 2.2   Teacher Checklist for Language Skills of Advanced Readers

Directions: Circle the appropriate number that applies to the individual student.

	Low				High
1. The student enjoys the subtleties and complexities of language.	1	2	3	4	5
2. The student demonstrates advanced understanding of language and uses an expansive vocabulary.	1	2	3	4	5
3. The student uses reading to acquire a large repertoire of language skills.	1	2	3	4	5
4 The student uses language for humor.	1	2	3	4	5
5. The student displays verbal ability in self-expression.	1	2	3	4	5
6. The student uses colorful and descriptive phrasing.	1	2	3	4	5
7. The student demonstrates ease in the use of language.	1	2	3	4	5

Figure 2.3   Screening Procedures for Evaluating Giftedness in Students

Screening (Assessment Measures)

- Direct observation
- Checklists of gifted characteristics
- Classroom work products
- Anecdotal records
- Group intelligence tests
- Group achievement tests
- Grades or curriculum-based assessment

Team Evaluation Approach in Screening and Identification of Giftedness

In using a team-evaluation approach in screening and identification, the determination of a student's giftedness is based on an examination of all areas of assessment without assigning special weighting to any one factor. This approach is accomplished through the efforts of a team—teachers, psychologists, gifted specialists, and parents—who make a determination that a student is gifted and needs special education and related services. Figure 2.3 illustrates the team evaluation approved in screening including assessment measures.

Figure 2.4 depicts identification procedures for intelligence, achievement, creativity, visual and performing arts, and leadership.

Figure 2.4   Identification Procedures for Evaluating Giftedness in Students

- Individualized intelligence test
- Individualized achievement test
- Creativity assessment
- Visual and performing arts assessment
- Leadership assessment

Renzulli Triad Model for Identification of and Services for Gifted Students

The Renzulli Triad model has evolved over 15 years of research and field testing into the Schoolwide Enrichment Model (SEM). In the SEM, a talent pool of 15 to 20 percent of above-average/high-potential students is identified in a school through a variety of measures, including achievement tests, teacher nomination, assessment of potential for creativity, and task commitment. Students may also nominate themselves, and their parents can nominate them. High IQ scores and/or high-achievement scores can place students in a talent pool; this is particularly helpful if the students are not performing well in the classroom setting (Renzulli & Reis, 1985).

Once students are placed in the talent pool, they can receive three kinds of service: (1) interest and learning style assessments; (2) curriculum compacting, which modifies their curriculum content by eliminating content that the students have already mastered and provides alternative work; and (3) engagement in the Type I, II, and III Triad Enrichment model. Type I enrichment includes general exploratory experiences such as guest speakers, field trips, demonstrations, interest centers, and the use of audiovisual materials designed to expose students to new and exciting topics, ideas, and fields of knowledge not ordinarily covered in the regular curriculum. Type II enrichment includes instructional methods and materials designed to promote the development of thinking, feeling, research, communication, and methodological processes. In Type III enrichment, the most advanced level of the Triad model, students identify topics they want to investigate or to use as the subject of artistic productions. In Type III activities, students take on the role of a firsthand inquirer, thinking, feeling, and acting like a practicing professional. Type I and II activities can be used with all students, and Type III works best with advanced readers and gifted students who can identify a problem to research and can work independently or collaboratively with a group of students.

Kaplan Layered Model for Differentiating Curriculum

Kaplan (1994) explored how to modify the core curriculum under a U.S. Department of Education Javits Grant for the gifted and talented, in a collaborative project with the California Department of Education and the California Association for the Gifted. An outcome of this project was the articulation of the importance of adding depth and complexity, the two ways Kaplan suggested to modify content in learning activities. Altering the content, process, or products of the curriculum was found to be an effective means of differentiating the curriculum for gifted students. Gifted students would be asked to develop a more complex product calling for greater depth. Figure 2.5 illustrates how the product can be modified for gifted students in a study of environmental ecology.

In Figure 2.6, the content is altered to provide for a more complex approach to the content. The gifted students would be asked to research and identify the patterns in global warming. In Figure 2.7, the core is altered by modifying the process: gifted students would be asked to interview an environmental ecologist.

Figure 2.5   Modification of the Core by Altering the Product

Process	Content	Process	Products
Thinking skills	The causes and effects of global warming	Research skills	~~Write a summary paragraph to share the information~~
Judge with criteria			Write an editorial and list effects of global warming

Figure 2.6   Modification of the Core by Altering the Content

Process	Content	Process	Products
Thinking skills	~~The causes and effects of global warming~~	Research skills	Write an editorial and pose the effects of global warming
Judge with criteria	The patterns in the behaviors of the people/nations that may have contributed to global warming		

Figure 2.7   Modification of the Core by Altering the Process

Process	Content	Process	Products
Thinking skills		~~Research Skills~~	Write an editorial and pose the effects of global warming
Judge with criteria	The patterns in the behaviors of the people/nations that may have contributed to global warming	Interview an Environmental Ecologist	

The Layered Curriculum approach or model emphasizes the acquisition of content. The first layer is the core curriculum or the basic curriculum, based on state or subject matter standards, that all students follow. The use of the dimensions of depth and complexity facilitates the differentiated core curriculum to meet the needs of individual students. The dimension of depth focuses on involving the students in increasingly difficult, divergent, and abstract qualities of knowing a discipline or area of study. Kaplan defines complexity as the means by which knowledge can be extended.

Dimensions of depth include language of the disciplines, details, patterns, trends, unanswered questions, rules, ethics, and big ideas. Language of the disciplines refers to learning the specific specialized and technological terms associated with a specific area of study. Details are the learning of specific attributes, traits, and characteristics that describe a concept, theory, principle, and facts. Patterns are recurring events represented by details, and trends are the factors that influence events. Unanswered questions are the ambiguities and gaps of information that the student may recognize within an area of study. Rules are the natural or human-made structure or order of things that explain the phenomena within the area of study. Ethics addresses the dilemmas or controversial issues that plague an area of study, and big ideas are the generalizations, principles, and theories that distinguish themselves from the facts and concepts under study. Another example of the Layered Curriculum model in action would be students in a biology class researching the question: When does life begin? This study would involve the students in the ethics of stem-cell research.

The dimensions of complexity, according to Kaplan (2005), include a focus on concepts over time, points of view, and disciplinary connection. When students engage in a study, they take into consideration that the passage of time changes our knowledge of things, and that there are different perspectives that alter the way ideas and objects are viewed and valued. Disciplinary connections refer to both integrated and interdisciplinary links in the curriculum. Disciplinary connections can be made within, between, and among various areas of study or disciplines. Examples are connections between math and music or between reading and science in which students engage in studying the similarities of the disciplines. In reading and science, they can use their critical reading skills to explore scientific discoveries in depth.

Activities in the following section provide opportunities for extension of the ideas presented in this chapter.

TEACHERS PUTTING IDEAS INTO ACTION

Reflect on your own educational experience. Did anyone ever indicate that you had talent in one or more areas? Were there gifted students in your classes or in your school? If not, why not? If you were identified as gifted, what experiences did you have? Find one other teacher and share your thoughts.

Rising Tide

Renzulli (1978) talked about the rising tide as an underlying philosophy for his SEM. What do you think that means? How does that philosophy fit in with current educational reform efforts, especially the emphasis on heterogeneous grouping? Think about your response, journal it, and then find two other teachers to discuss your points of view.

You Be the Advocate

In small groups, discuss the possibility of there being students in your school who need accelerated experiences. How would testing fit into your curricular planning for those students? Be prepared to share your group's ideas with others.

Out With Testing

A school board member recently stood up and said that he wanted to do away with all of the testing for the gifted program in his school. He quoted from a *Phi Delta Kappa* issue in which Wassermann (2001) said that we should be suspicious of the motives of those advocating standardized testing. Wassermann asserted that educators should omit testing from the assessment process and revert to the use of informed observations by teachers. This was just what the school board member wanted to hear, and he also quoted Wiggins and McTighe (1998):

> Students are tested not on the way they use, extend, or criticize knowledge, but on their ability to generate a superficially correct response on cue. They are allowed one attempt at a test that they know nothing about until they begin taking it. For their efforts, they receive and are judged by—a single numerical score that tells them little about their current level of progress and gives them no help in improving it. (p. 2)

The board member suggested that the district use portfolio assessment. List three to five points that you think would be a reasonable response to this board member.

Can the MI Theory Account for Traditional Gifted Students?

When Howard Gardner (1983) speaks about his MI theory, he often mentions that he was surprised at the positive reception that the MI theory received in educational circles. In small groups, discuss how the MI view of giftedness differs from a traditional IQ point of view. To what extent can a traditional view of giftedness account for or explain students who are gifted from an MI perspective? How might you develop and use a profile of MI abilities for all students in a classroom? Evaluate yourself on the intelligences: What do you conclude?

Find Your Advanced Readers

Use the checklist for advanced-processing language skills in Figure 2.3 of this chapter, with 1 representing low and 5 representing high, to assess the students in your class. Once you locate the advanced readers, what types of enrichment could you make available for them to help ensure that they experience advanced processing and continue to enjoy the reading process? Could you use the Triad Enrichment model of Renzulli (1978)?

SUMMARY

In this chapter, we provided a historical overview of giftedness and gifted education, exploring its beginnings in 1870, of mostly program efforts that focused on acceleration, and the positive impact of significant events such as *Sputnik* and various national reports on the field of education. We presented issues and challenges in the education of gifted students, including the high percentage of gifted underachievers and the poor performance of American gifted students in comparison to students from other countries in science and math. We introduced a number of models of intelligence, including Gardner's Multiple Intelligences, Sternberg's Triarchic Theory of Intelligence Model, Meeker's Structure of the Intellect, and Renzulli's Schoolwide Enrichment Model. We included the research base for the content of the chapter, which focused on the importance of early identification of giftedness being beneficial to later development of talent. We provided a case study as an example of the use of a psychoeducational assessment of a gifted youth who received radical acceleration.

The Ideas Into Action section provided recommended assessment practices of gifted students and advanced readers, and introduced the use of the team evaluation approach in screening and identification. We presented the Renzulli Enrichment Triad model, which has evolved into the Schoolwide Enrichment Model, as an example of a model for identification and educational services for gifted students, and we introduced the Kaplan Layered Curriculum model as a program adaptation focusing on curriculum with examples of instructional strategies used in the field of gifted education that can be used in collaborative literacy efforts with all students. The Teachers Putting Ideas Into Action section provided a number of engaging activities to extend the content of the chapter.

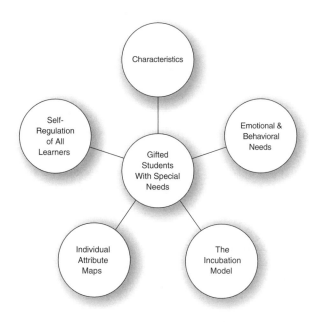

Diagram circles: Characteristics, Self-Regulation of All Learners, Gifted Students With Special Needs, Emotional & Behavioral Needs, Individual Attribute Maps, The Incubation Model

3

Strengthening Instruction of Gifted Students With Special Needs in a Collaborative Literacy Environment

Dorothy A. Sisk

Rebecca, a troubled, gifted teenager, experienced bouts of depression and was involved in an ongoing power struggle with her mother, often resulting in abusive language and physical abuse. In a counseling session, Rebecca was asked to examine a picture of a dolphin swimming in the ocean, with a smaller dolphin nearby. After a few moments of reflection, she was asked to visualize the two dolphins together and to allow the images to flow of their own accord. She was guided to "Become aware of any sounds that you might hear, to note the colors, the dialogue between the two dolphins, to hear what they are sharing, and to gather insight from their interaction."

In her journal, Rebecca wrote:

> One day the young dolphin saw her mother floating with her eyes closed. When the young dolphin sounded to her, her mother did not seem to hear her. The young dolphin became upset because she could not awaken her mother. A number of minutes later, the mother dolphin awakened from her trance.
>
> "Why didn't you hear me, mother?" asked the young dolphin. "I was in the sea of tranquility," said the mother. "How is that possible?" asked the young dolphin, "You were right here." "My child, the sea of tranquility is within me," explained the mother. "Everyone has a sea of tranquility."

COLLABORATIVE LITERACY AT WORK

This chapter examines gifted students like Rebecca who have special needs, and focuses on two areas of special-needs students, the twice-exceptional student: (1) the gifted student with emotional behavior disorders, and (2) the gifted student with learning disabilities, as well as the special needs of the under-achieving gifted student, and the creatively gifted student. We discuss the characteristics of gifted students with special needs and provide the research base for strengthening instruction to meet the needs of these students in a collaborative literacy environment, followed by Ideas Into Action, Teachers Putting Ideas Into Action to extend the content of the chapter, and a summary.

The chapter goals are to

- Develop awareness and understanding of the characteristics of gifted students with special needs—the twice-exceptional students, who are emotional behavioral disordered and gifted or learning-disabled and, gifted.
- Develop awareness and understanding of the characteristics of both underachieving gifted students and creatively gifted students as students with special needs.
- Develop knowledge of research-based instruction of gifted students with special needs in a collaborative literacy environment.
- Develop awareness and knowledge of program adaptations that incorporate collaborative literacy strategies to strengthen the instruction of gifted students with special needs.

RICH RESEARCH BASE: CHARACTERISTICS OF GIFTED STUDENTS WITH SPECIAL NEEDS

David Goldman, a senior at Cherry Creek High School and a debater and presenter on the topic of twice-exceptional students, said he remembers an incident in second grade when the whole class was sitting in a circle taking turns reading a book. He quietly watched as each student took a turn, and as the number of students between the reader and himself slowly dwindled, his pulse rate quickened. Everyone read so fast! Finally, it was his turn, and he told himself that if he slowly sounded out each word, it would be fine. But despite his best efforts, he got stuck on the five-letter words that everyone else read with ease. The entire class started laughing. He finished reading a few sentences in what seemed like three hours, but at last it was over, and the torture ended. Then he said he realized that the circle was going around again. Students who are twice-exceptional like David often hold themselves to high performance expectations, whether they are gifted and learning disabled or gifted and emotional behavior disordered, and it is difficult to balance the expectations of being gifted while trying to overcome learning difficulties (Strop & Goldman, 2002).

Gifted students with disabilities may be the most underserved and least understood of all gifted populations. An article in *Education Week* on twice-exceptional students reported that there are more than 45,142 gifted students with learning disabilities (Fine, 2001).

Silverman (1998) described gifted students as having complex thought processes and emotions that are mirrored in the intricacy of their emotional development:

> Idealism, self-doubt, perceptiveness, excruciating sensitivity, moral imperatives, desperate need for understanding, acceptance, and love—all impinge simultaneously. Their vast emotional range makes them appear contradictory: mature and immature, arrogant and compassionate, aggressive and timid. Semblances of composure and self-assurance often mask deep feelings of insecurity. The inner experience of the gifted is rich, complex and turbulent. (p. 84)

Gifted Students With Emotional Behavioral Disorders

There is no one definition of emotional behavior disorders; however, three features are found in most definitions:

1. Behavior that goes to an extreme; that is, behavior that is not just slightly different from the usual.

2. A problem that is chronic; that is, one that does not disappear.

3. Behavior that is unacceptable because of social or cultural expectations (Leu & Kinzer, 2003).

Students with emotional disturbance achieve substantially below expected levels, and their behavior can be classified into three behavior patterns: withdrawal, anxiety, and aggression. Rebecca, the youngster in the personal reflection, exhibited all three patterns. A twice-exceptional gifted child with an emotional behavior disorder may be without friends, have difficulty working with groups, daydream a lot, and appear secretive. Rebecca's anxiety was manifested by crying more frequently than normal and appearing tense and nervous, overly sensitive to criticism, easily embarrassed, depressed, sad or troubled, reluctant to work independently, and afraid of making mistakes in the classroom.

Learning-Disabled, Gifted Students

The term "learning disability," as first introduced by Samuel Kirk in 1963, referred to children with normal ability level who have difficulty learning in school (Nelson, 1993). Since then, a variety of definitions has been used, including the following:

- A substantial gap between expected achievement levels based on intelligence scores and actual performance in at least one academic subject area.
- An uneven achievement profile, with very high achievement in some areas and very low in others.
- Low achievement levels that do not result from environmental factors.
- Low achievement levels that are not due to mental retardation or emotional disturbance. (Nelson, 1993, p. 549)

Gifted students with learning disabilities may be identified as neither gifted nor learning disabled because the discrepancy between their ability level and their achievement may be small. The twice-exceptional gifted, learning-disabled student may be thought of as an underachiever or as a student who just doesn't try. Many school districts require the demonstration of a need for services, which may also eliminate special services for the gifted, learning-disabled student.

Willard-Holt (2002) said that gifted students with learning disabilities constitute the largest group of twice-exceptional students; they are also the most diverse group because of the many types of learning disabilities. Figure 3.1 depicts positive characteristics common to many such students.

Figure 3.1 Positive Characteristics Common to Gifted Students With Learning Disabilities

• High abstract reasoning ability	• Imaginative and creative thinking
• Good mathematical reasoning ability and spatial skills	• Good problem-finding and -solving skills
• Advanced vocabulary	• Perfectionism
• Sophisticated sense of humor	• Speed in grasping metaphors, analogies, and satire
• Exceptional ability in geometry, science, arts, music	• Comprehension of complex systems
	• Wide variety of interests

Willard-Holt (2002) also identified a set of difficulties common to these students:

- unreasonable self-expectations and negative helplessness
- asynchronous development
- high levels of frustration and learned helplessness
- emotional sensitivity
- problems in relationships with peers and/or teachers
- distractibility and/or disorganization, often leading to failure to complete assignments
- difficulties with sequential tasks, such as memorization, computation, phonics, or spelling

Underachieving, Gifted Students

The National Commission on Excellence in Education (1983) reported that half of gifted students do not perform to their tested abilities, and Carnegie Corporation *Years of Promise: A Comprehensive Learning Strategy for America's Children* (1996) report stressed the seriousness of underachievement in the United States:

> Make no mistake about it, underachievement is not a crisis of certain groups; it is not limited to the poor; it is not a problem afflicting other people's children. By the 4th grade, the performance of most children is below what it should be for the nation and is certainly below the achievement levels of children in competing countries. (p. 2)

Underachievement of gifted students may be indicative of a number of causes. Some causes may have origins in the environment and others in the child; it might also result from a combination of the two or what has become known as a mismatch of the unique needs of the gifted student and the environment (Reis & McCoach, 2000). The underachievement of gifted students represents a loss of valuable resources for the nation, as well as unrealized fulfillment for the individual student.

Creatively Gifted Students

Creatively gifted students may appear odd to their age-mates; they may have interests and passions that are different from the mainstream of students, and their unique thinking and self-expression may set them apart. Torrance (2002) said that creatively gifted students require a variety of social and emotional support mechanisms to develop their creativity, including environments in which risk-taking is valued and promoted and in which they are not pressured to conform.

Many creatively gifted students' behaviors may be included in characteristics lists used to identify learning and behavior problems. Cramond (2005) compared lists of characteristics of creative individuals and of those who have been diagnosed with ADHD; she noted many similarities, including daydreaming, high energy, impulsiveness, risk-taking, preoccupation, difficult temperament, and poor social skills.

Davis (2003) identified the following characteristics as related to creativity and consequential behaviors:

Original	Imaginative, resourceful, unconventional, challenges assumptions, asks, what if? Irritated and bored by the obvious.
Aware of creativeness	Creativity conscious, values originality, values own creativity.
Independent	Self-confident, individualistic, sets own rules, unconcerned with impressing others, resists societal demands.
Risk-taking	Not afraid to be different or try something new, willing to cope with hostility, willing to cope with failure.
Motivated	Adventurous, sensation seeking, enthusiastic, excitable, spontaneous, impulsive, goes beyond assigned tasks.
Curious	Questioning, experimenting, inquisitive, wide interests.
Sense of humor	Playful, plays with ideas, freshness in thinking, childlike.
Attracted to complexity	Attracted to novelty, asymmetry, the mysterious; is a complex person; tolerant of ambiguity, disorder, incongruity.
Artistic	Artistic and aesthetic interests.
Open-minded	Receptive to new ideas, other viewpoints, new experiences, and growth, liberal, altruistic.
Needs time alone	Reflective, introspective, internally preoccupied, sensitive, may be withdrawn, likes to work alone.
Intuitive	Perceptive, sees relationships, uses all senses in observing.

We now discuss the research base for program adaptations and use of strategies to strengthen the instruction of gifted students with special needs.

Research Base for Gifted Students With Special Needs

Research literature suggests that a realistic estimate of K–12 students with emotional behavioral disorders is 3 to 6 percent of the total school population, although current programs serve slightly less than 1 percent of this population (Kaufmann & Castellanos, 2000). Most students with emotional behavior disorders encounter problems in regular educational classrooms because they lack study skills and appropriate social skills; instruction in these areas can lead to skill improvement that also enhances their achievement (Sugai & Lewis, 1996).

The most common behavior disorder in gifted children is ADHD (Zentall, Moon, Hall, & Grskovic, 2001). Colangelo and Davis (2003) reported that dual exceptionality or twice-exceptional children and youth are at risk for under-achievement, since there are barriers to achieving at their level of giftedness. Colangelo and Davis (2003) summarized this view:

> Gifted students by their very advanced cognitive abilities and intensity of feelings deal with issues about self and others in ways that are different from those of the general population, and therefore require specialized understanding. (p. 173)

Colangelo and Assouline (2000) said that there is a sizable minority of gifted students who are psychologically at risk and need counseling focused on their needs. Using the prevalence figures for the population of 3 to 6 percent, the number of gifted students who may be classified as having emotional behavior disorders is sizable—in particular, when there is a poor fit between their unique needs and the school and/or home environment, it increases the likelihood that they may become disturbed.

In a study of learning-disabled students in Tampa, Florida, 7 percent of the identified learning-disabled students were gifted students with IQs of 132 and higher. However, because of their underachievement, these students were referred to the learning-disability program for services instead of to the gifted program (Sisk, 1989).

In addition to perceptual motor problems, gifted, learning-disabled students may manifest attention problems and lack effective learning and problem-solving strategies, which may lead to little or no self-regulation. Working with gifted, learning-disabled students to build their self-regulation has shown considerable promise (Reis, 2004).

Research indicates that the interaction between giftedness and learning disabilities is a confusing and perplexing situation for gifted students and young adults. This confusion may create problems for them as they try to understand why they do well in some things but struggle in others. In a research study of academically successful, gifted college students with learning disabilities, all of the participants shared negative, and in many cases painful, memories of school experiences (Reis, Neu, & McGuire, 1995). These experiences included repeated punishment for not completing work on time, retention of a grade attributed to the student's learning disability, placement in a self-contained special education class in which most of the students were developmentally delayed, and negative, inappropriate treatment by peers and teachers.

Baum, Owen, and Dixon (1991) found that when schools implement com-prehensive programs to identify and develop the individual gifts and talents of students, the gifted, learning disabled students begin to improve socially, emo-tionally, and academically. Bender and Wall (1999) found similar results when educators focused more on the gift than on the disability. Providing instruction in higher order thinking, problem solving, and information processing was found to be helpful in the development of academic coping strategies and improved students' self-esteem and academic performance (Hansford, 1987; Reis, McGuire, & Neu, 2000).

Olenchak and Reis (2002), examining case studies of gifted, learning-disabled students, found that differentiation in which the curriculum was adjusted around the needs of gifted students with respect to programming and teaching had negative ramifications for these students. The gifted, learning-disabled students expressed feelings of greater disparity from their peers than before the differentiation was implemented, and they exhibited anxiety and depression. When the differentiation strategies were adjusted to meet the unique needs of gifted, learning-disabled students, the students reported substantial improvement in both social and emotional status and academic performance.

Underachieving Gifted Students

According to the research of Renzulli, Baum, and Hébert (1995), under-achievement can sometimes be reversed through the implementation of positive adult encouragement, a focus on strengths, and self-selected interests in enrichment projects as suggested by the Renzulli Enrichment Triad. These Type III activities include independent research on self-selected topics of interest. McCoach, Kehle, Bray, and Siegle (2001) found in their research that gifted underachievers often view school negatively and report that they don't fit into the system. According to Cross (1997), gifted students' underachievement may represent a coping strategy, whereby they strive to adapt to a nonintellectual school environment. Reis and McCoach (2000) suggest interventions that enhance self-efficacy or develop self-regulation, which may complement other intervention strategies and increase these students' effectiveness.

Creatively Gifted Students

Russ, Robins, and Christano (1999) found that specific educational interventions like providing time in school for imaginative or fantasy play and for role-playing enhanced the performance of creatively gifted students, who are then able to use their ability for ingeniously attacking problems. Torrance (2002) said that the best way to nurture these students is to recognize and value their creativity. In a 22-year follow-up of individuals identified as creatively gifted in elementary school, he found that teachers who made a difference were those who enabled students to hold on to their creativity.

Two strategies that meet the needs of creatively gifted students are taking risks in writing and manipulating or otherwise toying with ideas. Students who used these strategies were found to be better at problem-solving tasks (Cramond, 2005). These tasks are included in the Torrance Incubation model.

IDEAS INTO ACTION

Incubation Model to Develop Creative Thinking

The Incubation model (Torrance & Sisk, 1997) is ideally suited to teaching the creatively gifted student and, with adaptation of the process, pace, and product, is also useful for all students in the regular classroom. All students are

Figure 3.2   The Incubation Model of Teaching

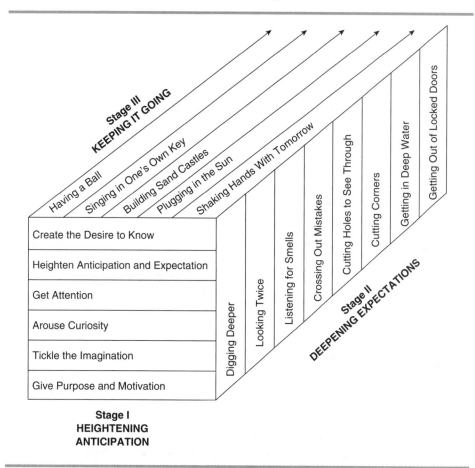

curious and want to learn; they anticipate what is coming, and this anticipation is heightened when they begin to dig in and start learning. Exploratory activities motivate students to reflect on what is learned, to find out more, to ask questions, to experiment, and to apply and use what they have learned.

Torrance developed the Incubation model as a way of addressing the whole of creativity. Its purpose is to open students' minds through creative activities and to keep their minds open to learning about a given topic, even when a formal lesson is completed. There are three stages to the model: Stage 1 is called "Heightened Anticipation"; Stage 2 is "Encountering the Expected and Unexpected, and Deepening Expectations"; and Stage 3 is "Going Beyond and Keeping It Going." Stage 1 consists of 15 strategies in which the teacher focuses on creating the desire to know, building heightened anticipation and expectation, getting attention, arousing curiosity, tickling the imagination, and providing purpose and motivation. Figure 3.2 depicts the Incubation model.

In this chapter, we will focus on Stage 1 of the Incubation model. The 15 strategies are listed below:

Stage 1: Heightened Anticipation

1. Confronting ambiguities and uncertainties.

2. Questioning to heighten expectation and anticipation.

3. Creating awareness of a problem to be solved, a possible future need, or a difficulty to be faced.

4. Building on the students' existing knowledge.

5. Heightening concern about a problem or future need.

6. Stimulating curiosity and the desire to know.

7. Making the strange familiar or the familiar strange.

8. Freeing from inhibiting mindsets.

9. Looking at the same information from different viewpoints.

10. Provocative questioning to encourage thinking about information in new ways.

11. Predicting from limited information.

12. Making the purposefulness of the lesson clear, showing the connection between the unexpected learning and present problems or future careers.

13. Providing only enough structure to give clues and direction.

14. Taking the next step beyond what is known.

15. Physically or bodily warming up to the information to be presented.

Collaborative Literacy Activity for Middle-School Gifted Students With Special Needs

Let's look at an example of a collaborative literacy activity for middle-school students using strategies #3 and #9 in Stage 1 of the Incubation model. This activity calls for the students to work in collaborative literacy groups of four students. Each group decides on a famous person they want to know more about—someone who is making a difference and addressing a problem the students agree needs to be solved. The students locate at least two biographies or articles about the selected individual that are written by two different authors, then they compare and contrast each writer's perspective. This activity uses such skills as note-taking, paraphrasing, developing outlines, comparing conflicting information, writing bibliographies, constructing displays, compiling character traits of the people selected for study, and summarizing ways the individuals affected or are affecting a problem or issue on a local, state, national, or international level.

The use of the individual attribute map depicted in Figure 3.3 will be helpful in guiding the students, particularly the gifted, learning-disabled students who will benefit from the structure of an attribute map, to graphically organize the information or evidence from the collaborative group effort.

To encourage creatively gifted students to use their higher order thinking, compare and contrast, infer, analyze, and synthesize, summarizing statements provide opportunities for them to personalize the information from their study. After completing the statements, the students can plan action steps to apply

Figure 3.3 Individual Attribute Map

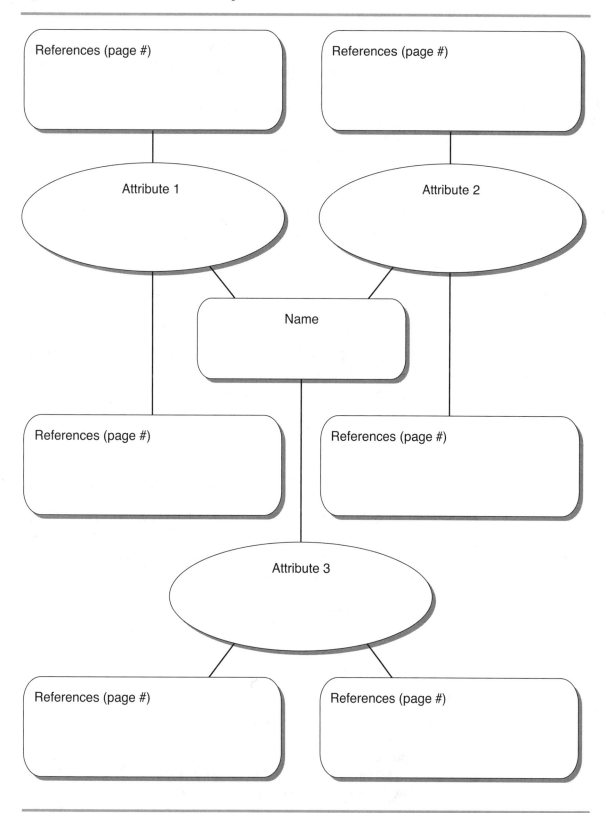

the information to their own self-regulation. The following are examples of summarizing statements:

EXAMINE THE INFORMATION ON EACH PERSON YOU HAVE STUDIED. ARE THERE SIMILAR CHARACTER TRAITS OR ATTRIBUTES AMONG THE BIOGRAPHIES? IF SO, WHICH ONES?

_____

_____

_____

DO YOUR SUCCESSFUL PEOPLE HAVE SIMILAR ATTRIBUTES? LIST THE SIM-ILAR ATTRIBUTES.

_____

_____

_____

SELECT ONE OF THEIR STRONG CHARACTER TRAITS AND REFLECT ON HOW YOU COULD USE IT TO BE MORE SUCCESSFUL IN YOUR SCHOOLWORK AND IN SOCIAL SITUATIONS. LIST ONE OR TWO IDEAS.

_____

_____

_____

SELECT ONE PERSONAL TRAIT THAT YOU WOULD LIKE TO STRENGTHEN. WITH YOUR PARENTS, GUARDIAN, OR TEACHER, IDENTIFY TWO GOAL-SETTING TECHNIQUES THAT YOU THINK WOULD BE HELPFUL FOR YOU TO HAVE A SUCCESSFUL SCHOOL YEAR.

_____

_____

_____

Before the students write the biographies, they will need to decide how they will go about completing their first draft; for example, who in the group will do the editing? Do they want to construct a display or model to share their findings? A comparative biography sheet, shown in Figure 3.4 (see the next page), can provide additional organizing structure for the gifted, learning-disabled students, as well as for the underachieving gifted student.

The next activity has proved very successful with creatively gifted students who love to ponder and discuss abstract meanings of literature. This activity, which refers to the Statue of Liberty, focuses on the Torrance Incubation model's strategy #7, "Making the strange familiar or the familiar strange."

Figure 3.4   Comparative Biography Sheet

Name _____   Due date _____

DIRECTIONS: Circle the correct information or fill in the blanks below about your biographee.

I. BACKGROUND Poor Middle Class Wealthy   2. NUMBER OF SIBLINGS _____

3. PARENT OCCUPATION   Mother _____   Father _____

4. MARITAL STATUS _____   5. NUMBER OF CHILDREN _____

6. MILITARY SERVICE _____

7. VOLUNTEER WORK (Peace Corps etc.) _____

8. RELIGIOUS/ETHNIC BACKGROUND _____

9. EDUCATION (highest grade, degree obtained) _____

10. HOBBIES/Sports/Activities _____

11. OCCUPATION (Jobs) _____

12. LAST OCCUPATION _____

13. IMPORTANT ACHIEVEMENTS _____

14. WHO OR WHAT HELPED YOUR BIOGRAPHEE ACHIEVE HIS/HER GOALS? (inspirations)
_____

15. FAILURES OR SETBACKS _____

16. CHARACTER TRAITS (2-3) _____

17. LIST EXAMPLES OF WAYS YOUR BIOGRAPHEE SET GOALS _____

18. LIST SIMILAR CHARACTER TRAITS YOU AND YOUR BIOGRAPHEE SHARE _____
_____

Paraphrasing: A Collaborative Literacy Activity for Elementary Creatively Gifted Students

This collaborative literacy activity can be successfully accomplished by fourth-grade students. It will help prepare them for completing future individual research projects. Many students have difficulty putting information into their own words, and this activity will introduce and teach this skill prior to using paraphrasing in their independent research. In addition to strategy #7, this activity makes use of strategy #9, "Looking at the same information from different viewpoints," and strategy #3, "Creating awareness of a problem to be solved, a possible future need, or a difficulty to be faced." The lesson teaches a number of skills, including dictionary skills and locating keywords. Working in collaborative literacy groups, the students can work to reach consensus and then plan their work in order to complete a group project.

The materials needed for the lesson include a copy of the Emma Lazarus poem "The New Colossus," white construction paper, a dictionary or thesaurus, markers, paper, and pencils. As students work in collaborative groups of three, each student will receive a copy of the poem. Each group is to think of two thoughts or connections they can make regarding the poem. This activity involves the students in the preliminary use of paraphrasing as a literacy skill.

"The New Colossus" by Emma Lazarus

Not like the brazen giant of Greek fame,

With conquering limbs astride from land to land;

Here at our sea-washed, sunset gates shall stand

A mighty woman with a torch, whose flame

Is the imprisoned lightning, and her name

Mother of Exiles. From her beacon-hand

Glows world-wide welcome; her mild eyes command

The air-bridged harbor that twin cities frame.

"Keep, ancient lands, your storied pomp!" cries she

With silent lips. "Give me your tired, your poor,

Your huddled masses yearning to breathe free,

The wretched refuse of your teeming shore,

Send these, the homeless, tempest-tost to me,

I lift my lamp beside the golden door!"

The groups, working for approximately 20 minutes, are to circle unfamiliar or colorful words in the poem with the colored markers; then they can decide who is going to look up the unfamiliar words, and then each student writes down at least two thoughts or interpretations of the words and shares them with the other two group members. The students may need to share their interpretations with the teacher if they need assistance. Then the students write the exact words of the poem on construction paper in quotations. Some students may want to illustrate their two thoughts, which will engage the creatively gifted students. The group's thoughts can be compiled to make a class book that the students may want to share with another class or with their parents.

The following example is from Law (2005). The lines of the poem are in quotations, followed by the students' thoughts in italics.

"Not like the brazen giant of Greek fame,

With conquering limbs astride from land to land;"

Not like the shameless Greek giant

That overcame country after country

"Here at our sea-washed sunset gates shall stand

A mighty woman with a torch, whose flame"

At sundown in the ocean, tall gates will stand

A strong woman with a flame of glowing light will greet newcomers of foreign lands

"Is imprisoned lightning, and her name

Mother of Exiles. From her beacon-hand"

The Statue of Liberty welcomes refugees world-wide.

While her light guides them to her

"Glows world-wide welcome; her mild eyes command

The air-bridged harbor that twin cities frame."

From the torch she holds gleams a greeting and welcome to the world

Her serene eyes watch over the harbor that two cities surround

"Keep, ancient lands, your storied pomp!" cries she

With silent lips. "Give me your tired, your poor,"

Keep your lands that you boast of with your stories and traditions,

she says to the older countries that surround her.

But bring in your weary, your destitute, those who want freedom.

"Your huddled masses yearning to be free,

The wretched refuse of your teeming shore,"

All people wanting freedom and independence

The unwanted of your country.

"Send these, the homeless, tempest-tost to me.

I lift my lamp beside the golden door!"

Send me your troubled people seeking a new life

I welcome them to freedom in America

Abstract Nursery Rhymes

This activity can be successfully accomplished by students from kindergarten to second grade; it involves gifted students with learning disabilities and underachieving gifted students in sequencing and develops their skill in making symbolic abstractions and relationships. It builds on strategy #8 of the Torrance Incubation model, "Freeing from inhibited mindsets." It engages the high energy of the creatively gifted student and the gifted student with emotional behavior disorder, and the active fun inherent in the activity makes it a successful lesson. The following case study presents an example of the activity.

Case Study

Mrs. Foster meets her first graders at the door and begins reciting "Humpty Dumpty sat on a wall, Humpty Dumpty had a great fall. All of the King's horses and all of the King's men couldn't put Humpty Dumpty together again." By the time all of the children have entered the room, all are eagerly chanting the nursery rhyme. Then Mrs. Foster calls the students to the story rug and asks, "What is a symbol?" Mark says, "It is a sign," and Tom says, "It's like a stop sign." Molly says, "It's like a smiley face." "Or a frowning face," adds Steve. Mrs. Foster holds up a square, and asks, "Is this a symbol?" They all agree, and then they add that a triangle is a symbol as well. Mrs. Foster gives Molly a yellow circle and Tom a red circle, and asks, "What do these colors make you think of?" The students begin to respond: fire, blood, danger. Then Leah says, "It makes me think of happy. I like red."

Mrs. Foster then asks the students to go to their writing center and work in collaborative groups of four. Each group receives a copy of the nursery rhyme and several paper shapes (circle, square, triangle, rectangle), and Mrs. Foster asks them to think of how they can use the shapes to recite the rhyme.

Mrs. Foster moves among the five groups and encourages the students to recite "Humpty Dumpty." One group puts the circle on the square. "That's a good idea," she says, "What are you thinking?" "The rectangle looks like a wall, and the circle can be Humpty," says Melanie. At this point, when the other students hear Melanie's response, they all begin to reproduce Humpty as a circle, and the wall as a rectangle. Mrs. Foster asks the children to decide what colors and shapes they would like to use to represent each character and event. When they finish, they share their work with one another. Then each group decides on another rhyme, and they try to guess the title of the new nursery rhyme. Figure 3.5 on the next page contains an example.

Fleith (2000) and Rejskind (2000) have suggested a number of ways to demonstrate the creativity consciousness and creative attitudes that Mrs. Foster demonstrates in the case study.

- Maintain a psychologically safe classroom environment.
- Help students become aware of their creativity.
- Recognize and reward each child's creativity.
- Encourage fantasy and imagination.
- Accept students as they are.
- Give positive, constructive evaluation.
- Help students resist peer pressure to conform.
- Recognize students' strengths, abilities, and interests.

Figure 3.5   Humpty Dumpty Example

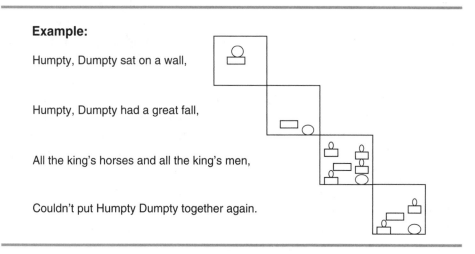

- Encourage questions, different responses, humor, and risk-taking.
- Be aware that a child's difficult behavior could be a manifestation of creativity.

In discussing the lesson, Mrs. Foster shared that she was able to use all of the ideas of Fleith (2000) and Rejskind (2000) except helping students resist peer pressure to conform. When Melanie gave her idea, all of the children quickly followed her response. Mrs. Foster's introduction of using colors steered the activity toward a new direction and encouraged the students to make more than one response.

For twice-exceptional students who have emotional behavior disorder, there are behavioral strategies involved in self-regulation that can involve them in checking their own progress or quality of work—for example, examining their actions during the learning process.

SELF-REGULATION

Students with emotional behavior disorders can learn to evaluate and understand the consequences of their actions. In self-evaluation and reflection, gifted students with emotional behavior disorders can learn to analyze task to determine what the teacher expects and to decide if they want to put in the time and effort necessary to complete it. It is equally important that students with special needs learn to reflect on their self-instructions, feedback, attentiveness, and self-talk (Reis, 2004).

Self-regulation enables students to develop and learn constructive behaviors that can positively affect their learning. Students with high levels of self-regulation are able to focus on the process of learning and feel that they are in control of achieving their goals. Self-regulation includes organizing and transforming information, planning and setting goals, and keeping records (Reis, 2004).

For twice-exceptional students who are gifted and learning disabled or gifted and emotional behavior disordered, self-regulation strategies can include learning how to memorize more efficiently and how to improve their written and verbal language. Many twice-exceptional students are under-achievers; however, not all underachievers are twice-exceptional. Examples of skills to help build self-regulation include using mnemonics to memorize important material by remembering the first letter of each word, and using imagery to remember diagrams or to visualize concepts. Another strategy that builds self-regulation is assisting other students by teaching the material to them, or making sample questions that can be used in collaborative study sessions. Performance rubrics for self-regulation are helpful in providing direction for self-assessment and teacher assessment, as indicated in Figure 3.6 on the next page.

When twice-exceptional students think about the consequences of their action, they may want to ask themselves: What will happen if I do not complete my assignment? Through reflection, they can come to understand that if one fails to turn in homework, there are serious consequences.

It is also important that twice-exceptional students learn how to provide themselves rewards for becoming more self-regulated and meeting their goals. They can identify the rewards that they enjoy, such as playing video games, talking on the phone, or watching television. Upon completion of a task, they can reward themselves for their positive action and for delayed self-gratification. Self-talk is helpful, such as "If I read this chapter in history, I can watch one half-hour of television, and then go back to study the questions at the end of the chapter."

Strategies that work well for gifted students with emotional behavior disorders, such as Rebecca in the personal reflection at the beginning of this chapter, include visualization, contract reading, bibliotherapy, and Book Buddies. Visualization provides the twice-exceptional student a creative and quieting activity that can stimulate personal insight, and journal writing similar to Rebecca's journal entry can lead to meaningful insights. Contract reading, in which students agree to read for a purpose with definite dates for completion, is also very helpful. Figure 3.7 (see page 64) shows a reading contract for Rebecca.

In her reading contract, Rebecca agreed to read *Hope for the Flowers* by Trina Paulus, and to read it to a fifth-grade class at an adjacent elementary school. She and her teacher developed criteria for self-evaluation, and Rebecca generated her questions for the fifth-grade students on the basis of the Taylor model (1963). She reflected on her own thoughts about the book, including striving for no clear goal and following the crowd without thinking, which represented personal problems for her. In a sense, Rebecca was engaging in bibliotherapy as she read and planned the questions for the younger students. D'Alessandro (1990) said that reading about others with similar problems and seeing how the characters in a story solve their difficulties can provide important insights for students, particularly gifted students, with emotional behavior disorders, who read from an aesthetic stance that personalize their reading.

Figure 3.6   Self-Regulation Performance Rubric

Name: Date:	Self		Peer		Teacher	
Item	Quality Effort	Not Yet	Quality Effort	Not Yet	Quality Effort	Not Yet
1. Worked toward goals established by the group						
2. Helped resolve conflict within the group						
3. Individual contributions were on time						
4. Individual contributions were of high quality and displayed high level of effort						
5. Was a leader when the group needed direction and a follower when the group needed cooperation						
6. Showed respect for ideas and points of view of others						
7. Helped others when they asked for it and it was appropriate						
8. Followed the established rules that helped maintain order in the class when working in groups						
9. Tried to improve the team product						
10. Remained on task and helped to get the group on task						
11. Displayed high standards and expected the same from other group members						
12. Had fun while learning						

Figure 3.7 Reading Contract

Name: Rebecca   **Date work to be completed:** 4/22/04

Description of work to be completed:

Read the Trina Paulus book *Hope for the Flowers* and plan an activity that can be introduced to elementary school students (grade 5). Read to the students once a day for a week to complete the book. and then do the activity on the last day. I will make 5 questions using the Taylor model of Academic. Predicting. Conununicating, Creative, and Evaluation questions.

Signed *Rebecca*

Self-Evaluation: Did I read slowly and distinctly. show the pictures. and answer questions? Did I plan an activity to extend the story that was doable? I will journal my activity.

My questions: Academic: Who wrote *Hope for the Flowers?*
Answer: Trina Paulus

Predicting: The caterpillars are climbing up the tower, do you think they will reach the top?
Answer: They do and there is nothing there.

Creative: If you were to change this story to make it more interesting, what would you add?
Answer: Any response is OK.

Communication: If Yellow and Stripe were to try and tell someone what happened, what would they say?
Answer: We saw everybody climbing, so we started climbing too—we didn't know why we were climbing, and when we got there, there was nothing on top.

Evaluation: What do you think Trina Paulus was trying to tell us? What is the big idea in the book?
Answer: Sometimes when we follow the crowd and do what others do, we may not know why. In the end, there is no result, or answer. The story emphasizes the importance of thinking things through.

Teacher Evaluation (Rubric):
Plan appropriate lesson and carry it out with 5th grade lesson based on Taylor model.

Parent comments and signature: _____

Why Not Use Gifted Literacy Strategies for All Students?

Teachers can extend the self-regulation student performance rubric: Younger students can use this form by creating pictures to portray the criteria being evaluated.

Teachers can adapt strategies by grade levels: Older students can use the assessment to evaluate their peers. Teachers can adapt the language of the assessment by adding the words "My Peer" to the beginning of each statement.

Teachers can use strategies across content areas: Content-area teachers can easily use the performance rubric by adding content specific statements such as, "Organized the science or math manipulatives prior to beginning my work."

TEACHERS PUTTING IDEAS INTO ACTION

What Does It Mean to Be Learning Disabled?

Select one of the books below to read and reflect on how a gifted, learning-disabled student views the world. Find one other teacher and share your new insight.

Albert, L. (1976). *But I'm Ready to Go.* Scarsdale, NY: Bradbury Press.

Gibson, J. (1980). *Do Bananas Chew Gum?* NY: Lathrop.

Hunter, E. (1969). *Sue Ellen.* New York: Houghton Mifflin.

Lasker, J. (1974). *He's My Brother.* Chicago: Albert Whitman.

Smith, D. B. (1975). *Kelly's Creek.* New York: Crowell.

Figure 3.8   Student Choice Menu

Explore a State	Explore Exploration	Explore a Place
Write to the state tourism office or visit their Web site to create a travel brochure for the state.	Using refdesk.com, find out all you can about the word *exploration:* what does it mean? What are its translations, synonyms, or rhyming words?	Take a virtual tour of the White House, Mars, or the human body by visiting the bookmarked exploration sites. Write a review of the site you visit.
Explore the Famous Investigate the life of a famous woman by visiting the National Women's History Web site. Imagine you are her and write a diary entry.	**Explore Your Own Idea** Find out about anything you'd like to know about exploration. You decide the content, process, and product. See me for a contract.	**Explore a Book** Read an e-book by or about an explorer or one that involves an exploration. Create a review, diorama, bookmark, or any other product for keen readers.
Explore a Topic Venture on a Webquest with 2 or 3 friends. Follow the instructions and explore a topic: animals, people, places.	**Explore Art** Take a tour of the National Gallery of Art. In the role of an art critic, choose an artist or style of art and write a critique.	**Explore an Explorer** Using the *Kids' Address Book* or an ask-an-expert Web site, get in touch with an explorer. Ask them five interesting questions about their explorations.

Student Choice

Creative students thrive on choice, and Winebrenner (2001) suggested that a Choice Menu be used to open the door to individual student interests. Select one of the items from the Choice Menu in Figure 3.8 above and plan a lesson for a special-needs child. Tell why you think your selection meets the needs of the gifted and learning-disabled student, the gifted student with emotional behavior disorder, the underachieving student, or the creatively gifted student. Winebrenner said that teachers can bring the world right into their own classroom, opening doors for students and making learning more exciting than ever.

Questioning the Author (QtA)

This activity uses strategy #10 of the Torrance Incubation model, "Provocative questioning to make the students think of information in new ways." Gifted students enjoy this strategy, which helps to personalize the material for them. Think of a book that you have recently read for pleasure, and focus on the author's intent. What was the author trying to say? This type of abstract thinking is a well-developed skill that most gifted students have, but it can be further developed with a series of questions like the ones below. Using the most recent book that you have read, answer these questions:

- What was the author trying to say?
- What was the author's message?
- What was the author talking about?
- What did the author assume that you already knew?
- What did the author want you to discover?

When gifted students have opportunities to use the questioning the author (QtA) strategy with literature, they quickly see the connection between becoming more critical when listening to the radio or watching television and becoming aware of how important the intent of the author is in the message.

Humpty Dumpty Has a Friend: You Choose

Recall the graphic depiction of Humpty Dumpty in this chapter and select a nursery rhyme that you remember listening to as a child. Plan how you would introduce a lesson to a group of creatively gifted students, using the strategies in the Torrance Incubation model as a resource. Draw your own depiction of the nursery rhyme that you select and share your drawing with another reader.

Who Has Seen the Wind? An April Rain Song

Poetry can stimulate the creative thoughts of gifted students, and reading and comparing two poems written about the same theme, such as weather, can be a useful way to stretch their minds. This activity uses strategy #9, "Looking at things from a different point of view," from the Torrance Incubation model. Read the two poems and think about how each poet describes the weather. Which one do you prefer? What seasons do you think the poets might be describing? Try writing your own poem about your favorite season. Share your poem with someone who loves poetry.

"Who Has Seen the Wind?" by Christina Rossetti

Who has seen the wind?
   Neither I nor you.

But when the leaves hang trembling,
   The wind is passing thro'.

Who has seen the wind?
   Neither you nor I:

But when the leaves bow down their heads,
   The wind is passing by.

"April Rain Song" by Langston Hughes*

Let the rain kiss you

Let the rain beat upon your head with silver liquid drops,

Let the rain sing you a lullaby

The rain makes still pools on the sidewalk

The rain makes running pools in the gutter

The rain plays a little sleep-song on our roof at night

And I love the rain.

When you use this activity with gifted students with special needs, gifted students with learning disabilities, or underachieving gifted students, you may want to have them dictate their poem to you. Creatively gifted students may want to illustrate their poems.

Incubation Model Application

Select one of the strategies from Stage 1 of the Torrance Incubation model, identify the gifted student with special needs whom you want to engage in an activity, and plan a lesson that uses the strategy you chose. Share your lesson with another teacher. Reflect on the use of the model for planning lessons for gifted students with special needs.

SUMMARY

In this chapter, we presented the characteristics of special-needs students or twice-exceptional students, including gifted students with emotional behavior disorders and gifted, learning-disabled student. In addition, we listed and discussed the special needs and characteristics of the underachieving gifted and the creatively gifted student. We demonstrated and validated that the ideas and suggestions for activities are research-based. We introduced the Torrance Incubation model (Torrance & Sisk, 1997) and demonstrated activities for gifted students with special needs through the use of selected strategies from Stage 1. We presented the concept that an ill-fitting environment, including home and school, may be part of the problem for many students with special needs who are underachieving and having difficulty in social situations. We provided engaging activities for teachers who want to extend the knowledge and strategies introduced in the chapter with the expressed intent that teachers can modify and use these activities with their special-needs, gifted children, and in most cases with all students.

---

*From *The Collected Poems of Langston Hughes* by Langston Hughes, © 1994 by the Estate of Langston Hughes. Used by permission of Alfred A. Knopf, a division of Random House, Inc.

PART II

Building Collaborative Literacy Communities in the Regular Classroom

Developing and Creating an Enriched Literacy Collaborative

Sheri R. Parris and Cathy Collins Block

PERSONAL REFLECTION

Before beginning this chapter, we interviewed several gifted students to collect their opinions on how their schools could better serve the special-needs and gifted students. Three of their answers, shown below, summarize the ideas we gleaned from these valuable interviews.

Student 1

In an ideal educational setting, I would be able to choose each of my professors [or teachers] for any of my subjects from any college [or school] in the world. For example, if I wanted to study . . . with a world-renowned philosopher teaching in Spain [I could. I could use] my interactive computer monitor (complete with an English-speaking translator). I would be able to not only see and hear the professor, but participate in classroom discussions as well. In an ideal setting, there would be no age minimums for participation in research programs. I could use my anthropological knowledge by assisting on international archeological digs. In an ideal setting, there would be no traditional grading system. Quarterly student evaluations in my program would be based on a point system, wherein points would be deducted from a 100-point scale for incomplete work, truancy, etc. In order to remain in my program, a minimum of 90 points [would have to] be maintained at all times. Allowing every student to begin the school year with a perfect score of 100 points is psychologically very productive, as all students are on an equal footing. [It would also] make everyone essentially a top student . . . verifying the confidence that the school places in each of its students. By creating a noncompetitive learning environment, students [would] work together in harmony to maintain their top [100 point] scores.

I have always found our current grading [and evaluation] system [which requires that each person has] to claw [their] way to the top, where only a limited number of As are available, [is] antiquated and counterproductive [because it pits] student against student, thereby destroying any cooperative and/or harmonious atmosphere that would make learning exciting and fun. In my 100-point system, everyone [would] begin at the top, so [that] the school is telling you that you are the best before you even begin, [and everyone would have] no reason to think otherwise. In our current grading system, we are conditioned to fight for an A from the first grade, bringing discord into the classroom in the crucial formative years of a student. It also destroys the joy that the camaraderie of learning [in a literacy collaborative] can bring.

Student 2

[Students want more of the following:] availability of courses; wide options for AP and honors classes; three levels of classes (regular education, honors, and advanced placement); advising to make you aware of what counts in college and how to stay ahead, [as well as] open discussion.

Student 3

[I want all schools to reduce] class sizes, but not to make them too small. English needs to be a small class. The school needs to take into consideration who they are staffing [as teachers. There should be] high standards to get in as a teacher.

COLLABORATIVE LITERACY AT WORK

This chapter introduces an instructional model that incorporates highly effective instructional strategies (often reserved for gifted and talented programs) that can be incorporated into the basic lesson plans that teachers already use. This model is called CLIMB (Parris & Block, 2006). It enables teachers to create and enrich literacy collaboratives by infusing collaborative gifted and talented ideals into daily literacy instruction.

RESEARCH BASE FOR COLLABORATIVE LITERACY ENVIRONMENTS

In response to the often asked question, "Is there a special environment and curriculum needed for gifted students vs. all other students?," Sandra Kaplan (2003), a leader in the field of gifted education, responded:

> A review of the literature indicates that pedagogical practices such as Socratic Dialogue, Inquiry Training, and Creative Problem Solving are essential to teaching gifted students. . . . However, the idea that these pedagogical strategies are appropriate for gifted students does not imply that they were designed only for gifted students (p. 1).

> The crest from whence we teach,
> How to use this fleeting time?
> Dreams determined—within reach.
> We offer footholds for to climb.
>   *"Climb"*—Sheri R. Parris, 2005*

CLIMB (Parris & Block, 2006) is an acronym that provides a simple way to remember the five essential components of this model. We have coined the term Collaborative Literacy Inquiry (CLI), to express a collaborative approach to literacy that incorporates best practices from gifted and talented curricula into daily instruction for all students. The first three letters designate the type of activity being implemented, **C**ollaborative, **L**iteracy, and **I**nquiry. The final two letters express the other key components in collaborative literacy activities: **M**anagement and **B**ridge. CLIMB is a model designed to increase the potency of any literacy unit.

The CLI component is partially based on research from the National Research Center on Gifted and Talented (Reis et al., 2003). A summary of these strategies that have proven successful for differentiating instruction and curriculum for talented readers appears in Table 4.1. This model is also partially derived from research that supports Shared Inquiry (SI), a group study technique made prominent by the Great Books Foundation (www.greatbooks.org). SI is a method of learning that involves students reading a literature selection and then developing a collective understanding by incorporating prior experience, analysis, and reasoning. Deizmann and Watters (1995) conclude that the most effective programs for gifted and talented students foster environments in which "they are able to share experiences with their peers" (p. 9). CLIMB supports these learning principles while providing for more in-depth projects that require additional structure and more extended thinking processes.

With CLIMB, students work as teammates to investigate and then create a meaningful outcome based on a specific literacy objective. Collaborative group

---

*SOURCE: The poem, "Climb," is used by permission of Alfred A. Knopf, a division of Random House, Inc. Contributor, Sheri R. Parris, Doctoral Candidate in Reading Education at the University of North Texas.

Table 4.1   Differentiated Instructional or Curricular Strategies to Challenge Talented Readers

1	Substitution of regular reading material with more advanced trade books or basal material	Durkin, 1990; Renzulli, Smith, & Reis, 1982; Savage, 1983; VanTassel-Baska, 1996
2	Appropriate use of technology and the Web	Alvermann, Moon, & Hagood, 1999; Leu, 2000; 2001
3	More complex assigned reading	Baskin & Harris, 1980; Halstead, 1994; Hauser & Nelson, 1988
4	More complex assigned writing	Dean, 1998
5	Independent reading choices	Guthrie & Wigfield, 2000; Savage, 1983
6	Independent writing options	Davis & Johns, 1989
7	Independent study opportunities	Feldhusen, 1986; Renzulli, 1977; Treffinger & Barton, 1988
8	Grouping changes (within class or across classes)	Kulik & Kulik, 1991; Rogers, 1991; Sandby-Thomas, 1983
9	Independent project choices based on student interests	McPhail, Pierson, Freeman, Goodman, & Ayappa, 2000; Reis & Renzulli, 1989; Renzulli, 1977; Renzulli & Reis, 1997
10	Substitution of regular reading instructional strategies with other options	Bates, 1984; Baum, 1985; Dean, 1998; Dooley, 1993; Levande, 1993; Mangieri & Madigan, 1984; McCormick & Swassing, 1982; Reis & Renzulli, 1989; Renzulli & Reis, 1997
11	Great Books	Daniels, 1994
12	Advanced questioning skills	Bloom et al., 1956
13	Interest assessment and interest-based reading opportunities	Reis & Renzulli, 1989; Renzulli, 1977; Renzulli & Reis, 1997

work allows students to become actively involved in the learning process (Kauchak & Eggen, 2003). It is important to remember that, in general, groups with more than four members can be difficult to manage and are not recommended (Cohen, 1986). In addition, a basic characteristic of collaborative learning is that students are not grouped according to ability levels, achievement, interests, or any other characteristic, as homogeneous grouping can deny all students the opportunity to share unique questions, ideas, and solutions with each other. A key feature of a collaborative literacy environment is that all students should contribute evenly to the group. Also, educators must ensure that gifted or more advanced students are not pressured to serve as tutors or "junior teachers" for struggling students. Such "instructional aides positions" have been demonstrated to limit the growth of more advanced students (Robinson, 1990). To combat this tendency, teachers should structure the CLIMB so that all group members must prepare individual responses for each of the major components in a project before they share their ideas with other group members. In addition, all members should be required to explain the reasoning behind this input. One way to ensure this happens is for students to keep a record, or journal, of each group member's input.

Barbara Clark (2004) recommends the following guidelines for group literacy activities for gifted children. They should (a) have access to intellectual peers, (b) share ideas verbally in depth, (c) have a longer incubation time for ideas, (d) pursue ideas and integrate new ones without forced closure or product demands, (e) build productive thinking abilities, and (f) draw generalizations and test them.

IDEAS INTO ACTION

When using collaborative group activities for the first time, teachers should initially limit students' choices and steadily scaffold the groups toward independent functioning. Supportive supervision should focus on the following components:

- How to select a collaborative literacy group topic (when applicable).
- How to develop an effective, incremental timeline.
- How to establish group inquiry and management procedures.
- How to plan, create, and present the outcome of their work so it becomes a "bridge" that leads beyond the immediate project outcome.

CLIMB—Instructional Component

The planning stages of CLIMB involve several steps. First, teachers introduce the common unit of instruction and literacy objectives. Next, teachers provide background information and preview activities to activate students' prior knowledge. Literature or other text selections that will be common reading for this project should be read by all students at this time. To ensure basic comprehension of the material, students should respond to a selection of base questions (see Figure 4.1) in a small-group or whole-class setting. Such questions will assess pupils' understanding of the teachers' introductory content. This initial exchange will launch the circulation of ideas among students.

Individual groups may now choose a path of inquiry that is compatible with their interests, talents, and learning styles. Each group sets its own goals and writes an outline of the activities they propose for their path of inquiry. During the pursuit of an original question, more valuable inquiries may surface. These can also be explored, but the original questions create the focus and driving force for the present CLIMB project.

The CLIMB project's bridge will also explicitly state (or demonstrate) how all learners generated, explored, and discussed their own questions, and employed characteristics of mindful learning, which is the continuous creation of new categories, openness to new information, and an implicit awareness of more than one perspective (Langer, 1997).

Groups should be instructed to maintain a risk-free environment for all members in order to foster an atmosphere in which it is safe to challenge other members' reasoning and ideas, as well as give constructive feedback to each

Figure 4.1   Question Types and Examples

BASE QUESTIONS	**REACH QUESTIONS**
Memory (recall of information)	**Evaluative (making judgments)**
Literal questions: who, what, when, where, why.	How would you feel if _____ happened?
Does this make you think of anything else you have read?	What do you need to do next?
Would you like to be one of the people in this? Who? Why?	Can you think of another way we could do this?
What parts of this did you especially like or dislike?	How did you solve this problem?
What did you mean by _____? Can you give me an example?	How did you come up with this, and what helped you the most?
Did the author make you feel any specific emotion?	How could we go about finding if this is true?
Can you describe the _____ ?	Do you have good evidence for believing that?
If you had a chance to talk to this author, what would you speak to him or her about?	Do you think this story could really happen? Explain.
Why do you suppose the author gave this title? Can you think of another appropriate title?	
Why is this an important story to share?	
Convergent (connecting information)	**Divergent ("What if . . .?")**
Yes, that's right, but how did you know?	What were your thoughts when you decided whether to _____ or _____? How did you decide?
What are your reasons for saying that?	Who do you think would benefit from reading this book? Why?
What do you (or author) mean by ____ ?	
Why does this go here instead of there?	If you were (name a character in the book), what would you have done differently? Why?
How did you know that?	
If _____ happened, what else could happen?	Is there an idea in this book that you would like to see happen in your school or community? Why?
Does this story remind you of any other ones? Why? What specific characteristics do they have in common?	
What do you know that you did not know before reading this?	
Did your thoughts and feelings change as you were reading? How and why?	
Did you have to remember anything that you already knew? Why?	

other. Encourage students to comment on the responses of classmates before summarizing or moving to another question (Metts, 2005).

Designing Questions

CLIMB is designed to use four common question types, as described by Metts (2005). These types are described below, and sample questions are listed in Figure 4.1.

Memory questions: Recall of information.

Convergent questions: Connection of known details to infer relationships among pieces of information.

Evaluative questions: Making judgments as to the logic, reasonableness, or worth of an idea or argument. Evaluations might also be based on ethics, practicality, values, etc.

Divergent questions: Imagining new possibilities; original thinking that cannot be tested directly against known information. "What if" types of questions.

Base and Reach Questions

These four categories of CLIMB questions can be grouped into two levels, "base questions" and "reach questions," as described next. Elementary students need only understand the two main concepts (base and reach) and the types of questions found in each category. Secondary students will benefit by additionally understanding the four types of questions found within the above two levels of questions (see Figure 4.1).

Base questions (Parris & Block, 2006) provide the foundation for inquiry learning. They require a mastery of the basic content to be answered correctly. For example, a base question could begin with who, what, when, where, or why. These inquiries are generally journalistic or factual questions and have a relatively limited range of answers, which require little, if any, creativity or higher level thinking skills to answer. These questions include, but are not limited to, the "memory" and "convergent" categories listed above. Base questions should require that learners have become familiar with the content area information relevant to their CLIMB study.

Reach questions (Parris & Block, 2006) require learners to do just that— reach and stretch their capacity to use creative and analytical thinking skills. They enable students to use available data, conduct research, and explore other resources relative to the present inquiry. Reach questions are open-ended (Johnson, 2003). Students use these higher level thinking questions to generate their own discussions. They require learners to seek information from outside the required texts. Reach questions include, but are not limited to, the "evaluative" and "divergent" categories listed above. They enable learners to express and test their views against the insights and perspectives of their peers. In addition, they assess new information for its validity and applicability to the group's goal or goals. Figure 4.2 presents a summary of all these steps in the CLI instructional components of CLIMB.

Sample of a CLIMB Literacy Collaborative

Throughout the planning, implementing, and evaluating components of CLIMB, students should have copies of Figures 4.1 and 4.2 to reference. These figures can be enlarged and mounted in a place in the classroom where all groups can see them easily. Alternatively, every student could receive a copy of each.

Through every CLIMB literacy collaborative, students use the questions in Figure 4.1 to move them through each step in the CLIMB process described in Figure 4.2. When CLIMB is in action, the classroom will be filled with vibrant

Figure 4.2 Summary of Steps in the CLIMB

Model for Literacy Collaboratives

STEP 1: Introduction of topic, literacy objective, and assigned list of base questions related to the project.

STEP 2: (INQUIRY—BASE): Initial reading of assigned text(s) and answer the list of base questions. Base questions must be correctly completed before progressing to step 3.

STEP 3: (INQUIRY—REACH): Teacher introduces list of reach (open-ended) questions. Group members discuss the reach questions and begin formulating additional questions of their own. Each group member is responsible for keeping a log of the questions that he or she generates from the conversation, as well as all plausible responses to the question. Text(s) should be used during all discussions.

STEP 4: Group management strategies should be applied throughout the activity. Specific strategies and protocols will vary from classroom to classroom. The critical factor is that all students understand and are held accountable for the group management processes.

STEP 5: (BRIDGE): Implementation of the extended thinking component of the activity.

---

literacy collaborative, high-level, purposeful, goal-attaining conversations. Tinzmann et al. (1990) provide a description of such ideal discussion:

> Members discuss their approaches to solving a problem, explain their reasoning, and defend their work. Hearing one student's logic prompts other students to consider an alternative interpretation. Students are thus challenged to re-examine their own reasoning. [For instance,] when three students in a group ask a fourth student to explain and support her ideas, that is, to make her thinking public, [the principles of CLI will be enacted.] [To participate, this fourth student must] frequently examine and develop her [own] concepts [for herself] as she talks [aloud. A second example occurs] when one student has an insight about how to solve a difficult problem; the others in the group learn how to use a new thinking strategy sooner than if they had worked on their own. Thus, students engaged in interaction often exceed what they can accomplish by working independently.

CLIMB—Management Component

They see the pattern, understand the order, experience the vision.

—Peter Drucker (as cited in Gerber, 1995)

The term management is defined as the act of handling or controlling something successfully, as well as the skillful handling or use of resources (Encarta World English Dictionary, 1999). In CLIMB, all students are given increasing responsibility to "manage" their own learning experience. Whereas many gifted and talented programs espouse the idea of reaching for a potential without limits and for a challenging and stimulating activity that invites creativity, CLIMB gives learners the opportunity to have responsibility. It does so because success in any endeavor demands the ability to manage it. The term management, however, is in no way intended to imply that "order" in some way trumps "knowledge and creativity." All three are necessary components in CLIMB.

Figure 4.3   The Management Component of CLIMB

STEP 1: Create a timeline, including establishment of progress checks (benchmarks). Identify group goal(s) and strategies.

STEP 2: Provide a record or summary of key points as they emerge. Leave time at the end of group sessions for students to write key points from the discussion or list important questions that remain for them.

STEP 3: Research—Draw connections between the literacy objective, present knowledge, and incoming knowledge. Includes reading, discussing, seeking outside sources of information to expand, alter, or confirm hypotheses or opinions; brainstorming; preliminary project plan. Focus on long-term, open-ended ideas and solutions rather than short-term "let's find an answer and finish this."

CLIMB management demands three abilities. First, students develop the skills of providing a structure and maintaining order. It is precisely these competencies that provide the foundational support for growth and the ability to "climb" to higher levels of achievement. These abilities are developed through self-regulating activities such as monitoring progress, adjusting, and maintenance of productive questioning. Because objectives are reached more easily within a group that shares responsibility for learning (Tinzmann et al., 1990), during CLIMB activities students are asked to keep a record of their own contributions and the corresponding responses of their teammates. When students are required to record this process, dialogue is more likely to stay on-track, meaningful, and directed toward the group's objective. They also keep track of the amount of time they spend on certain activities to ensure that they will meet their group's and class's deadlines. This "time log" makes individual management strengths and weaknesses visible, documents the activities taken to manage the group-defined literacy experience, records research, creates a research "trail" or bibliography using APA format, and shows how ideas developed to answer the group's questions. The steps in the M component of CLIMB (Effective Management) are listed in Figure 4.3.

CLIMB—Bridge Component

The term bridge is defined as something that provides a link, connection, or means of coming together (Encarta World English Dictionary, 1999). It is typical to use the term "product" to describe the concluding component of a group project or activity. Unfortunately, too many times, this term denotes and becomes a boundary for learning when students prepare a project's outcome. With CLIMB, we propose a concluding component that removes this finality connotation. The B component of CLIMB provides more room for extending the positive ripple-of-learning possibilities of a project because it focuses on long-term effects and ramifications (extensions) of student effort and knowledge gain. A bridge need not be a huge project, as it is constructed on the basis of the time and resources available. The teacher may pose one or more "bridge" questions at the onset of a group project, such as "What would happen if your ideas were applied throughout our school [community, nation]?" Students should keep the question(s) in mind as they pursue the CLIMB project, then revisit the question(s) as they begin to create the bridge component of the activity. These questions guide students' ideas to higher levels of universality and application. As a result, pupils (of all ability levels) begin their project explorations with application as well as content goals. Some additional questions may include:

- How can our work be distributed to help others outside our group?
- What must we consider as we begin our research so that people from all walks of life can improve their stations because of the time we will spend exploring solutions to this problem?
- What else needs to be added to our list of tasks to ensure that we will have taken all perspectives into consideration before we present our plan of action to the city council?

Even when the time is very limited and resource constraints are huge, as will be inherent with many projects, bridges can still be constructed as written plans for future action that identify and express possibilities for ongoing learning or solutions from the group's work.

Why Not Use Gifted Literacy Strategies for All Students?

How a teacher can extend the CLIMB strategy: This strategy can easily be extended by having students at all levels create their own collaborative learning analogy.

How a teacher can adapt strategy by grade levels: The size of the groups can vary depending on the classroom environment or ability levels of the students. CLIMB experts in the classroom can be trained to help more capable peers set up their own CLIMB communities.

How a teacher can use strategy across content areas: Teachers from different content areas can work together to look at current-events issues or problems and organize students to prepare a bridge project that will benefit the community.

In summary, a bridge focuses students' thinking on long-term ideas and their ramifications, rather than on merely, "Let's find an answer and finish this." Using the words "create a bridge to future learning or solutions" instead of "present your end product or conclusion" better enables groups to engage in critical inquiry and refection throughout a literacy collaboration. They will no longer be simply charged with "getting it right," but with generating outcomes that are thoughtful and meaningful for others. Building a bridge also makes it easier for them to see their work as an addition to humanity's body of knowledge, as a bridge others can cross with them into new territories, so their work continues in some way. Bridges are the outcome of the inquiry process and include elements of reflection, review, and/or enrichment as it relates to each group of student creators (Fluellen, 2003). The group "presentation" thus becomes a "progress celebration" (unveiling the bridge and the plan for the continuation of positive possibilities). After all, literacy is the tool designed to bring all people together.

Student Self-Management Assessment

It is important for students to be given opportunities to self-assess. This is a vital component in the development of independent thinkers and learners. Ee, Moore, & Atputhasamy (2003) found that students who reported knowledge of self-regulated learning had a significantly greater disposition to initiate self-regulated learning. In turn, self-regulated learning was positively linked to significantly higher literacy achievement.

SELF-EVALUATION FOR STUDENTS

The following eight evaluative objectives have been demonstrated to increase students' self-regulated and self-initiated learning in literacy collaboratives. The eight questions will help students internalize some general principles needed for success in any CLIMB activity. Teachers can give this evaluation, entitled the Literacy Collaborative Self-Management Assessment, to each student at the beginning and at the end of CLIMB projects, and vocabulary can be altered to fit the age level of the students. By receiving this assessment before a literacy collaborative activity, most students will begin to build a "compass" within themselves about how to engage in effective group interaction, which is also the cornerstone for effective group inquiry. To test younger students, kindergarten to grade 5, teachers can read Figure 4.4 orally to them individually or in small groups. Teachers can then identify which item each pupil needs to improve to become a stronger self-regulated learner and help them to develop a method of overcoming their lowest self-regulated ability.

To administer the Literacy Collaborative Self-Management Assessment in grades 6–12, copies of Figure 4.5 are distributed to all students. Teachers tell everyone to cover their answers so no one else can see what they wrote. Each item is read orally, and students circle the number that best represents their answer. When all items have been answered, students tally their total scores and place a star beside the items that have the lowest scores. Then they complete the last three statements on the assessment. Papers are returned to students after the CLIMB project is finished, at which point students are asked to reread their answers on the test. Teachers advise students that each item reflects a "negative" trait, and a low answer means that they need to increase that part of their responsibility as a group member. By decreasing the number of low answers and increasing the number of high answers during the course of the CLIMB project, students become more self-regulated and powerful learners. We suggest that a class discussion be held to ensure that everyone understands why these traits are so important to learning.

TEACHERS PUTTING IDEAS INTO ACTION

1. What are the recommendations you would make to implement collaborative learning at the grade level that you teach? List the three most important recommendations that would improve instruction in your building and tell why.

Figure 4.4   Literacy Collaborative Self-Management Assessment for Kindergarten to Grade 5

NAME: _____   DATE: _____

1. How I feel when someone else has a different idea from me.

   ☺   😐   ☹

2. How I feel when I am asked to discuss different ideas.

   ☺   😐   ☹

3. How I feel if I think I'll have to ask for help on a problem.

   ☺   😐   ☹

4. How I feel when I am in a group activity and I need to ask a question.

   ☺   😐   ☹

5. How I feel when I can do a project on my favorite topic, but it is not an easy project.

   ☺   😐   ☹

6. How I feel when I have thought of a good idea, but I still have to listen to everyone else's idea, too.

   ☺   😐   ☹

7. How I feel when I first start a long project and I have to decide how to get it done on time.

   ☺   😐   ☹

8. How I feel when I think up an idea for a project and then the teacher tells me to write out a plan for how to do it.

   ☺   😐   ☹

Figure 4.5   Literacy Collaborative Self-Management Assessment for Grades 6–12

NAME: _____   DATE: _____

1. When someone challenges my belief, I become even more resolved to retain it.

1	2	3	4	5
Always	Usually	50/50 chance I will	Sometimes	Never

2. When new ideas are presented to me, I am not interested in discussing them.

1	2	3	4	5
Always	Usually	50/50 chance I will	Sometimes	Never

3. When faced with a problem or challenge, I often wait for someone else to solve it or to help me before I start working on it.

1	2	3	4	5
Always	Usually	50/50 chance I will	Sometimes	Never

4. When I am in a group and become confused about what is said, I will remain silent and hope that someone else will ask questions, or that I can figure it out on my own.

1	2	3	4	5
Always	Usually	50/50 chance I will	Sometimes	Never

5. When I have the option to choose an assignment, I often choose the one that seems easiest, or in which I have the most prior knowledge.

1	2	3	4	5
Always	Usually	50/50 chance I will	Sometimes	Never

6. I believe that statements made in group meetings should be intended to forcefully persuade others that the perspective of the person speaking is correct.

1	2	3	4	5
Always	Usually	50/50 chance I will	Sometimes	Never

7. I have trouble meeting deadlines.

1	2	3	4	5
Always	Usually	50/50 chance I will	Sometimes	Never

8. I am better at thinking up ideas than planning how to get them done.

1	2	3	4	5
Always	Usually	50/50 chance I will	Sometimes	Never

9. To improve in my self-management during the next CLIMB project, I need to create a method to

_____

_____

[Students, write a paraphrase of the item 1–8 to which you had the lowest score.]

10. The methods I will use to improve my abilities in this area are _____

_____

_____

11. I will know I have improved in this area by / because / when _____

_____

_____

2. Implement CLIMB in your classroom. Keep a journal about the change it produces and why.

3. Use the following helpful Web sites to continue thinking about how to build a collaborative literacy environment.

> National Association for Gifted Children
> http://www.nagc.org
>
> The National Research Center on the Gifted and Talented
> http://www.gifted.uconn.edu/nrcgt.html
>
> World Council for Gifted and Talented Children
> http://www.worldgifted.org
>
> Council for Exceptional Children
> http://www.cec.sped.org
>
> Hoagie's Gifted Education Page
> http://www.hoagiesgifted.org
>
> Great Books Foundation (Shared Inquiry)
> http://www.greatbooks.org
>
> Rubric for Shared Inquiry
> http://www.stantoncollegeprep.org/explore/rubrics/sharedinquiry rubric.htm
>
> Fostering Effective Classroom Discussion: Online Resources
> http://www.mhhe.com/socscience/english/tc/pt/discussion/resources .htm

SUMMARY

There are many effective teaching strategies known to enhance instructional effectiveness for gifted and talented learners. This chapter describes a model (CLIMB) that combines teaching strategies often used in gifted and talented classrooms. More specifically, CLIMB is designed as a way to bring successful gifted and talented strategies to any collaborative literacy activity. The first three letters, **CLI**, define the activity component, collaborative literacy inquiry. The final two letters express the other key components in implementing the model: **M**anagement and **B**ridge. Thus, students gain experience in managing their own collaborative group during a CLIMB activity. The bridge component allows students to expand their critical thinking skills by finding a way in which their project could reach out and connect with the school or community. In contrast to the concept of a "final product," a bridge is the culmination of the group's efforts, which also include a plan or an actualization of future possibilities. In summary, CLIMB activities build a solid learning foundation for students by allowing them to develop strong individual and group management skills, giving them a foothold from which they can stretch their critical thinking and climb to higher levels on the literacy development continuum.

Building Collaborative Literacy in a Multicultural Classroom

Dorothy A. Sisk

Rosa, a child of migrant Mexican American parents, was selected by the school counselor to attend Saturday enrichment seminars for high-potential students at a nearby university. Rosa attended three courses in the semester-long program: creative writing; hands-on science, focusing on biology; and art, in which the students constructed puppets and wrote and produced a show for the parents and other students. Rosa was eager, attentive, and responsive, but when she was asked to return the next semester, shared her feelings of excitement concerning the new ideas she had experienced, particularly exploring who she could become. But Rosa also compared herself to a crab in a crab barrel. When she went back to her school, she said the students teased her about being "uppity." They wanted her to be like them. Rosa shared that being different, acting different, was too high a price to pay, and she decided not to return to the enrichment program.

COLLABORATIVE LITERACY AT WORK

This chapter examines the multicultural heritage of the United States and the need to view diversity in the classroom as a strength; the importance of multicultural education; and program adaptations with specific strategies that will meet the needs of advanced readers and gifted students like Rosa who face unique problems in developing their talents, and how those strategies used in gifted education can be used with all students. We discuss the research base for these program adaptations, followed by examples of Ideas into Action and Teachers Putting Ideas into Action to extend the content of the chapter.

The chapter goals are to

- Build an understanding of the multicultural heritage of the United States.
- Develop awareness of the growing diversity in the classrooms of today, and that diversity represents a rich resource.
- Develop awareness and knowledge of three program adaptations that have proved successful in multicultural settings.
- Develop awareness of the following characteristics of gifted students: ponders with depth and multiple perspectives; exhibits feelings and opinions from multiple perspectives; infers and connects concepts; enjoys self-directed learning; and anticipates and relates observations (Kingore, 2003).
- Develop knowledge of research-based literacy strategies that are appropriate for advanced readers and gifted students who may be culturally diverse.

RICH RESEARCH BASE: MULTICULTURAL HERITAGE

When the United States was founded, the population included speakers of many different languages, including French, German, Spanish, and hundreds of Native American languages, yet the founding fathers declared no official language. Over the past several decades, immigration patterns have changed; the number of immigrants from Europe has declined, and the number of immigrants coming from Central America, China, India, Korea, Laos, Mexico, the Philippines, and Vietnam has increased. According to the 2000 census, by the turn of the century, nearly 20% of all students will be considered limited English proficient (LEP), living in non-English-speaking homes, and receiving family assistance. Currently, the United States has approximately 30 million Latinos, making it the fifth-largest Hispanic country in the world (Romo, Bradfield, & Serrano, 2004).

Few teacher preparation programs have made modifications to adequately prepare teachers to change their curriculum, instruction, and assessment to accommodate the needs of the increasing number of multicultural students and classrooms (Crawford, 1999). Consequently, it is essential that school administrators step forward to build an understanding of the positive aspects inherent in a diverse student body, and to create opportunities for teachers and students to experience cultural diversity as a resource. One significant challenge for administrators to address is how to reduce the intolerance, bias, and racism that exist in classrooms. No one is born intolerant, biased, or racist; however, many children soon become aware that people around them are different, and they quickly surmise that human differences are in some way related to power and privilege (Ryan, 2003). A key to turning these early misconceptions around is engaging students in positive learning activities and experiences with diverse groups. This is particularly important for advanced readers and gifted students, who are sensitive and concerned about inequities (Kingore, 2003; Tolan 2003).

The rich diversity found in today's classrooms calls for teachers to consider ways of adapting the curriculum to ensure that all children can learn and develop to their full potential, including refugee students, who are making a transition to a better life (McBrien, 2003). In this chapter, we will discuss three program adaptations that have proved successful in multicultural settings. The first is the Two-Way Bilingual Program; the second is the Village English Activity, which places a great deal of emphasis on the home language of students and guides them in seeing relationships between the use of language and social and professional realities. The third, called Project Step-Up (Systematic Training of Educational Programs for Underserved Pupils), focuses on active learning to increase vocabulary and content knowledge.

RESEARCH BASE

The research base for Two-Way Bilingual Programs focuses on increasing the vocabulary and word knowledge of English language learners in dual-language programs. Slavin and Cheung (2004) reported that there is considerable evidence that teaching students to read in both their native language and in English is successful in closing the achievement gap. In Texas, students randomly assigned to classes in which instruction was primarily in Spanish in kindergarten and English in first and second grades performed higher on the Comprehensive Test of Basic Skills (CTBS) than students who were taught English only.

The Village English Activity links multicultural experiences with vocabulary development (Delpit, 1988). It is recommended as a strategy to help students see relationships between language use and the social and political realities in the United States (Au, 1993).

Project Step-Up (Sisk, 1994) encouraged wide reading as a means to develop vocabulary and engaged high-potential students in active learning. The students were provided opportunities to read self-selected books independently, and they received daily critical-thinking lessons. Reutzel and Hollingworth (1991) found that allowing children to read self-selected books 30 minutes every day resulted in significantly improved scores on reading comprehension tests. According to research, vocabulary instruction that provides only definitional information, such as dictionary activities, fails to improve comprehension significantly. However, active learning opportunities such as word webs, playing word games, and discussing new words in small groups or literature circles are more effective in building new knowledge and improving comprehension (Stahl, 1999).

The final Project Step-Up report to the U.S. Department of Education described the success of the collaborative program effort among the universities of Arizona, Arkansas, and Lamar in increasing the achievement of the participating students, with over 50% of the students demonstrating high achievement and high ability to qualify for the gifted programs in their schools (Sisk, 1994).

IDEAS INTO ACTION

Two-Way Bilingual Program

Two-Way Bilingual Programs have proved quite successful in developing dual-language proficiency in the participating students. Miami-Dade County Public Schools established a Two-Way Bilingual Program at Coral View Elementary School to develop fluent bilingualism in both their Spanish- and English-speaking students. The mostly Cuban Spanish-speaking students would begin each morning with lessons in Spanish, and have recess, lunch, art, and other content-area classes with English-speaking students in the afternoon. Conversely, the English-speaking Floridian students would begin each morning with English, and have recess, lunch, art, and content classes in Spanish in the afternoon. On standardized reading achievement tests, the English-speaking and Spanish-speaking Coral View students did as well as their counterparts at all English-speaking schools. Coral View administrators and teachers report that bilingualism enriches every student, and that developing the ability to communicate in more than one language enriches both the cognitive and social growth of the students as they develop an understanding of diverse people and cultures. The program also helps teachers and students to realize that cultural diversity is a positive resource. Similar programs have been implemented in Houston and El Paso, Texas, with positive student gains in achievement (Sisk, 1994).

High-potential students in Worsham Elementary School in Houston worked together in a collaborative literacy activity called family tree that asked them to share stories from home and to gather information about their family members. The students shared their immigrant stories, talking about their countries of birth, how they finally arrived in Texas, and why. Each student brought in a family picture to place on the class family tree. Many of the pictures included family relatives who still live in Central America and Mexico; the children were encouraged to tell stories about their relatives and to write their stories on the computer in both Spanish and English. Newspapers in Spanish and English were available in the classroom, and time was provided for the students to share selected items of interest with one another from both papers in small collaborative groups. The students were taught how to be good listeners with five guidelines: (1) be interested and attentive, (2) make eye contact, (3) be patient, (4) don't interrupt, and (5) be aware of nonverbal messages.

The teachers made regular one-on-one appointments with their students for 5–10 minutes to further reinforce a supportive classroom atmosphere and to find ways of modifying their teaching strategies to meet the needs of the individual students. The teachers asked the students three questions: What do you like most in class, and why? Which class activity/project do/does your parent/parents/guardian like the most, and why? How can your classmates and I help you in class?

Another example of a two-way bilingual program is the Morgan Academy of fine Arts in Galveston: The Academy with an enrollment of 680 students is located in an economically disadvantaged area of Galveston, with 59% African Americans, 27% Hispanics, 11 % Anglos, and 2% Asians. The Academy is a magnet school that offers dance, art, and drama for all of the students. Teachers are selected by their interest in the program, educational training, and fluency in Spanish and English. The students are provided opportunities to expand their vocabulary, and to build literacy first in their native language, and then to transfer these skills to a second language.

Village English Activity

The second program adaptation, the Village English Activity, works well in multicultural settings, and it respects and encourages the home language of the children. Delpit (1988) used the activity with Native Alaskan students, and it was used in Project Step-Up with Navajo, Hispanic, and African American students. The Village English Activity begins with the teacher generating common expressions to list on a chart under a topic entitled Our Language Heritage. The teacher then explains to the students that at home, we speak a language with our families and friends that is informal. Then the teacher explains that at other times, we speak a more formal language. The teacher stresses the importance of recognizing that in the United States, the American people speak in a number of different ways, which makes the language similar to a colorful patchwork quilt.

As the students list words and expressions in their native language on the Our Language Heritage chart, the teacher encourages them to think of ways to say the same word or expression in a more formal way under the chart entitled Standard American English. These two charts are placed on a Word Wall for the students and teachers to refer to as they experience new vocabulary and learn to value their native language and the language differences. Gifted students ponder with depth and multiple perspectives, and they exhibit feelings and opinions from multiple perspectives; consequently, they are quick to infer and connect concepts in the Village Activity.

An extension of the Village English Activity is the use of a word map (Schwartz & Raphael, 1985), a graphic rendering of words that the students select using the Visual Self Select (VSS) strategy. Students can choose one of the English words or phrases that may be new to them and define it to the best of their ability, using the words on their list as clues from their own background. When the word or phrase is presented to the entire class, the students can take turns explaining when it is used and why they think the class should know and use it.

If the students choose to do a word map, they can address the questions of "What is it?" "What is it like?" and "What are some examples?" Answers to these questions help students link the new word or phrase to their prior knowledge and experience, which has a positive effect on comprehension (Stahl, Hare Sinatra, & Gregory, 1991). In addition, word maps address gifted students' characteristics of anticipating and relating observations, and advanced readers' characteristic of being highly alert and observant. Figure 5.1 contains an example of a word map created by the Step-Up Mexican Americans students.

Figure 5.1   Word Map

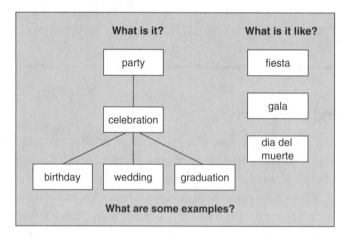

Project Step-Up

Project Step-Up is a program adaptation that identified high-potential multicultural students in Arkansas, Arizona, Florida, and Texas, and provided activities to help them become adept in two languages (Spanish/English and Navajo/English). The program was funded through the U.S. Department of Education Javits program for the Gifted and Talented; it encouraged wide reading to help the students acquire new vocabulary independently and increase their content knowledge. The students read many multicultural "Pourquoi" tales, which gifted children and advanced readers, with their natural curiosity, enjoy reading. Pourquoi tales or fables explain a natural phenomenon, such as how the Milky Way was formed or how the leopard got its spots. The Step-Up children were challenged to find the similarities and differences between the cultures, and they soon discovered that different cultures may have different tales for the same phenomenon lesson.

> I don't know what you've done, but it is magic—my son wants to help. When I asked him why he was so helpful, he proceeded to tell me the fable about the wolf and the porcupine that he read in Project Step-Up. He shared that just like the wolf, when he does something for others, it feels good. He told the story in great detail to his two younger sisters, and even asked them, "What are some favors you could do for others?" When he saw that I was listening, he said, "That's what my teacher asked us." I couldn't help but marvel at the power of one lesson.
>
> —Parent of a third-grade student

At the end of the third year of the Javits project, more than 50 percent of the participating high-potential Step-Up students were able to qualify for the gifted programs in their schools on standardized achievement and ability test scores. Project Step-Up teachers were evaluated on seven criteria using a Likert scale of 1 (low) to 5 (high). Figure 5.2 shows a completed Step-Up checklist. Teacher #1 was evaluated with 5 on all teacher behaviors. Teacher #3 was considered high and above average (3) on most behaviors. Teacher #2 was evaluated as average (3) and below average (2).

Figure 5.2   Project Step-Up Teacher Checklist

Criteria:	T1	T2	T3
Presents clear, consistent, and sincere messages	5	3	4
Communicates high expectations	5	3	4
Communicates commitment through actions	5	3	4
Uses continuous assessment	5	2	4
Cares about individual student learning	5	3	5
Models that all students/cultures deserve respect	5	2	4
Uses democratic processes	5	2	5
Adapts instructions for culturally diverse students' needs	5	2	5
Uses a variety of teaching strategies	5	2	3
Involves parents in educating their children	4	2	4

The Step-Up teachers maintained an individual interest sheet (IIS) of their students, which is displayed in Figure 5.3. A useful resource to help match

Figure 5.3   Individual Interest Sheet

Name: <u>Mira</u>   Date: _____

1) What are the titles of the last two books that you have read?
<u>Ramona and Her Mother, Too Many Tamales</u>

2) Who is your favorite author and why?
<u>Beverly Cleary – her books are interesting</u>.

3) Check the type of book that you most want to read: 1 for first, 2 for second, and 3 for the third choice.
Folk Tale <u>1</u>   Fantasy <u>2</u>   Adventure <u>3</u>   Biography <u>4</u>

4) What things are you interested in knowing more about?
   a. What is your favorite TV program?
      <u>Discover</u>

   b. What do you like doing when there is nothing else to do?
      <u>Read a book, play with my game cube</u>

   c. Which type of sport do you like?
      <u>Tennis</u>

   d. List hobbies that you have
      <u>Sketch book (draw)</u>

   e. If you could read one favorite book over, which one would you choose?
      <u>Ramona and Her Mother</u>

Figure 5.4   Collaborative Writing Center

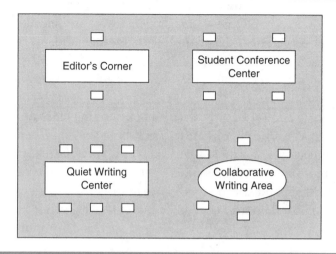

student interest to books was *Through the Eyes of a Child: An Introduction to Children's Literature* (Norton, 2002), which provides descriptions of main storylines on a wide variety of topics.

Case Study

The 18 second- and third-grade students in Mrs. Correll's Project Step-Up class were selected from the English as a Second Language (ESL) program; seven had been in full-time ESL classes in first grade, and 11 were ESL students who were being transitioned or mainstreamed. Most of the students are children of Mexican American migrant workers in Volusia County in Florida. The students were nominated using the Sisk Minority Check List and test scores on the Structure of Intellect (SOI) inventory, and designated as high-potential students. The Step-Up class spent 75 minutes after lunch each day focusing on increasing vocabulary and building word knowledge in reading and writing workshops. Mrs. Correll focuses on reading workshops for one week and then on writing workshops the next week. She has a center in her room that serves as both a writing center and reading center; Figure 5.4 above depicts the writing center.

When the children, mostly Mexican Americans and one Asian American, come in from lunch, they begin reading the books they have chosen, with little or no direction from Mrs. Correll. The books they are reading include Numeroff's *If You Give a Moose a Muffin*; Carle's *Have You Seen My Cat?*; Wells's *McDuff Moves In*; Soto's *Too Many Tamales*; Garza's *Family Pictures*; Cazet's *Born in Gravy*; Lionni's *Three Frogs*; Waters's *Lion Dancer: Ernie Wan's Chinese New Year*; Cleary's *Ramona and Her Mother*; and Barrett's *Cloudy with a Chance of Meatballs*. Several students are trying to decide on a new book from the classroom library provided by the Step-Up project. The students are responsible for selecting their own books, and this freedom to choose is very important to them. The children have each filled out an individual interest sheet, which helps Mrs. Correll provide guidance and instruction when needed.

Mrs. Correll talks briefly with four students who are selecting a book and then goes to the conference table to meet with another student. When students complete books, Mrs. Correll meets with each individually; frequently, when several students have read the same book, she meets with them in a small group.

Mira has read several Beverly Cleary books and has just finished *Ramona and Her Mother*. Mrs. Correll asks Mira to tell about the book, her favorite part, and what connections she makes with her life. Mira shares that she would never make more work for her mother: her mother is so busy with younger brothers and sisters, and putting toothpaste in the sink would be wasteful. She shares that she, like Ramona, would like more of her mother's attention, but her mother is always very busy. Mrs. Correll spends 15 minutes with Mira, checks her reading contract (see Figure 5.5), and talks briefly with her about her new tennis lessons.

Figure 5.5   Reading Contract

Date: 2/1/05   Name: Mira

Work to be completed (Content, Process, Product)

Content (1) Read Strider by Beverly Cleary.

Process (2) Decorate a box to look like Strider.

Product (3) Things to Do Boxes with activities to develop creative thinking.

Completion Date 2 weeks

Self Evaluation I did a good job. The class liked it.

Teacher Evaluation Mira completed her Things to Do Box, complete with activities.

Parent Comments and Signature Mira worked hard and enjoyed it.

Mrs. Ruiz

Mrs. Correll conducts mini-lessons based on student needs that she observes in her Step-Up students, and today she has planned a 15-minute mini-lesson, so that the books the children read will become more personalized. In the mini-lesson, Mrs. Correll identifies "making connections" as the topic and then asks the students to give examples of making connections with the books they are reading. She points out that talking about a book and reflecting on our feelings about it strengthen our comprehension. In the mini-lesson, Mrs. Correll asks the students to read a section from each of their books and to share the connections that they can make with themselves. Several students have read Barrett's *Cloudy with a Chance of Meatballs*, and they all agree that they like the make-believe, which Mrs. Correll calls fantasy.

Mrs. Correll notices that in her class that when one student reads a book, other students show interest in it, and they often begin to spontaneously discuss the books with one another. Mrs. Corell also introduces new books to the students by reading parts of them, which builds further interest (Delp, 1975).

When the reading time is over, Mrs. Correll calls the class together for sharing time. The students who have finished reading a book conference with her, and they have the option to give a book talk. Today, two students are prepared to give a brief presentation of no more than three to five minutes. Each student shares the title of his or her book, the author, and a summary. They tell why they think other students might like the book, read a short excerpt, and show illustrations. The students are quite proficient at giving book talks because they have observed Mrs. Correll modeling how to do it. One student, Mira, indicates that she would like to do a Things to Do Box, a strategy that is similar to Book Boxes, but includes a variety of activities that younger first-grade students can do (Sisk, 1985). The activities, listed in Mira's reading contract, are based on five levels of the Taylor (1984) model: Academic, Predicting, Creative, Communicating, and Decision Making. The box will be decorated to depict the book; Mira's was *Strider* by Beverly Cleary, and she plans to decorate the box to look like Strider. Mira, like many gifted students and advanced readers, enjoys self-directed learning, and decorating the box will provide an opportunity for her to use her creativity. When she shares the box with the first-grade students in a collaborative literacy activity of reading the book and engaging the younger students in questions, she will reinforce her own English and reading skills.

Mrs. Correll spends the last 15 minutes reading aloud to the class from *Strider*, since many of the students have indicated they want to read it. Several of her students have pets, and others want to get a pet, but it is difficult for them with their parents moving from place to place so often. The students predict how Leigh might change after he gets his dog Strider, and several students ask if they can begin reading the five class copies of the book.

When the reading time ends, Mrs. Correll often provides time for the students to write about their book, make illustrations, or do a Quick-Write (Elbow, 1973) in their collaborative writing center, which is depicted in Figure 5.4. Most of the students read two to three books a week, and over the year, Mrs.Corell says that many students read as many as 150 books. Of Mrs. Correll's 18 students, 10 were able to qualify for the gifted program on the basis of high performance scores on the Stanford-Binet and on the ITBS after the first year of the Step-Up program. The supervisor of gifted education and the reading supervisor described the students' growth in English, vocabulary, and content knowledge as remarkable.

TEACHERS PUTTING IDEAS INTO ACTION

Ideal Classroom

The following activity was suggested by Paula Bradfield (Romo, Bradfield, & Serrano 2004). Visualize the ideal classroom, and then find another teacher to create a web of activities that you would like to have students experience. When a school is in a poor community, teaching becomes noticeably different than in middle- or upper-class schools (Anyon & Wilson, 1997). Students in urban schools, which are primarily culturally diverse or in poverty-stricken areas, see and experience teachers asking questions, giving directions, making assignments, monitoring seat-work, reviewing assignments, giving tests, reviewing tests, assigning homework, settling disputes, punishing noncompliant students, marking papers, and giving grades (Haberman, 1995).

How does this differ from your vision of the ideal classroom? What is the message to the students as to what matters? What are they being taught to do? Does this teacher behavior address the needs of advanced readers and gifted students? Read Martin Haberman's article, "The Pedagogy of Poverty versus Good Teaching," that is located on the Eisenhower National Clearing House Equity Section at http://www.enc.org/topics/equity/articles/documents/0.1946 .ACO-111376.003shtm and discuss the article in small groups.

Making a Commitment to Read Multicultural Books

Make a commitment to read at least one book that chronicles diverse culture, religion, or gender. Here are some books to review:

Angelou, M. (1969). *I Know Why the Caged Bird Sings*. New York: Bantam (African American)

Esquivel, L. (1992). *Like Water for Chocolate*. New York: Doubleday (Latino)

Garcia, C. (1992). *Dreaming in Cuban*. New York: Ballantine (Latino)

Morrison, T. (1987). *Beloved*. New York: Signet (African American)

Tan, A. (1991). *The Kitchen God's Wife*. New York: Putnam (Asian American)

Taylor, M. (1981). *Let the Circle Be Unbroken*. New York: Bantam (African American)

Wong, J. S. (1950). *The Fifth Chinese Daughter*. New York: Harper (Asian American)

Being Treated as an "Other"

When culturally diverse students write narratives of "otherness," the experience challenges them to reflect on student harassment and what conditions promote the "othering" of students. As a teacher, think about an incident, period, or time in your school-life or education in which you experienced "otherness" or were "othered." Share your thoughts in poetry, letters, or an autobiography.

The Voice of Poverty

Many students who are culturally diverse also live in poverty. Ruby Payne (1998) suggests the following activity for teachers to explore the "voice of poverty." Role-play these voices with two other teachers and discuss what you discover about yourself and others.

Adult voice: Nonjudgmental, free of negative statements or nonverbals, factual, focused on behavior and not the person, often couched in a question format, with a win-win attitude.

Examples: In what ways could this be resolved? What factors will be used to determine the quality, effectiveness, outcome, etc.? I would like to recommend _____. What are the choices in this situation? I am (un)comfortable with _____. Options that can be considered are _____.

Child voice: Defensive, victimized, emotional, whining, losing attitude, strongly negative, nonverbal, powerless, and helpless.

Examples: Quit picking on me. You don't like me. You want me to leave. Nobody likes me. I hate you. You are ugly, stupid, or boring. You make me sick. It's your fault. You make me mad. You made me do it.

Parent voice: Authoritative, directive, judgmental, evaluative, win-lose mentality, demanding, punitive, sometimes threatening, can create shame or guilt in others, can be very loving and supportive.

Examples: You should or (shouldn't) do that. It is wrong (right) to do it. That is stupid, immature, out-of-line, or ridiculous. Life is not fair, get busy. You do as I say. Why can't you be like _____? You are good, bad, thoughtless, or beautiful (any judgmental word).

After role-playing, try to decide which voice you most often use, and when or where. Discuss the voices and how they are different.

Quote and Reflect

In small groups, discuss the following quotation, and as an individual write a one-page reflective paper.

> *If education is growth, it must progressively realize present possibilities, and thus make individuals better fitted to cope with later requirements. Growing is not something which is completed in odd moments, it is a continuous leading into the future.*
>
> —Dewey (1916)

Exploring Globalization

Paul Spies (2004), in *Reclaiming Democracy*, suggests the following teacher activity: Create a list of interdependence by examining a variety of things that you own, and note where these items were manufactured. When you have a substantial list, examine the lives of the people with whom you are linked as a result of this global exchange. Check the Web sites of the Global Exchange

Organization (www.globalexchange.org) and Free the Children International (www.freethechildren.org). Critically examine the material that is available, and in small groups discuss how our lives are intertwined and interdependent with people and events around the world. What are the implications for infusing meaningful multicultural education in the classroom across subject areas?

Kaleidoscope of Ideas or Melting Pot

In small groups, discuss the idea that meaningful multicultural education can be described as a mosaic or kaleidoscope of ideas and people or as a melting pot. What are the implications of instruction using the metaphor of people as a kaleidoscope and/or as a melting pot?

Transformative Teachers

A fourth-grade teacher made the following comment:

Transforming into a multicultural teacher takes time. I remember when I was asked to reflect, and to do a self-examination, I was stymied. I was totally unprepared to examine how educational decisions are made. I always assumed they were made on theory, and to find out that many decisions were made, and are still being made, on ideology—like the decision to focus on one language in the United States is mind boggling for me. The fact that Oregon, California, Washington, and Arizona have just recently passed English-only laws is incredible.

Find one other teacher and share your response to her statement. Do you feel that you are a multicultural teacher?

SUMMARY

This chapter explored the multicultural heritage of the United States and discussed the change in immigration patterns, specifically the increase in the number of immigrants from Central America, China, India, Korea, Laos, Mexico, the Philippines, and Vietnam. The rich diversity found in today's classrooms calls for teachers to consider ways of adapting curriculum to ensure that all children can learn and develop their potential. We discussed three program adaptations:, the Two-Way Bilingual Program; the Village English Activity, with emphasis on the home language of students and guiding them to seeing relationships between the use of language and social and professional realities; and Project Step-Up, a U.S. Department of Education Javits program to develop giftedness in high-potential underrepresented students. These programs represent the research base for building collaborative literacy in a multicultural classroom.

We introduced a case study to demonstrate the Step-Up program in action with migrant Mexican American students. Mrs. Correll's classroom represents an in-depth "how" to implement the collaborative literacy strategies in a multicultural classroom. Teachers Putting Ideas into Action introduced engaging ways to extend the literacy activities introduced in this chapter, including the "voice of poverty" based on the work of Ruby Payne, since many students who are culturally diverse live in poverty.

Building Collaborative Literacy During Reading and Writing Instruction

Susan E. Israel

TEACHER REFLECTION OF PRACTICES BENEFITING TALENTED READERS

I use flexible grouping patterns to enable me to have students read trade books at different instructional levels based on similar themes. I vary my use of explicit instruction, omitting some from the work done by talented students, as they already know the skills, and I provide higher-level independent writing options. I also use enrichment opportunities jointly with the enrichment teacher to challenge my talented readers.

—A teacher from the regular classroom
at Strong Porter School (Reis et al., 2004, p. 330).

Designing differentiated instruction in reading is often time consuming and difficult to implement. Not only are teachers faced with finding reading material at the appropriate instructional level for all students, they are faced with the decision making of grouping. In the case of the regular-classroom teacher at Strong Porter School, working collaboratively with the enrichment teachers helps him or her more effectively meet the needs of all students in the regular classroom, including gifted students and advanced readers; this positively responds to the call for high-quality curricula for the gifted and for all students (VanTassel-Baska, Zuo, Avery, & Little, 2002).

COLLABORATIVE LITERACY AT WORK

This chapter focuses on helping regular-classroom teachers understand how to build collaborative literacy reading instruction that promotes opportunities for continuous progress that benefits not only talented readers, but all readers in the regular classroom. Following is a summary of the chapter goals:

- To develop an awareness of strategies to differentiate reading instruction that builds collaborative literacy instruction in the regular classroom
- To evaluate current reading instructional practices to ensure high levels of effective differentiated instructional practices
- To build an understanding of how to implement literary circles in the regular classroom
- To develop an awareness of research-based differentiated strategies for gifted and talented readers

RICH RESEARCH BASE: CREATING A LITERACY FRAMEWORK IN READING AND WRITING INSTRUCTION

Thus far, you have been introduced to the theoretical framework of collaborative literacy, how to create an environment that is conducive to building collaborative literacy, and how to identify gifted and talented readers. The purpose of this chapter is to build on previous knowledge gained in this text and apply this information to help regular-classroom teachers learn effective methods for organizing reading instruction around research-based differentiated instructional strategies.

What Are Attributes of Effective Reading Programs?

According to VanTassel-Baska and Sher (2003), an effective reading program that supports gifted and talented readers should be integrated and provide opportunities for acceleration that extends beyond what the teacher provides in the regular classroom. Regular-classroom teachers can reflect on the following questions when evaluating reading instruction that is appropriate for talented readers:

- Do I provide my students with opportunities to use advanced reading materials?
- Do I allow my talented readers to participate in inquiry-based programs and children's literature discussions appropriate for developing higher level thinking?
- Do I include writing that encourages elaboration and incorporation of ideas from literature into stories?
- Do I provide supplementary materials for the development of vocabulary skills?
- Do I provide opportunities for talented readers to select biographies and texts that deal with multicultural issues?
- Do I use spelling and vocabulary words from both basal and literary reading selections?
- Do I allow time for talented readers to tell stories and read personal works?
- Do I allow time for talented readers to pursue reading material that is based on the children's interests?

VanTassel-Baska and Sher (2003) emphasize appropriate selection of text based on developmental levels, regardless of the grade level. This requires that the teacher have a strong knowledge of the reading abilities of talented readers, as well as knowledge of reading skills already mastered (Stainthorp & Hughes, 2004).

Should Educators Use Homogeneous or Heterogeneous Grouping?

Because building collaborative literacy in the regular classroom requires opportunities for social interaction, teachers in the regular classroom are faced with deciding how to go about grouping gifted and talented readers. Despite the controversies surrounding decisions on whether to engage groups with only talented readers (homogeneous) or connect groups with different levels of reading ability (heterogeneous), the outcome is to provide students with high-quality differentiated reading instruction with regular opportunities for creative expression and build on students' interests and growing expertise (Bernal, 2003). Teachers can also be aware of gifted students' perceptions about groups. According to Adams-Byers, Whitsell, and Moon (2004), most gifted students in the regular classroom preferred to be grouped with other identified gifted students for educational purposes, but a portion of the gifted students also preferred to have contact with nongifted peers during the course of the school day. This finding suggests that regular-classroom teachers offer a broad array of services that provide both homogeneous and heterogeneous grouping opportunities. When designing reading programs, teachers should consider the following (Adams-Byers, Whitsell, & Moon, 2004; Cramond, 2004; Cross, 2002):

- Homogeneous grouping ensures that gifted students have access to social and emotional support and opportunities to be with peers who share similar literacy-related interests.
- Heterogeneous grouping provides gifted and talented readers with an opportunity to take on leadership roles during discussion time. However, gifted and talented readers might also need social and emotional strategies on how to deal with peers who do not understand or share similar abilities and interests.

What Research-Based Strategies Can Be Used to Build Collaborative Literacy and Differentiate Instruction?

Collaborative literacy reading instruction supports opportunities for differentiated instruction. Reis et al. (2004) observed 12 third- and seventh-grade reading classrooms and found that talented readers received some differentiated reading instruction, but appropriately challenging books were not available to talented readers; also, many of the teachers lacked the proper training on how to differentiate reading instruction. On the basis of a review of the literature by Reis et al. (2004), differentiated strategies that can be used to build collaborative literacy and challenge talented readers include.

- Curriculum compacting
- Acceleration
- Using more advanced trade books
- Utilization of technology
- More complex reading and writing tasks
- Independent reading and writing options
- Grouping changes
- Tiered reading for thematic units
- Independent project choices
- Substitution of regular reading instruction with other options
- Great books or literature circles
- Advanced questioning skills
- Interest assessment and interest-based reading opportunities

As summarized by Reis et al. (2004)

Talented readers should have opportunities to work together and engage in critical reading and analysis, advanced vocabulary development, challenges such as comparing themes across fiction and nonfiction, and consistent exposure to advanced reading opportunities. The use of available materials such as Great Books or strategies such as literature circles can help make these opportunities easier to implement. (p. 334)

In summary, building collaborative literacy reading instruction requires teachers to gain knowledge about attributes of effective reading programs that support talented readers, flexible grouping, and differentiated strategies that challenge talented readers.

Problems That Keep Educators From Building Collaborative Literacy in the Regular Classroom

I try to get to them at least once a week, but I am not always able to do that. You see, so many of my students read below grade level that it is hard to justify not working with them. Many of these lower readers will be retained in this grade if their scores do not improve. The top group already reads at grade level, so I rarely have any instructional time to give to them.

The problem I have with gifted kids in literacy or reading is helping them stay organized to complete follow-up assignments or reading independently. My solution is to offer them a graphic organizer or to-do lists that helps them stay on task. For students who really struggle with organization and focus, I have them work with a partner to complete certain tasks or at least check in periodically with a buddy to discuss progress, etc. (Heather Kogler, third-grade teacher, Dayton, Ohio; Reis et al. 2004, p. 329)

COLLABORATIVE TOOLS TO HELP DIFFERENTIATE READING INSTRUCTION

According to Block and Israel (2005), reading instruction should provide opportunities not only for learners who excel, but for all learners in the regular classroom. Therefore, meeting the needs of all learners continues to be a challenge for teachers. Literature circles are an effective instructional approach to help meet the needs of gifted and talented readers, as well as readers with varying levels of ability in aspects of reading such as decoding and comprehension. Chapter 1 in this book, Reis et al. (2004), and VanTassel-Baska & Sher (2003) suggest using literature circles to help build collaborative literacy in the regular classroom and help develop literary students. Research also suggests that challenging reading instruction for gifted and talented readers should emphasize higher level thinking tasks, provide opportunities to read fiction and nonfiction, and introduce themes based on interests and ability levels. On the basis of the insight from the case study in Chapter 7, helping students move from being literate to being literary should be a goal. In Chapter 7 of this book, Mary and Joe LaMagna, parents of gifted children and advanced readers, state:

As our children progress, however, I think it is also important to help them become "literary." Appreciation for great writing involves tackling a level of complexity, intellectual challenge, and emotional involvement greater than any other form of entertainment. Guiding them in selecting material and discussing the merits of this material is sic essential to that progression. Personal favorites, based upon an American literature minor in college, include *The Adventures of Huckleberry Finn*, *The Great Gatsby*, *The Eighth Day*, and *The Scarlet Letter*. Not only are these works accessible to a relatively young reader, but they contain thoughtful plot lines. Further discussion relative to themes, authors' points of view and the stature of the work within the body of literature begins to create an appreciation in these young readers for great writing and writers. Suggesting additional reading conducive to critical assessment of these works helps to sharpen their understanding of the content. A further recommendation in this area is to obtain critically annotated versions of these works, which often include analysis. By gaining this deeper appreciation for the potential of literature, the young reader is less likely to see only the superficial value of reading as a form of entertainment. (p. 125, See Chapter 7)

Literary circles are a highly effective method to build collaborative literacy reading instruction in the regular classroom. Helping students become literary is the design for differentiated reading instruction and the goal of collaborative literacy.

Building Collaborative Literacy Reading Instruction Using "Literary Circles"

Literary circles provide an opportunity for teachers to differentiate reading instruction and meet the needs of learners with varying levels of reading abilities. In addition, literary circles enable students to engage in differentiated reading instruction by making decisions about curriculum through (1) cooperative group meetings (Feldhusen & Feldhusen, 2004); (2) thematic engagements across text types (Smith & Weitz, 2003; Stein & Beed, 2004) by being exposed to critical reading and analysis, advanced vocabulary development, and challenges such as comparing themes across fiction and nonfiction; and (3) tiered literacy lessons (Pierce & Adams, 2004; Tomlinson, 1999). Figure 6.1 provides a summary of theme-based text selections that can be used during literary discussions. More literary selections can be found in the resource section of this book. In literary discussions, teachers can guide students in each collaborative group to prepare mission statements, which can be used throughout the school year to help guide students and keep them focused during literacy activities.

Cooperative Group Meetings

Cooperative group meetings take place prior to the beginning of a literary discussion. Peer-led discussants, selected by the students, organize the group's discussion. The cooperative group meetings are a time for collaborative groups to discuss issues they might face in the text they are reading, problems or solutions with difficult text, directions for future research, or any other issues or concerns related to the group's success in the literary circle. Feldhusen and Feldhusen (2004) believe that group meetings provide opportunities for students to learn leadership skills and engage in cooperative learning to enhance their learning of subject matter, and for gifted and talented students to master higher level cognitive and social skills.

Figure 6.1   Literary Collection: Learning About Our Place in the World

Selection compiled by Kim Burr, Elizabeth Metz, and Alison Pleiman
University of Dayton

Building Collaborative Literacy Using a Mission Statement: Through academic and personal development, students will learn to respect each other in and out of the classroom. Students will learn from characters in the literature to act compassionately, accept diversity, and promote justice.

Alexander, Lloyd, et al. (1990). *The Big Book for Peace*. New York: Dutton Children's Books.
The various stories and illustrations in this book promote peace and nonviolence in all of its forms.

Aliki. (1986). *How a Book Is Made*. New York: HarperTrophy.
Students are able to expand on reading books by learning how books are made.

Florian, Douglas. (1994). *Beast Feast*. New York: Harcourt, Brace & Company.
In these poems, readers learn amazing facts about animals.

Florian, Douglas. (1998). *Insectlopedia*. New York: Harcourt, Brace & Company.
In these poems, readers are introduced to a magical world of insects.

Johnson, D. B. (2002). *Henry Builds a Cabin*. Boston: Houghton Mifflin.
The author presents, in a fun environment, the historical tale of Henry David Thoreau's experience with simplicity and nature.

Lewis, J. Patrick. (1998). *The Little Buggers: Insect and Spider Poems*. New York: Dial Books for Readers.
Students are able to learn about all types of insects and spiders from this collection of clever poems.

Livingston, Myra C. (1987). *I Like You, If You Like Me: Poems of Friendship*. New York: Margaret K. McElderry Books.
These poems teach acceptance of different types of friends.

Lowry, Lois. (1989). *Number the Stars*. New York: Bantam Doubleday Dell.
As Annemarie learns about friendship and courage, readers can learn about a fascinating and dangerous time in history.

Merriam, Eve. (1985). *Blackberry Inc*. New York: William Morrow & Company.
This book explains life experiences children go through.

Prelutsky, Jack. (1984). *The New Kid on the Block*. New York: Greenwillow Books.
This book is a collection of poems that introduces children to new animals and food and finds ways to relate these topics to their lives.

Saint George, Judith. (2000). *So You Want to be President*. New York: Philomel Books.
This book provides interesting facts about the various presidents in the past and makes it possible for students to relate to them as people.

Seuss, Dr. (1963). *Dr. Seuss's ABCs*. New York: Random House.
This book helps beginning readers understand the alphabet through poetic writing.

Seuss, Dr. (1971). *The Lorax*. New York: Random House.
Readers will learn from the Once-Ler's mistakes to treat the environment with respect and to make a difference in the world.

Thematic Engagements Across Text Types

In literary circles, students select from a variety of reading materials. For example, students in a literary circle may be focusing on understanding issues related to social justice. A group of five or six students may be reading several different books based on the social justice theme. Teachers provide collections of themed-based materials on social justice, from which students choose the types of text they want to read. Figure 6.2 provides a sample list of text selections that can be included in a thematic unit on social justice. Primary teachers can use the literary selections by focusing on picture books and nonfiction.

Figure 6.2   Text Selections for Literary Circles Focusing on Social Justice

---

Unit: Social Justice (Book selections from Herbeck, 2004)

Teacher Read Aloud: *A Single Shard* by Linda Sue Parks (2001) published by Scholastic.

Literary Text Selections:

Picture Books: Bunting, Eve. *December,* illus. by David Diaz (1997), Harcourt.
Bunting, Eve. *Fly Away Home.* Illus. by Ronald Himler (1991), Clarion.
Gunning, Monica. *A Shelter in Our Car,* Illus. by Elaine Pedlar (2004), Children's Book Press.

Novels: Fox, Paula, *Monkey Island.* (1991), Yearling.
Johnston, Lindsay Lee. *Soul Moon Soup.* (2002), Front Street.
Mathis, Sharon Bell, *Sidewalk Story.* (1971), Puffin.

Nonfiction: Ayer, Eleanor, H. *Homeless Children.* (1996), Lucent.
Chalofsky, Margie, and other. *Changing Places: A Kid's View of Shelter Living,* Gryphon.
Roman, Nan. *The Way Home: Ending Homelessness in America.*

Supplemental Students can bring in newspaper articles to share with their literary groups,
Materials: as well as poetry and journal articles from *Time* or *Newsweek* that might be appropriate to share.

Teachers can obtain additional text selections from Herbeck (2004).

More advanced readers in the primary grades can read from chapter books. Intermediate teachers can use the literary selections with all groups of students. Everyone can benefit from the picture books, as well as the nonfiction material, which helps all students, regardless of ability level, think critically about issues related to social justice.

Peer leaders can be selected for each discussion. Figure 6.3 provides an example of a peer-led discussion form that members of a literary discussion group can complete prior to the discussion.

Tiered Literary Lessons

Tiered lessons help teachers respond to a broader range of abilities and academic needs. According to Tomlinson (1999), tiered lessons address specific standards, key concepts, and generalizations. Tiered lessons also provide students with several pathways to explore a specific area of interest. There are no rules to state how many tiers a lesson can have. However, the number of tiers depends on the number of ability levels within the classroom or the type of interests or learning styles (Pierce & Adams, 2004). Tiered lessons can be used with students in literary circles by ability levels when using heterogeneous groups or by interest level when using homogeneous groups. Figure 6.4 provides an example of a tiered lesson based on learning styles.

Metacognitive Teacher-Reader Groups

Metacognitive teacher-reader groups are adapted from a scientifically based trade book reading method called teacher-reader groups (Block, 2004; Block & Israel, 2005). The following procedures can be used to implement them.

Figure 6.3   Peer-Led Discussion Forms and Planning Guide for Literary Circles

Organizational Session:

Title of Books (Overview Contents)

Group Participants: Individual purpose and goals for reading text selections:

Group Plan for Reading:

Session# and Readings to Complete	Peer-Led Discussant(s)	Peer-Led To-Do List
Session #1:		Plan for reading outline with names of peer discussants
Session #2:		Plan for literary presentations
Session #3:		General outline for presentation
Session #4 (Optional Outside of Class)		

Book groups may schedule time during recess if more time is needed.

Responsibility of Peer-Led Discussant:

1. Organize group discussion by preparing questions or topics from assigned readings. Use peer-led discussion form and prepare for session.
2. Keep discussion on task and monitor allocated time.
3. Complete peer-led form and submit to teacher.
4. Have fun! Bring in any outside resources to enhance discussion!
5. Peer-leader is in charge of choosing discussion location and communicating that to professor by writing on the board: Book/Location.

Peer-Led Discussion Form for Literary Circle Discussions: Session #_____

Peer-Leader: _____   Date: _____

Group members present:

Readings discussed during session:

Questions or topics to be addressed during discussion (done before class):

New ideas generated from readings (done before book discussion):

Brief summary of key points (done before or after book discussion):

Lingering thoughts:

Signature means members were actively engaged during book discussion and made contributions that helped enhance the overall meaning construction of the book:

_____ Group Member Name

Figure 6.4   Tiered Lesson for Literary Circles on Social Justice for Middle-School Students Tiered in Process According to Learning Styles

---

Literary Circle: Social Justice

Key Concept: Character Analysis

Generalizations: Students compare and contrast various characters within text selections and the teacher reads aloud.

Background: This would be the second or third lesson in the unit on social justice. Students should have already discussed the different texts they are reading.

Tier I: *Kinesthetic Learner:* Students in a literary circle work in pairs to locate places in the community that provide services for homeless people. An adaptation to this would be to invite a guest speaker to the classroom and role-play how it feels to be homeless.

Tier II: *Visual Learner:* Pairs of students in the literary circle watch different age-appropriate documentaries on homelessness. Student meet to compare and contrast the characters from the documentaries and the texts being read. Further reflection can be done in journals.

Assessment: Students in the literary circles can create questions for use on an oral or written text.

Step 1: Teacher models strategic processes that good readers use (Block & Israel, 2005).

Step 2: A student is selected to become the teacher-leader of the metacognitive teacher-reader group, which can be the same group as the literary discussion group or specific strategy-focused selected group. The teacher-leader will reteach the lesson originally taught by the teacher.

Step 3: Students in the group are asked to verbalize the steps of the strategy being taught, putting the strategic process in their own words.

Step 4: The teacher-leader will always end each discussion with another student with one question: "Why did you say that?" or "Why did you respond that way?"

Having the students explain their answers makes them think metacognitively (Israel, Bauserman, & Block, 2005).

Why Not Use Gifted Literacy Strategies for All Students?

How a teacher can extend the collaborative tools in reading and writing: Teachers can extend literary circles by inviting guest discussants to join the group and provide new knowledge about the subject matter. This gives gifted and talented readers an opportunity to observe someone who might be a role model in the community.

How a teacher can adapt the collaborative tools in reading and writing: Literary circles can easily be adapted to any grade level by selecting books and themes that are more appropriate. Because literary circles are based on themes and a wide variety of reading materials on that theme, struggling readers have an opportunity to learn about the topic and at the same time read books appropriate for their ability level.

How a teacher can use the collaborative tools in reading and writing: Teachers can use the concept of literary circles across all content areas. Themed related text can be used in science, social studies, or math. In addition, literary circles can be used at any grade level.

TEACHERS PUTTING IDEAS INTO ACTION

Following is a summary of ideas that teachers can use to build collaborative literacy reading instruction in the classroom, school community, and with parents.

1. Provide students with an opportunity during each class period to set goals that they want to achieve during reading, as well as an opportunity to reflect on their goals. Students should also be given an opportunity to celebrate achievements when they meet goals.

2. Teachers who want to expose students to more advanced reading material can offer to trade class libraries with an upper-level class. New books are always exciting, and having classes swap book collections is another way to build collaborative literacy across grade levels.

3. Invite parents to attend several literary circle discussions. This will help parents learn more about the types of reading materials students are being exposed to, as well as effective instructional strategies they can model at home with other family members.

SUMMARY

This chapter focuses on helping the regular-classroom teacher design reading instruction that enables all students to be motivated during reading, as well as realize achievement and the ability to excel in reading. Teachers have learned how to organize literary discussion groups, hold cooperative group meetings, organize theme-based selections across text types, design tiered literacy lessons, and integrate metacognitive teacher-reader groups.

Building Collaborative Literacy With Parents

Susan E. Israel

PERSONAL REFLECTION

When my son Seth was much younger, he played the piano. I was very happy that he played the piano. I play the piano, I like the piano, and I was happy to see him following in my footsteps. After a while, he stopped practicing, and then he quit. I was disappointed. A few months later, he told us he wanted to start the trumpet. He asked us to buy him a trumpet. I told him to forget it—he was a quitter and no way we were going to buy him a trumpet. Then I thought about how harsh I had been and realized that I was being a jerk. When he wanted to follow in my footsteps by playing the piano, that was fine. But when he wanted to do something different, I did not accept it. I did not like the idea of a Sternberg kid playing the trumpet. But of course, what a parent of any child, especially a gifted child, should do, is not to try to turn the kid into a junior version of oneself, but rather, into whatever he or she should be. So I apologized and we ended up buying him a trumpet. He then began lessons. After a short while, he quit that, too. So he was a quitter after all! Well, not really. In my theory of successful intelligence, the key to successful intelligence is figuring out one's strengths and weaknesses, and then capitalizing on the strengths and compensating for or correcting the weaknesses. A role of parents is to help their children figure out their strengths and weaknesses. It is a slow, arduous process, full of wrong turns. The piano and trumpet were not for Seth. Today as an adult he is in business: He has found his niche. But it usually takes a while for children to find that niche, and we as parents need to be as supporting and loving and patient as can be, guiding the children but never steering them so that they meet our needs rather than their own.

—Bob Sternberg

COLLABORATIVE LITERACY AT WORK

Parenting a gifted or talented reader is not an easy job (Riley, 1999). As Dr. Sternberg stated, "A role of parents is to help their children figure out their strengths and weaknesses. It is a slow, arduous process, full of wrong turns." At early stages in development, some children demonstrate abilities that are beyond the average skill level for their age range. This chapter focuses on helping classroom teachers understand and develop collaborative literacy strategies with parents, with the goal that all parents working with teachers can help their child excel in reading, regardless of the child's developmental level. Following is a summary of the chapter goals:

- To develop an awareness of the importance of nurturing reading in the home environment
- To develop awareness and knowledge of the components of the No Child Left Behind Act and literacy in relation to parents and teachers
- To build an understanding of what effective parenting might look like for the next generation
- To understand effective strategies that parents can easily implement to enrich literacy experiences in the home

RICH RESEARCH BASE

The No Child Left Behind (NCLB) Act, signed into law by President George W. Bush on January 8, 2002, established Reading First as a new, high-quality, evidence-based literacy policy and national program to provide excellent literacy instruction to all primary-aged students in America. The NCLB demonstrates that it is of critical importance to the president and the nation that more children receive effective reading instruction in the early grades (Block & Israel, 2005). According to Cramond (2004), the NCLB emphasizes three areas of reading and instruction related to support for students of all ability levels, including gifted and talented readers:

1. Raise reading levels of underperforming students

2. Increase demands on students for reading in different ways

3. Assess reading abilities

As summarized in Chapter 1, building collaborative literacy with parents should be the goal of all teachers in the regular classroom. Teachers can help parents respond to the NCLB legislation in three ways. First, parents should have high standards that are motivating. Understand that reading is not a superfluous activity; rather, it is one that requires understanding of the nature and needs of gifted students as well as the teaching of reading. Second, learn multiple strategies for reading different types of texts and varying types of sources of information, such as Internet reading. Third, determine what skills are strong and what skills need to be nurtured by working with the teacher. Some assistance in the following may be needed: choosing appropriate literature, choosing books to help students deal with affective issues, and lessons that incorporate higher level thinking. Figure 7.1 summarizes some effective strategies that teachers can communicate to parents.

In the opening reflection, we learned that it is important to nurture talents and interests in the home environment. Parents are usually the first teachers of advanced readers. Some of my favorite categories and books are listed below. All can be read as guided-reading side-by-side books, or independently. Figure 7.2 lists books that have challenging material that are appropriate for advanced readers. Parents whose children might struggle with decoding can use the books during read-aloud and discuss the challenging material. This helps promote critical thinking as well as worldly knowledge and vocabulary development.

Figure 7.1   Parent Strategies

Set High Standards: Determine weekly reading goals. Avoid task or curriculum that demands so little. Consider joining activities with other advanced readers who share similar interests and goals.
Learn Multiple Strategies: Read *How to Read a Book* (1972) by Adler and Van Doren and learn how to categorize reading into four levels: elementary reading, inspectional reading, analytical reading, and syntopical reading.
Read to Achieve: Permit children to progress through skills as quickly as they can. Do not hold them to doing repeated skills they have already mastered.

Figure 7.2   Books for Advanced Readers

Books with Distinctive Language	*Buried Onions* by Gary Soto (1997) *When Pigasso Met Mootisse* by Nina Laden (1998) *The Z Was Zapped* by Chris Van Allsburg (1987)
Books with Challenging Structures	*Whirligig* by Paul Fleischman (1998) *The View from Saturday* by E. L. Koningsburg (1996) *The Three Pigs* by David Wiesner (2001)
Books with Unusual Perspectives or Point of View	*Witness* by Karen Hesse (2001) *Go and Come Back* by Joan Abelove (1998)
Books with Ambiguous Endings	*I See a Song* by Eric Carle (1973) *The Stranger* by Chris Van Allsburg (1986) *The Jazz Man* by Mary Hays Weik (1977)
Books with Role Models	*Mango Elephants in the Sun* by Susana Herrera (1999) *The Most Beautiful Roof in the World: Exploring the Rainforest Canopy* by Kathryn Lasky (1997) *Kids on Strike!* by Susan Campbell Bertoletti (1999)

Another resource that teachers can share with parents is a booklet published by the International Reading Association titled *Your Gifted Child and Reading: How to Identify and Support Advanced Literacy Development.* Ideas on how to build collaborative literacy in the home environment include:

- *Collaborative read-aloud* is a joint activity to do with a child at any age. Parents and children can select books to read together and discuss its quality and complexity. Even if the child can read, it is still important to be actively involved in home literacy experiences.
- *Develop critical reading through collaborative discussions.* Parents and children can participate in their own book discussions at home by responding to specific problems or issues in the book or posing their own challenging questions. Parents can also introduce children to a variety of texts on the same topic.
- *Collaborative family discovery discussions.* Discovery discussions (Block, 2003) can be used at home by parents to engage their child in conversation. Parents give their child an opportunity to share his or her ideas and reflect on literacy development. Parents should give their child full power in the conversation and act as a conversational guide, not a director. The conversation can be moved by prompting information about character associations, sharing their own literary voice, constructing their own reasoning, and asking questions.

PROBLEMS THAT KEEP US FROM BUILDING COLLABORATIVE LITERACY IN THE REGULAR CLASSROOM

As a teacher in the regular classroom, I am faced with having to individualize my instruction to meet the needs of all my students. More and more curriculum mandates are being pushed on teachers, and I have very little time to focus on all my students. Based on the NCLB legislation, I am having to spend more time helping struggling readers. I really need the help of parents in the classroom and at home. I feel if we could work together more, it would help me meet the needs of not only the struggling readers but the talented readers as well. I need parents to take more ownership and I need resources that can easily be used so that we can work together and be more effective in the regular classroom.

—Third-grade teacher

Solutions

Host small-group parent workshops early in the year and provide resources that will enable parents to learn strategies on how to help their child.

Help parents learn about the NCLB by informing them about the free publications they can obtain from the Department of Education at www.edpubs.org

IDEAS INTO ACTION

This section details specific ideas to help parents build collaborative literacy at home and with teachers. In each example, we explain how gathering information from parents can be useful to plan and implement reading and writing activities. Second, we give an assessment that can be used to gather information from parents to better understand their child's perceptions and attitudes toward reading. Third, we discuss strategies to help teachers work with small groups of parents to plan activities.

Gathering Information From Parents

As an author of this book and a mother of three advanced readers, I (Susan Israel) am frequently asked questions on what I did to help nurture literacy in my children. I would like to share some of these strategies by providing the questions that I am frequently asked, as well as my responses. This question-response model can be used by all parents when gathering information from other parents with the goal of planning and implementing reading and writing activities at home.

What types of books do you read at home?

When I first started reading books to the girls, we began to develop a stack of very favorite books. We read daily together, and we always started with their favorites. These were also the first books they began to read on their own.

How did you nurture reading at home?

Because I had more than one young child at the same time, I had to pay attention to all of them all the time. We always sat side by side and read the books together. We would take turns reading pages. I always read the harder pages. Having them read easier pages at an early age helped build their self-confidence with the task of reading. Building confidence related to reading was always one of my goals.

I always gave books or other literacy-related gifts, such as "Talking Mother Goose," a talking stuffed animal that reads stories. I also gave them storybook-making computer software. I had the girls tell me which books they would like to have, and I also took them to the bookstore to create book wish lists. At birthdays and holidays, we gave the lists to family members, who used them to buy books for the girls.

What other activities did you do at home to help them with reading and writing?

Before the girls could read, I always helped them make books. Sometimes it was a matter of just stapling blank construction paper together and calling it a book. Once I started this, the girls would always make their own. At first the books were filled with pictures and no words. Once the girls began reading, they began making books on poetry or books with just lists of their favorite words. As they became more proficient in reading, they started designing their own books with computer software. They were always making books.

How do you promote reading at home?

At an early age, I decided that the girls could check out as many books from the library as they wanted. I would carry my largest laundry basket to the library and fill it with books. I never said "no" to any book because we had too many already. I always said, "We have plenty of room." This strategy continues today. When the girls are working on large research projects, they do the same thing. They check out all the books they like on their topic and take them home. I did pay a few fines because of overdue books, but I didn't mind. When I was first married, we didn't have a lot of shelf space, so I put the books in the toy box. Most of the time, I bought interactive books with things they could move or touch. The girls were used to playing with their books and toys.

How did you develop vocabulary?

When my oldest was born, Richard Scarry books were very popular. I purchased a Richard Scarry big book that had a lot of big words in it. Before she could read, she looked at the pictures with all the words and we talked about them together. We also learned how the words fit together to tell stories. I continued buying books with big words. I always purchased picture dictionaries or picture rhyming books. The girls also had an old collection of encyclopedias that I purchased at the library book sale. I let them cut up the old encyclopedias, because I knew they were learning about words.

What other actions do you take to promote reading and writing?

Summer reading programs were very popular when the girls were young, and I signed them up for several. When they received a prize or a coupon for something free, I always made sure they received the prize on the same day as the coupon. The rewards were very motivating for the girls, but earning them frequently and immediately made a difference. We always went every week to collect their prizes. I never made them wait. Because the girls were such dedicated library users and readers at an early age, they were frequently the top readers at the library. When our youngest daughter couldn't read, she still participated in the reading program. She looked at many picture books and earned points. The other girls would read to her as well. No matter how simple the reading task or how challenging, I always took the time to acknowledge their achievements. I considered anything related to reading an achievement, and I always tried to give immediate and positive feedback. I had to be very observant of them, and when they finished reading a book, I made a point to tell them I was proud of them. I still do that today.

Perceptions and Attitude Assessment

Teachers can benefit by collaborating with parents to better understand a child's perceptions and attitudes about reading. This information can be used at home to help parents understand strengths and weaknesses, as well as strategies they can implement to help minimize frustrations about reading and reading materials being used. One test that parents can easily administer at home is the Reader Self-Perception Scale (RSPS) by Henk and Melnick (1995). This assessment tool measures how children feel about themselves as readers.

Results from this assessment can help both teachers and parents understand the child's general perceptions about reading, progress, observational comparisons, social feedback, and physiological states.

Small-Group Parent Collaboratives

Parents can work together to form small groups to help build collaborative literacy opportunities. They can be started to discuss issues and concerns, as well as be a means to avoid a feeling of aloneness. Parents can also use the small-group collaboratives to read and discuss research on topics such as acceleration (Howley & Howley, 2002) or policies related to gifted education (Robinson & Moon, 2003), or simply to seek support (Rash, 1998). Parents can read the following books in a small-group setting to learn about strategies to implement at home to help their child in literacy:

What Kids Need to Succeed: Proven Practical Ways to Raise Good Kids (1998) by Peter L. Bensen, Judy Galbraith, and Pamela Espeland.

Why Bright Kids Get Poor Grades: And What You Can Do About It (1995) by Sylvia Rimm.

The New Public School Parent: How to Get the Best Education for Your Elementary School and Middle School Child (2002) by Bob Chase.

Reading First and Beyond: The Complete Guide for Teachers and Literacy Coaches (2005) by Cathy Collins Block and Susan E. Israel.

Why Not Use Gifted Literacy Strategies for All Students?

How a teacher can extend the collaborative tools: One way would be to hold monthly meetings with parents of talented readers. Both parents and students can attend the meeting. Parents can take turns sharing ways they are helping their child at home, books they are reading, or strategies to help assist talented readers. Teachers are very busy, and holding group meetings will help minimize the time spent meeting with all the parents individually. In addition, allowing parents and students to organize the meetings will also encourage more collaboration between parents, students, and the teacher. Guest speakers can be invited to discuss their knowledge of talent development in literacy.

How a teacher can adapt the collaborative tools: Parents can use praise at home when things at school are going well. If parents are too busy to attend the collaborative literacy discussion groups, on-line discussions can take place. Schools can create a Web site for parents that shares enrichment materials and ideas for book selections.

How a teacher can use the collaborative tools: The RSPS can also be used with students who are struggling. Teachers and parents need to understand their attitudes and perceptions about reading in order to provide high-quality reading instruction.

Case Study

Build Collaborative Literacy at Home From a Parent's Perspective:
Nurturing a Love for the Written Word

By Mary Morris LaMagna and Joseph C. LaMagna
Parents of gifted children and advanced readers

As the mother of five young children (spanning ages six through fifteen), I spend a great deal of time thinking about how best to help each child reach his or her potential. As parents, it can be difficult to be objective; that is, we wish to set high standards for achievement and yet to be realistic in our expectations. We want our children to enjoy learning, to expand their horizons, and to maximize the "gifts" they have been given. At the same time, we must balance *our* desire to see them excel under our terms with their interests and goals. We hope to help form happy, healthy, productive, and fulfilled young adults. That is the challenge. I would like to share how my husband and I are working to meet this challenge in our home. For the most part, most of our strategies have evolved either from our own childhood experiences or through trial and error with our children.

I am the second oldest of six children. My father spent thirty-five years as a teacher in a public school system. My mother is a nurse who was primarily at home rearing the family. From early on, my siblings and I knew that education was a priority in our home. Schoolwork came before sports and outside activities. There was an emphasis on vocabulary, increasing word power, and correct usage of grammar. My mother is an avid reader, and there were always books and periodicals around, as well as frequent trips to the local public library. We had places to study and time every evening set aside for schoolwork, with no electronic distractions (at that time, no television during "study hours").

I learned early on that reading would be the key to my academic achievement. In my first-grade class, our teacher would call on a handful of students to read aloud. She consistently chose those whom she considered to be the "best" readers—and I was not among them. Even as a six-year-old, I could see that if I wanted to achieve in the classroom, reading was my ticket.

Our grandmother was a kindergarten teacher, and she would read to us or have us read to her. Our parents and other relatives would help us to "sound out" words and begin to read more and more challenging material. I dedicated myself to books and reading. I fondly remember biking to the library and spending hours browsing the aisles of books, discovering new things to read. This mastery of reading has lead to a lifetime of reading pleasure.

Eventually, reading led to academic success in other subject areas, including math. My competitive nature, combined with proper emphasis and structure at home, allowed me to earn an academic scholarship to a private college-preparatory high school. My secondary-school experience was excellent. In addition to our coursework during the school year, we were required to read eight to ten books each summer, and we were held accountable for the material. I took advantage of the Latin classes that were offered, which contributed greatly to my ability to continue building vocabulary and better reading comprehension. Through the efforts of a caring and dedicated faculty, my classmates and I were challenged to master subject areas and to value academic accomplishment. I applied myself to my studies and school activities and graduated as valedictorian of my class. I believe that this early love for reading and learning created a desire for knowledge and a way to achieve academic success. In partnership with my husband, I am attempting to create a home environment for our children that fosters a love for reading and learning, as well.

Home Life

I have never been particularly comfortable with identifying certain children as "gifted" or "talented" because I prefer to believe that we *all* possess unique gifts and talents. This is apparent to me in our home. Each of our five children has different strengths, weaknesses, aptitudes, challenges, likes, dislikes, etc. This makes family life interesting and fun. Since we recognize the importance of reading and understanding the written word, we strive to have each of our children stretch to reach (or exceed) his or her "potential." Several of our children were able to read (with comprehension) before the age of four. It is not something that we worked on using flashcards or other early-learning techniques. In fact, we purposely chose nonacademic, part-time preschool programs for those of our children who attended school before kindergarten. Our challenge is to meet the needs of each child in the family and to encourage him or her to reach his or her personal best. Our experience has been that all have performed at, or in most areas above, grade level.

It has been important to establish a home environment in which the pursuit of knowledge is valued. We do this in several ways. First, through our example: We show our children that reading is important by modeling this behavior. They see us reading books, magazines, and newspapers frequently. We also read to them starting at a very young age. Once they became beginning readers, they read to us as well. Often, older siblings will sit with younger ones and read to them, too. Older siblings enjoy the sense of accomplishment that this provides. (In fact, our third child claims that she taught her two younger brothers to read. In large part, she is correct!)

Second, we have interesting reading material available. We try to make sure that our children are surrounded by (or have access to) many books and periodicals. It is fun to make trips to the library or bookstore to select books. They enjoy looking through the shelves and choosing books that interest them. As long as we consider the material to be appropriate, they have free reign to choose what they wish. It is much more fun to read a book that covers a topic of interest, whether that is sports, animals, dance, etc.

Third, we limit the amount of time spent using electronic devices. The computer can be a valuable learning tool if used properly. We are also not against television viewing or electronic games, within limitations. The difficulty is in striking a proper balance. When these devices are available, they take away from the amount of time spent reading or in creative pursuits (including play and exercise). With few exceptions, we "unplug," i.e., we do not use electronics, during the school week, and we limit the amount of time spent using them during breaks from school. We do make exceptions for school-related computer usage. Our system isn't perfect, but it is manageable.

Fourth, we find times in our day to discuss topics of interest. This may occur in the car, at the breakfast or dinner table, or wherever we happen to be. We talk about school, their studies, current events, and our daily experiences. This frequently provides the opportunity to validate the importance of schoolwork, make suggestions regarding any difficulties or challenges encountered, and generally keep abreast of our children's lives and activities.

Fifth, from the time that our children were very young, we spoke to them frequently and in regular "grown-up" language. It is not that we were attempting to turn them into "mini-adults" with adult super-vocabularies. Rather, we have found that by speaking to and with them as thinking, understanding, comprehending little beings, they naturally absorb language and grammar and integrate this with their normal language development. This is not based on any scientific studies that we have read; we have based this on what we instinctively believe and also the results that we have experienced.

Finally, I will admit that from early on we have set high standards for our children, and for the most part, they have responded in a positive fashion. There is no secret formula to this. The expectation is that our children will listen to us and behave appropriately. Over time, this helps children to develop self-discipline and concentration skills, which absolutely aid in learning to read and in mastering other academic areas.

Formal Education

Like most families, we have struggled with formal education choices. This began as early as preschool. We believe that our foundation at home is the most important component of future literary and academic success. (Of course, we recognize that there are important exceptions to this, in which early intervention is recommended for children with special learning needs.) Our three oldest children attended preschool, primarily for the chance to socialize with other children. We were new to our city and hoped that this would give them the chance to meet new friends. Our two younger children did not attend preschool, as I was able to spend more time with them without having to also meet the needs of younger infants at home.

I am not a proponent of formal teaching strategies at this age. I believe that most children will learn to read when they are developmentally ready. We should provide them with the material and the environment. I have found that asking a child to read when he or she is not ready actually creates unnecessary stress and anxiety for the child and becomes counterproductive. When something is fun, we are more inclined to participate; conversely, if something is too demanding, it becomes frustrating. I would prefer to have young children exposed to age-appropriate literature. This includes picture books with the alphabet and corresponding illustrations of objects that begin with each letter. By reading these types of books to children, they become familiar with the sound(s) that each letter makes. If young children are capable of imitating animal sounds for every creature known to man, then over time, they can learn the sounds that letters make as well. The key is repetition *over time*, done in a casual and playful fashion.

We have chosen a combination of parochial and public schools for our children. Each child's needs are different, and we have had to decide how best to meet these needs, in keeping with our particular family values. Generally, our preference would be schools that provide programs to enrich and challenge all students within the classroom. This would meet a very important social component of healthy development, as well as provide opportunities to raise the standards for all students. We respect that this is a challenge for classroom teachers and is not always supported by the prevailing philosophy of the school system. Our children have benefited from "pull out" type language arts enrichment programs, and we have had to weigh these benefits against the social consequences (such as isolation from peers and disruption from regular classroom routine, to name two). Throughout, we try to maintain an awareness of our children's needs and provide extra challenges at home when possible.

Once they're in school, it continues to be important for us to stay abreast of what our children are reading and studying. This enables us to assist them by encouraging their mastery of difficult subjects, as well as maintaining an awareness of the material to come. As our children are entering high school, we are better able to help them choose courses in anticipation of college. We become aware of their interests, aptitudes, and personal academic goals. We also recognize that they will need advice from others more closely involved in the school arena and can encourage them to seek guidance from teachers and counselors at school, as well as from colleagues and other associates.

Another important aspect in the collaborative education of our children has been to instill in them a healthy and proper respect for educators. This is important on several levels. First, teachers are adult authority figures whose role inherently demands respect. Second, our children must recognize that all teachers have unique perspectives, education, and experiences that will ultimately contribute to their own academic foundations. (Even if we disagree with certain perspectives, it provides us with an opportunity for discussion and further development of our own understanding of issues.) Finally, if our children do not view their teachers as essential to their overall academic success, they may allow this attitude to undermine their views of the importance of the learning process. Simply, if our children do not respect their teachers, they are less likely to respect the importance of formal education in general.

A final major component of the academic success of our children has been insisting that each child take ownership of his or her education. That is to say, we firmly believe that children should be encouraged to take responsibility for their own work. They are expected to complete assignments on time and to do their own work. Even our first grader can sit down and complete his homework with very little (or no) direction. Of course, we read with them, quiz them on spelling words, etc., if this is part of the assignment. We also read with the younger ones before bedtime. Our children have a sense of accomplishment and pride in their work when they have done it themselves. For parents, this can be difficult. We all like to see our children succeed, and sometimes we confuse our role as nurturers and facilitators with our vested interest in this success. However, we have all had our years in school. It is now our children's opportunity to perform. It can be all the more challenging to adhere to a "hands-off" policy when teachers assign projects that are virtually impossible for children to complete without considerable parental involvement. Ultimately, our children will be better off if they can approach an assignment and devise a strategy to bring it to successful completion on their own.

Mom's Final Thoughts

In conclusion, our children are all works in progress. We, as parents, are works in progress too. We continually remind ourselves of our ultimate goals for our children and ask ourselves whether we are headed in the right direction. There are specific, measurable academic goals (grades and test scores) and general education goals (helping children to attain their "personal bests"). Most important, we do not want to lose sight of the real goal of nurturing happy, well-adjusted, caring human beings. We can adopt (and adapt) strategies that will work in our home. We try to stay open to new ideas from other parents, healthcare professionals, and educators. A combination of education strategies and parenting techniques, custom-designed for our family, seems to work best in the long run.

Dad's Perspective

The fundamental building blocks to help our children become "literate" clearly began with encouraging reading. At early ages, this involved not only reading to them but also setting an example through personal habits. Spending time with a book, newspaper, or magazine instead of with a television is obviously a good influence. More important, sharing enthusiastic views about written material created an appreciation for the benefits of reading. At early ages, the nature of the material was less significant. Any subject that attracted their interest and enthusiasm—sports, movie stars, travel locations—helped make reading a form of entertainment, which encouraged its practice.

As our children progress, however, I think it is also important to help them become "literary." Appreciation for great writing involves tackling a level of complexity, intellectual challenge, and emotional involvement greater than any other form of entertainment. Guiding them in selecting material and discussing the merits of this material is *sic* essential to that progression. Personal favorites, based on an American literature minor in college, include *The Adventures of Huckleberry Finn*, *The Great Gatsby*, *The Eighth Day*, and *The Scarlet Letter*. Not only are these works accessible to a relatively young reader, but they contain thoughtful plot lines. Further discussion relative to themes, authors' points of view, and the stature of the work within the body of literature begins to create an appreciation in these young readers for *great* writing and writers. Suggesting additional reading conducive to critical assessment of these works helps to sharpen their understanding of the content. A further recommendation in this area is to obtain critically annotated versions of these works, which often include analysis. By gaining this deeper appreciation for the potential of literature, the young reader is less likely to see only the superficial value of reading as a form of entertainment.

HELPING PARENTS PUT IDEAS INTO ACTION

Suggestions From Mary and Joe LaMagna

1. Place a large magnetic chalkboard in a common area. We have ours in the kitchen. Post quotations or articles that are thought-provoking or lead to family discussion. We post excerpts from books, newspapers, the Bible, or other reading that encourages critical thinking and analysis (and sometimes future reading). Other times, the quotes are amusing or pertain to family issues at hand.

2. Have books and periodicals available at home. Create a family library, even if you have only one or two shelves available. Start with children's books and easy readers and add to the collection as your children grow. Eventually, introduce classics and books from well-known book lists (e.g., *New York Times* Bestsellers, literary award winners, guides to college reading lists, etc.). We have books in our "library" that we have been collecting since our own school days. Also, try to have reference books such as a dictionary, an atlas, and books on grammar in your family library.

3. Purchase a paperback dictionary for all children. Encourage them to keep it on their nightstand or wherever they like to read. Teach them to consult the dictionary when they come across an unfamiliar word in the text. This is a wonderful technique to build word power; it helps to ensure concrete understanding of words in context and helps to commit them to memory. Otherwise, they may only derive vague (and sometimes incorrect) meanings of new words.

4. Familiarize your children with lists of commonly misspelled words and common grammatical errors. This will help them to avoid these pitfalls. Do not allow yourselves to slip into lazy speaking habits (e.g., "yeah" rather than "yes") or colloquialisms and improper grammar (e.g., "You did good" rather than "You performed well").

5. Leave the daily newspaper open to interesting topics (e.g., sports scores, zoo facts, local school news, etc.) at the breakfast table. Rather than reading the backs of cereal boxes, your children will look forward to staying abreast of current events or their particular interests.

6. In your own reading of periodicals, clip out or mark articles of interest. I like to leave these items out on the kitchen table as well. When our children arrive home from school, they often read these clippings while having a snack. It can be something humorous, or something pertinent to a topic being studied in school, etc. This encourages our children to see reading as a tool to increase subject knowledge or simply to provide enjoyment.

7. Hang a large map of the world in a common area of your home. Years ago we framed a large world map and hung it by our kitchen table. Often, table discussions of current events include mention of other cities and countries. Having a map nearby encourages an interest in geography and reading names of places, which will then become familiar. Often, children will begin to study the map just to see where they are in relation to other parts of the world, and it expands their sense of the possibilities.

8. Before taking vacations, encourage your children to research your destination or points along the way. Find out more about the history of the city, its people, cuisine associated with the area, the industry and economy, etc. For very young children, this can be kept very simple. We have done this before summer vacations, and it has helped to keep minds active and sharp. Our destinations are often beach or recreation areas. Nonetheless, knowing a bit more about the particular region of the country has made these trips more meaningful for all of us.

9. During breaks from school, suggest books for your children to read. (This is especially important if your school does not require summer reading.) Your local library or teachers at your children's school can help with this. Make this easy for your child by picking up several of these books from your library and have them on hand. Allow your child to choose.

10. Play word games during the frequent opportunities to pass time, such as while waiting to be served in a restaurant or driving in the car. For young children, you can play "hangman" or "I am thinking of a word that starts with . . . or a word that rhymes with. . . ." For older children, have a contest by providing a word and see who can come up with the most words created only by using letters from the provided word. Trivia contests, crossword puzzles, and word searches are also

options. Be creative; consider using names of popular songs or movies as the basis for games, too.

11. Make a conscious effort to "unplug" from electronic distractions. These electronic devices may provide enjoyment on a limited basis, but may also discourage independent reading and creative pursuits if overdone.

12. Make schoolwork a priority. Be sure that your children understand that you value their education and academic growth. Help them to see that it is a key component of their future success, no matter what career path or vocation they choose. Our actions help to reinforce or to undermine this message. If we allow outside activities to take priority over quality homework time, we convey the message that school is not the priority. If we frequently miss school for trips or other family choices, we convey the same message. As parents, we must be convinced that quality work and regular attendance are critical to academic success. We, in turn, will convey this to our children through our resulting actions.

13. Read, read, read! Read to your children often and have them read to you. Have siblings read to one another. Read signs when driving in the car; read topics that interest your child; read menus, scorecards, lyrics, and music programs. You will know what topics interest your child; key in on this and feed their curiosity.

SUMMARY

This chapter focused on strategies to help teachers build collaborative literacy with parents. Because of the NCLB legislation and the goal for all students to be successful, teachers and parents are working together to build collaborative communities beyond the classroom. Mary and Joseph LaMagna have shared their personal experiences of what types of strategies they use to support their five children, who have all been identified as gifted or advanced readers. As Robert Sternberg states, "we as parents need to be as supporting and loving and patient as can be, guiding the children but never steering them so that they meet our needs rather than their own." The role of teachers and parents in the education process should mirror this philosophy: Guide but never steer. Building collaborative literacy with parents can be an arduous process, but the rewards will be manifested in the achievements of each child.

SOURCE: Personal Reflection by Robert Sternberg; used with permission.

PART III

Building Collaborative Literacy Using Gifted and Literacy Strategies

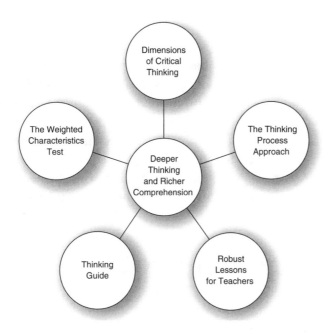

8

Using Gifted Strategies With All Students to Increase Higher Level Thinking and Develop Richer Comprehension

Jennifer Gilmore and Cathy Collins Block

When entering any 21st-century classroom, a teacher will be faced with numerous levels of literacy, ranging from students with special learning needs to those who possess extraordinary learning gifts and talents. In these teaching situations, exemplary teachers have learned how to effectively teach *all* students while at the same time creating a stimulating environment for gifted students. To assist you in achieving this goal, in this chapter we describe how to use various lessons and processes so all pupils of all literacy abilities successfully master higher level thinking and obtain a deeper, richer comprehension. As you will detect throughout this chapter, our methods are based on the promise that every student should be challenged to think critically about the work they are doing and learn how to communicate the knowledge they have gained.

COLLABORATIVE LITERACY AT WORK

By the end of this chapter you will be able to:

- Define the eight dimensions of higher-level thinking, which includes critical thinking, that you can teach, which will enable gifted students and their less able peers to think critically and creatively.
- Articulate and implement lessons and activities that encourage students to succeed in each of these eight dimensions.
- Define the limitations of present comprehension practices and problems that students face in achieving high levels of thinking.
- Use strategies of the Thinking Process Approach to Comprehension Development to increase the comprehension ability in all students.

RICH RESEARCH BASE: DIMENSIONS OF CRITICAL THINKING

Higher level thinking can be introduced to students in several ways. Regardless of the method chosen, however, research has found that every lesson can best develop the core elements of critical thinking when teachers model for their students their own thinking, and when this think-aloud is followed by specific, direct instruction in high-quality thinking processes (Block & Israel, 2004; Block & Mangieri, 1996). Table 8.1 shows eight teacher modeling samples that you can use to teach each dimension of higher level, critical thinking.

Table 8.1 offers a brief overview of the dimensions of higher level thinking and what students can expect from each dimension, as well as goals they can set for themselves. Along with expectations and goals, there are lessons that can be used with each dimension in order for students to learn more lucratively. For a few of the dimensions listed in Table 8.1, we will give one basic lesson to introduce the skills and goals and one "challenge" lesson for gifted students to lead in CLIMB project groups. For all eight of the dimensions of higher level thinking, we suggest that teachers give students a basic lesson before a CLIMB project, designed to develop the dimension of thinking assigned. Doing so will better shape students' understanding of the skill that was taught before asking them to apply it at a higher level of thinking. A description of the basic lesson for each dimension follows.

Table 8.1   Skills, Abilities, and Lessons That Develop Eight Dimensions of Higher Level Thinking or Critical Thinking

Dimension	Skills	Specific Abilities to Be Taught	Higher Level Comprehension Goals for All Students
Dimension 1: Basic Thinking Skills	To translate, relate, and order sensory, literary, and visual input	1. Mnemonic lists 2. Synonyms and examples 3. Condensing, summarizing	1. Evaluate facts 2. Draw conclusions 3. Reflect on what is truly the best
Dimension 2: Essential Thinking Processes	To detect patterns; infer next events; translate and interpret; note inconsistencies and why they exist	1. Organize and label information 2. Combine with two sets of facts 3. Judge credibility 4. Categorize and describe why	1. Infer 2. Categorize 3. Judge credibility of the source
Dimension 3: Decision Making	To make an effective decision by selecting from two or more alternatives	1. Anticipate consequences 2. Use outside resources 3. Fair judgment for all sides 4. Recognize truth and evidence vs. propaganda 5. Listen to various points of view and consider the well-being of all involved	1. Decide on the best decision 2. Search for truth, facts, reason, judgments, and opinion 3. Recognize and be able to evaluate propaganda
Dimension 4: Problem Solving	To analyze and solve difficult situations through multiple problem-solving strategies	1. Assess reasoning and quality of ideas 2. Reject poor reasoning 3. Explain assumptions 4. Use problem-solving strategies	1. Recognize good/poor reasoning 2. Recognize the quality of ideas 3. Solve problems effectively
Dimension 5: Developing Metacognitive Thinking Abilities	To master metacognitive thinking, including self-knowledge, and self-appraisal, self-regulation	1. NOT simply agreeing or disagreeing 2. NOT to accept/reject on the basis of egocentric attachment 3. NOT assume they are wrong if their reasons deviate from other students	1. Use social interaction to assist self-regulation 2. Understand personal beliefs and why 3. View thoughts from various points of view

(Continued)

Table 8.1 (Continued)

Dimension	Skills	Specific Abilities to Be Taught	Higher Level Comprehension Goals for All Students
Dimension 6: Creative Thinking	To think more creatively by engaging emotions and attention in order to produce original ideas and products	1. Explore logic 2. Discover multiple perspectives 3. Find a personal voice 4. Create original ideas and products	1. Enact stories based on experiences, literature, etc. 2. Participate in improvisational activities 3. Create individual and unique writing such as poetry
Dimension 7: Thinking More Effectively in Groups	To think effectively in groups and depend on the nature of thinking as it evolves in group settings	1. Mentoring 2. Networking 3. Listening carefully to others' ideas 4. Asking questions 5. Set challenging goals with others	1. Make statements of appreciation and give compliments 2. Set group goals and collaborate to achieve them 3. Ask meaningful questions
Dimension 8: Ability to Think Effectively When Alone	To pursue and use the power of students' own ideas	1. Set goals and direction 2. Set priorities 3. Present ideas clearly	1. Improve marginal performance 2. Self-stimulate intellectual curiosities 3. Meet goals and direction

SOURCE: Adapted from Block (2001).

Basic Lessons for Each Dimension of Critical Thinking

For Dimension 1, the goals are for students to gain mastery of basic critical-thinking skills, such as evaluating facts, drawing conclusions, and reflecting on what is the "true" best. In order for students to reach these goals, the first lesson they will do is to create a Venn diagram, which will start out simply and then become more complex. Teachers help students learn how to create a Venn diagram, explaining that they are useful graphic tools to show differences and similarities. Next, teachers model how to use one by putting two objects on a table in front of the classroom. Teachers will then draw one on the board or overhead and perform a think-aloud with students to report the critical, higher level thoughts they use to discover differences and similarities. Students practice these thought patterns until they can look carefully at each part of objects, ideas, or events to almost automatically deduce similarities and differences.

After completing a Venn diagram and performing a think-aloud together as a class, students should discover what they think about when making comparisons on their own. Assign students an activity to complete:

- Create a Venn diagram to show the similarities and differences between two ideas that confuse them or to identify why they like one sport or movie more than another.
- Choose two characters from the novel that is being read in class and compare and contrast them using a Venn diagram to discern qualities that can help students become more successful.
- Go to the book center and choose two books with a partner. Take the books and record on a Venn diagram how they are alike and how they are different, and use the diagram to identify authorial writing traits that students can use to improve their own writing.

To take this lesson in basic thinking skills a step further, teachers can have students lead a discussion on how this type of thinking can increase their ability to gain meaning from texts and can be used to improve their abilities. Students need to feel connected to what they are learning and realize that it is part of their everyday life.

Dimension 2 focuses on essential thinking processes and leads students toward the goals of drawing inferences, categorizing information, and judging the credibility of sources. As a basic activity to achieve these goals, teachers help students learn how to make inferences while they read. Students can use note cards or sticky notes as they read to write down their inferences. Teachers show students how to use what they know and what they have read to speculate about what is to come. The best way to do this is to have students cover a portion of what they are reading. If they are reading a novel, for example, have them cover the bottom of the page and read only the first few paragraphs. After they have read half of the page, students list on the sticky note what they know already and what they have read. By adding these two categories together, students attempt to predict what will happen next. If students do this often as they read, they will think more critically about what they have read and how it affects what is to come.

Teachers challenge students to go further in learning these essential thinking processes through another activity called "Small Group Juries." In this basic Dimension 2 lesson, students are placed in small groups and taught what it means to be on a jury. Teachers explain that students are to determine whether the on-line articles and sources they are given are credible. Next, the teacher selects a variety of on-line sources and prints them off, demonstrating how to determine whether each source is credible. While the students are in groups, teachers ask them to make lists of what they found to be credible and what they found implausible. When all groups are finished, the class comes back together to answer questions such as

- Did the site have a credible author? How do you know?
- Are the reasons and claims valid and supported with evidence?
- Does the speaker or writer have firsthand experience?

Figure 8.1   The Weighted Thinking Guide

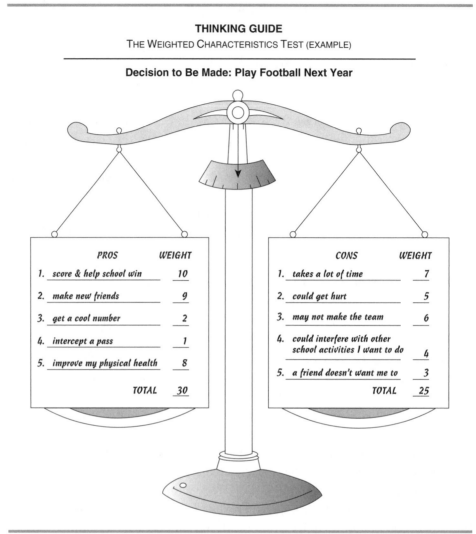

THINKING GUIDE
THE WEIGHTED CHARACTERISTICS TEST (EXAMPLE)

Decision to Be Made: Play Football Next Year

PROS	WEIGHT
1. score & help school win	10
2. make new friends	9
3. get a cool number	2
4. intercept a pass	1
5. improve my physical health	8
TOTAL	30

CONS	WEIGHT
1. takes a lot of time	7
2. could get hurt	5
3. may not make the team	6
4. could interfere with other school activities I want to do	4
5. a friend doesn't want me to	3
TOTAL	25

Answering these questions will further students' understanding of what a credible source is. Finally, students are given real cases and asked to research facts and determine the most just, even verdict. Books that contain such cases are *You Be the Jury* and *You Be the Jury II* (Miller, 1997, 1998).

Dimension 3, decision making, is a skill that students of all levels need to master. Whether it is making decisions on assignments in school or in the complexities of their lives outside of school, effective decision making is an important thinking process that must be taught. A basic lesson that can be used to build these abilities in Dimension 3 is helping students recognize and evaluate propaganda and how it affects the decisions people reach. For this exercise, teachers split students into groups of four or five. Each group receives a different piece of propaganda to evaluate, such as a newspaper editorial, a television commercial, a magazine ad, and so forth. Next, students watch or read their material and evaluate whether they think the information it contains is propaganda, and whether they agree or disagree with the message being sent. If the medium is trying to sell something, students write whether they would buy the product or service being pitched on the basis of the Internet research they completed. This exercise teaches students to recognize different types of propaganda and learn how to effectively evaluate fact and opinions before making decisions. Figure 8.1 provides a form that can be used for this lesson.

Dimension 4 moves students a step further in learning how to make tougher decisions and solve problems. To help develop thinking processes, students can use the "weighted characteristics test" to evaluate the pros and cons of any situation. In this lesson, students think of a decision that they are facing in their lives right now. It can be as simple or as complicated as they want. They will make a two-column chart, labeling the left column "pros" and the right column "cons"; then, they fill out the chart and assign values to each characteristic. Once they have filled out as many pros and cons as they wish, students add the number of pros and cons together. Then, they score the consequences on the basis of how important they are. For example, if they have five pros and five cons, for a total of 10, the highest value (10) will go to the most important consequence for them, 9 will go to the second most important, and so on. After assigning each characteristic a weight, the side with the highest number of points is likely to be the best decisions for the students at that time with the information that was available.

Why Not Use Gifted Literacy Strategies for All Students?

How a teacher can extend the weighted characteristics test: Teachers can use the same concept to weigh other aspects of the reading or lesson, for example, the plot, setting, or the solution.

How a teacher can adapt strategy by grade levels: Younger students will enjoy bringing the scale to life by placing students on different sides of the room and physically demonstrating what happens to the scale. Older students could build a scale and provide the responses with objects of different weights. Weights can actually be used to model the effects of the responses.

How a teacher can use strategy across content areas: Content-area teachers can use domain-specific criteria to change the issues being measured. For example, in social studies, historical decisions can be measured by research-based outcomes, and the strengths and weaknesses of those outcomes can be evaluated. Issues on slavery could be researched, or environmental concerns related to natural forces such as hurricanes.

Dimensions 5, 6, and 7 have similar basic lessons (see Table 8.1 for a description of several for each dimension). The basic lessons share the quality of increasing students' metacognitive skills (Dimension 5) by engaging them in creative thinking processes (Dimension 6) and/or inventive group-based CLIMB projects (Dimension 7). For example, when students must place themselves in someone else's shoes, assume the role of a literary character, or defend their beliefs with facts and reasoned judgments in a debate, they must use and enhance their metacognition, creativity, and group work skills to reach the optimum outcome. As also shown in Table 8.1, writing poetry, improvising, and creating insightful queries are equally effective basic lessons that develop students' Dimensions 5–7 or higher level thinking.

Although all dimensions of thinking critically are important to achieve higher level thinking, Dimension 8 and its basic lessons are becoming more important in this decade than in past ones. Students must move at a young age toward more effectively working alone because schoolwide tests carry larger consequences than in previous years. In order to evaluate students' success in working alone, a basic lesson is to teach them to set personal goals . One lesson that accomplishes this goal is to have as a constant in class a "Journal Fridays" activity to assess growth in individual work habits. This assessment could be a set of questions that each student must keep in a spiral notebook or a journal-based, free-writing exercise on which goals they achieved that week, where they fell short, and how many of their goals they will continue into the next week and why those goals took longer than expected to be attained. If teachers have a class syllabus or assignment sheet that prepares students for the week ahead, pupils can look at it in order to set their future goals. Self-assessment and evaluation of goals are also important skills connected to working effectively alone. Students must learn to be intrinsically motivated to achieve their best.

To expand on goal setting, teachers can show how to properly set goals and target dates through demonstrations of how they do so or by reading excerpts from biographies dealing with how famous people set their goals. This basic lesson for Dimension 8 begins when teachers give students a slip of paper they can place at the front of their notebook each week to record their goals. Students are taught that although it is important to make short-term goals, to achieve success in class it is also important to set long-term goals. Here are some easy guidelines to use when teaching goals:

- Start with the word "to"
- Follow it with an action verb
- Make the goal measurable
- Make the goal attainable and realistic
- Set a time frame in which the goal should be achieved

Limitations and Problems With Comprehension

From prior research, we have learned that highly effective comprehension lessons are cognitively, socially, and pedagogically richer than ever before (Block & Pressley, 2002). Teachers can no longer think of comprehension as a lone, static process. They much teach students to make meaning for themselves and address comprehension as an ever-changing interaction of thought processes, never too prescriptive or too free-flowing (Block & Mangieri, 1996). The following are possible problems that limit a student's ability to attain rich meanings from text:

- Instruction is sparse or unmonitored, which inhibits students from developing tools to think critically as they read
- Teacher is overbearing, which can lead to students not having the inability to apply skills without prompting
- Students often create vague meanings for words they do not know in order to move forward in the text; this makes comprehension a challenge, and eventually all meaning is lost

The Thinking Process Approach to Comprehension Development will push aside these problems and limitations and expand on what students know about comprehension. It will teach students how to use two processes simultaneously, to identify text-specific thinking processes, and to teach others the processes they used as well as describe what they want to learn next (Block & Johnson, 2004).

The Three Lessons of the Thinking Process Approach

Lesson 1 teaches students to set two process goals and coordinate two comprehension processes simultaneously. Doing this with every lesson will keep students' minds active and fully engaged, increasing the amount of text they comprehend and the depth to which they comprehend it. Throughout the process, teachers use think-alouds to explain the thoughts of expert readers as they read. The following are the steps to teaching Lesson 1:

- Teacher describes the two thinking processes that will be the goal for this lesson. He or she then performs a think-aloud for the first of the processes and writes the directions on the board.
- Teacher and students draw a diagram of the thinking process and practice using a motion to depict the process. For example, students could use a sticky note to draw an arrow to the next page of a text to represent inference.
- Teacher will do another think-aloud, this time for the second of the processes, and record directions on the board.
- Teacher and students repeat the second step for the second thought process, choosing a different way of diagramming.
- Teacher demonstrates each of the processes three times before asking students to split into small groups, and eventually has students work individually at their reading level.

The most important aspects of Lesson 1 are that it emphasizes the connection between the two processes and that students realize both will be happening simultaneously as they read in order for them to become more able comprehenders. There are various activities and strategies to illustrate this lesson to students in a variety of classroom settings; we will demonstrate one of them later in the chapter.

Lesson 2 teaches students the importance of finding the authors' intent and meaning rather than just guessing in order to keep moving forward. This lesson uses what Gee (2004) refers to as design grammar: the unique principles and patterns that writers use to communicate complex meanings. Lesson 2 contains five steps to be taught over several weeks; students should practice each step until it becomes an automatic process in their comprehension. Following are the five steps:

1. Use the first two pages to follow the author's train of thought carefully by looking at the connections between the sentences in the first few paragraphs.

2. Knowingly attend to the way the author connects his or her paragraphs, beginning with the third page, moving forward.

3. Diagram the method and frequency by which an author summarizes key themes or beliefs; this can be done mentally or literally.

4. Identify the depth of the author's writing style.

5. Visualize literal intratext and intertext connections.

This lesson allows students to gain comprehension because they will learn how to follow the train of thought from sentence to sentence and paragraph to paragraph. In addition to these five steps, teachers may also want to teach students how to "till the text" to find general meaning. Tilling the text asks readers to note three things: subheads and points of emphasis, level of density in ideas, and content flow. It works best with nonfiction, enabling students to predict what they will see on future pages as well as keeping them engaged so that they want to read further.

Lesson 3 puts the students at the center of what they will be learning. It starts with students letting the teacher know what they want to learn; in turn, the teacher will teach the processes. The next day, students will join a group in which a peer using a different book will reteach the process. Student-led comprehension process groups (SLCPGs) should occur about once a week. The first thing that will occur is that one student will share in his or her own words the processes taught in Lesson 1 or 2. All students in the group then share and ask questions about what they did to understand and accomplish the comprehension process. As students read sections from their book, they will perform think-alouds in order to discuss the processes they are using and how they are using them to gain better comprehension. The last thing an SLCPG will do is offer suggestions on how to overcome specific problems that may arise when using those comprehension processes. Various recording and reporting strategies can be used by groups to demonstrate what they discussed as well as the outcome of the processes. You will learn one of these later in the chapter.

Strategies and Activities to Increase Comprehension With All Students

For each of the three lessons of the Thinking Process Approach to Comprehension Development, there are various strategies and activities that can be used with all students to reach a higher level of comprehension. Table 8.2 describes a strategy for each of the three lessons, what to expect from students, and the goal(s) for the activity.

Although there are many different literacy levels in each classroom, an exemplary teacher will find ways of teaching critical thinking and comprehension that will enable students to perform at a higher level. Through the findings in this chapter as well as the lessons we provide, students of all levels will be able to think more critically and comprehend better. As teachers, we must ensure the education of all students to their highest ability. When thinking of how to

Table 8.2   The Three Lessons of the Thinking Process Approach

Lesson and Activity	Goals for Student	How to Execute the Activity and What You Will Need to Do So	Possible Outcomes/ Assignments
Lesson 1: Set Two Process Goals for Every Lesson **Activity:** Infer the feelings of characters in a text and combine literal meanings to build strong inferences	1. Using what they read plus what they know, students should be able to infer the feelings of characters from a text. 2. Recognize how inferences change as a result of the interrelationship of two comprehension processes (inferring feelings and drawing on literal meaning and clues). 3. Understand the use of comprehension and thinking processes to gain better understanding of text.	1. Describe the process of finding inference— "What I read + What I know = Inference"— and give 3 examples in a think-aloud. 2. Use the sticky note process (described early in the chapter) to mark inferences in the text. Cite examples of how characters are feeling and draw an arrow to what you can infer about the character. 3. Integrate clues from the previous paragraphs to draw meaning of what will happen next.	1. Students can write a continuation of the text they are reading based on the inferences hey have made. 2. Have students draw and/or write a descriptive paragraph about a character and a situation they might encounter (not in the text) based on the feelings they inferred. 3. Draw a graphic organizer to relate the concrete clues from each paragraph to the inferences the student made.
Lesson 2: Teaching Students Text-Specific Comprehension Strategies **Activity:** Diagramming an author's train of thought and continuing it into student writing	1. See relationships between sentences of each paragraph of an author's text. 2. Recognize main idea as well as details and description. 3. Recognize patterns in an author's summary style (how many paragraphs will be written before he concludes). 4. Describe the depth of style by using vocabulary, sentence structure, length of paragraphs, number of ideas, etc.	Execute these first as a think-aloud and then allow students to complete individually or with a partner. 1. Diagram sentence-to-sentence connections for the first several paragraphs. Note where the main ideas are as well as the details that follow. 2. Diagram paragraph-to-paragraph connections to determine type and number used to introduce, describe, illustrate, conclude, etc.	1. After executing steps through think-alouds allow students to go through the steps of diagramming with a partner, using different-colored highlighters to show main idea and details. Give instructions to put a box around summaries that the author makes. Tell students to underline words that add to the depth. Breaking text apart will show students how to better evaluate and comprehend what they are reading.

(Continued)

Table 8.2 (Continued)

Lesson and Activity	Goals for Student	How to Execute the Activity and What You Will Need to Do So	Possible Outcomes/ Assignments
		3. Diagram the author's summary method (e.g., determine how many paragraphs an author writes before he or she inserts a paragraph to summarize points to date). 4. Describe the depth of style by asking how deep is the vocabulary? How complex/simple are sentences? How many ideas per paragraph? 5. Diagram intratext and intertext connections.	2. After students are finished reading, have them write two paragraphs that they think would fit in with the author's style, asking them to pay attention to each of the steps in the diagramming process.
Lesson 3: Student-Led Comprehension Process Groups (SLCPGs) **Activity:** SLCPGs and Record Keeping	1. Describe in his/her own words the comprehension processes taught in Lessons 1 and 2. 2. Use the processes to gain meaning and use group think-alouds to demonstrate their ways of thinking. 3. Help each other to overcome specific problems related to comprehension processes.	1. Allow students to meet in their SLCPGs once a week to discuss the comprehension process being taught in relation to a specific text. 2. Have students write problems they are facing with the processes and predict what can help them overcome those problems. 3. Have students record their thoughts and questions through graphic organizers or lists.	1. Have each group of students predict two outcomes of the story after reading only half way through it. Allow them to organize their predictions through a graphic organizer that displays two possible ways the story could end and how they came up with their ideas (thought process). 2. Before reading, ask the group to generate a list of questions that they want answered when they are finished. Have them respond and cite where they found the answers.

SOURCE: Adapted from Block & Johnson (2004).

challenge students in critical thinking and comprehension, there are three things to consider:

First, students must be taught multiple processes to gain comprehension and higher level thinking. If students are led too much, they will never gain understanding on their own; if they are not given enough guidance, however, they will get lost in the text and never understand. It is up to you as a teacher to find the middle ground.

Second, students must be taught methods that will help them correct their own confusion as they read. These methods are described as the eighth dimension of thinking in the next section of this chapter. Third, students and teachers must realize that advanced comprehension and higher level thinking are possible for all students. When teachers use the strategies that follow with gifted students as well as the rest of their class, all students can be challenged and succeed in reaching their highest levels of thinking.

TEACHERS PUTTING IDEAS INTO ACTION

1. What are three ways to integrate the eight dimensions of critical thinking into your lesson plans? Name specific activities and goals.

2. Describe how you will use the Thinking Process Approach to Comprehension Development and state your expectations for students when participating in these activities.

3. What are some of the limitations that are present in current comprehension practices, and how can you help students overcome these?

4. Which of the eight dimensions of critical thinking do you believe to be the most important in your classroom instruction and why?

5. Provide an example of an activity you would use in order to help students analyze and solve difficult situations.

SUMMARY

As with any lesson, if teachers model the process before they ask students to participate, pupils will gain a better understanding of what they are supposed to achieve. Each of the eight dimensions of critical thinking will allow students to work on a high level of thinking prowess that is challenging yet achievable. They will learn the skills they need to think at a higher level throughout all lessons that you provide them.

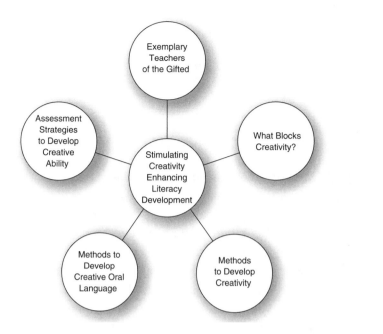

Exemplary Teachers of the Gifted

Assessment Strategies to Develop Creative Ability

Stimulating Creativity Enhancing Literacy Development

What Blocks Creativity?

Methods to Develop Creative Oral Language

Methods to Develop Creativity

9

Strategies to Stimulate Creativity During Reading and Writing

Nicole Caylor, Whitney Wheeler, and Cathy Collins Block

To introduce Lauren Brants, we would like to use the words of her principal, who described her as a caring and dedicated individual who is known not only for her intelligence but for her heart and her willingness to volunteer and to reach all levels of her creative capacity. Lauren is known equally for who she is as well as for how much she has accomplished on a superior level. Lauren describes the exemplary teacher like this: "An exemplary teacher possesses experience and portrays confidence. She should be comfortable in her own skin." Lauren goes on to say that exemplary literacy teachers of gifted students should be flexible and allow them room to fully develop each thought. She explains that teachers should be able to relate to students on the latter level. Teachers cannot relate if they do not know the content or how to teach it. As you will note in Lauren's vita, she has excelled in seven extracurricular activities or community-service activities, and at the same time she has received six high honors and awards.

Aaron Yamagata is the only student to be accepted to Yale Law School at the age of 14. He has compiled enough credits to transfer in as a junior. Aaron had already received honors and acclaims at the White House on two separate occasions before age 12. Aaron says this about exemplary teachers: "In my opinion, one of the most important qualifications that an educator of gifted students should have is dedication. It is paramount that educators of gifted children be realistic in helping each gifted student set realistic individual goals that will allow the gifted student to grow and experiment without a fear of failure. Educators should remember that no matter how gifted a student may be, gifted students are not superhuman. Educators must temper discipline with compassion. The most important qualities of all are: a selfless passion, love, and an appreciation for the individual differences and uniqueness of the gifted mind"(Yamagata, personal communication, 2005).

COLLABORATIVE LITERACY AT WORK

Teachers are responsible for building an enriched environment in which gifted children can thrive. In this environment, effective teachers are able to promote the growth of creativity among students. Through proper guidance, gifted students will learn how to draw from their own imagination and originality. This chapter also provides direction in assisting students with communication apprehension.

By the end of this chapter, you will be able to:

1. Define and replicate the qualities and actions of the exemplary teachers who build all students' creativity.

2. Create, modify, or use several informal measures that can increase students' creativity.

RICH RESEARCH BASE

Exemplary literacy teachers for gifted students stand out from ordinary teachers (Clark, 2003). Similar to gifted students, a truly gifted teacher realizes the importance of being creative and engaging higher level thinking skills while incorporating these aspects into the classroom. This teacher also recognizes his or her role as a facilitator of change and an advocate for individual students.

These teachers continuously develop their students' highest thinking abilities by providing everyone multiple opportunities to use knowledge creatively. In addition, by providing an atmosphere of acceptance, these teachers stimulate and receive significantly more unprompted expressions (Block & Mangieri, 2003). Knowing the value of asking proactive questions like those described in earlier chapters in this book, the teachers invite creative-thinking skills that include consistency, originality, elaboration, and purposeful idea finding. In every week's work, exemplary teachers also know that they too are continual learners and, therefore, understand the importance of self-educating and remaining current with the latest research. These teachers continue to strive for excellence by attending workshops, taking courses on gifted and individualized education, and following up on new techniques with background reading (Block & Mangieri, 2003).

Research has shown that exemplary teachers of the gifted student perceive behaviors in a constructive and motivating manner. They view students as able rather than unable oral communicators, knowledgeable rather than uninformed, interested rather than uninterested, and capable of unique and highly creative invention rather than incapable of higher level thought. These teachers help their students realize their creative communication capability by internally rather than externally motivating them to set high goals. Rather than viewing teaching as a controlling, concealing, and uninvolved task, they view their profession as enlightening and use it as an encouraging process to achieve goals.

How do these teachers promote the growth of an inquisitive mind? They begin most days by instigating a process that encourages students to guess or hypothesize about the unknown or untested. Not only does action allow teachers to better understand the student, it also enables the student to fully develop his or her own thoughts and ideas. While providing students the time to develop their thoughts, an exemplary teacher also asks them to personalize the support for their answers and opinions. Teachers can demonstrate this technique by dividing students into small groups to make predictions about future events at the end of each chapter of the book being discussed. By the end of the second and following chapters, the difficulty increases by having them also create proverbial or metaphorical sayings for their predictions. When each group finishes making predictions, students write proverbs that state their opinion about the moral of the book (Block, 2004a).

It is important to learn how such teachers instinctively value the extent to which self-respect must be extended. The methods in this chapter show how exemplary teachers move freely among students and show genuine interest in the rich literacy experience for every student. Additionally, they support group discussion in which feelings can be articulated productively. The methods examined in this chapter also demonstrate how teachers engage in positive redirection so that the blocks that stifle creative and effective oral communication described next can be overcome.

What Blocks Creativity?

Creativity is the wellspring that generates original ideas and products. Other factors that inhibit this creativity include the need for success, limiting the pursuit of the unknown, and conformity to peer groups and social pressure. Too often, an increasing amount of pressure to succeed is placed on gifted students. Not only do teachers pressure students, but also the students have a strong need to be successful in everything they do. This amount of anxiety weighs children down and becomes their main focus in life. The need for success limits students' ability to be creative. Gifted students will oftentimes hesitate to venture out into areas that are unfamiliar to them. This fear of failure also limits their creativity. Thus, in brief, it is valuable for literacy teachers of gifted students to encourage imagination and exploration every day.

The following six values held by individual students could limit their creativity. Because many students are not aware that they hold these values, teachers must take special steps to make them aware of them and provide methods by which students can alter these limiting values.

1. Everything you read must be practical.

2. Everything must be successful.

3. Everything you write must be flawless.

4. You must be well-liked.

5. You must have concentrated attention.

6. You must not overly express yourself emotionally through writing.

IDEAS INTO ACTION

What Are Methods for Developing Aspects of Creativity?

In this section, we present two major methods of helping students to increase their creativity. These activities are entitled "Who I Am" and "Living in the Now." Teachers who provide these activities help creativity surface in individual gifted students as well as other pupils in their classrooms. The following methods demonstrate how teachers develop individual aspects of creativity among students in each of the four activities presented below.

Who I Am: In using "Who I Am" with K–2 students, the teacher can have students draw pictures of themselves using their favorite colors. Tell the students to pay close attention to detail. They can draw only things that represent who they are: things they enjoy doing, eating, wearing, etc. This activity could also be effective for grades 3–5. In addition to drawing, have students use the letters in their name to describe characteristics about themselves. Have high-school students write out their first, middle, and last names, and identify characteristics to fit the letters in their names to create an acrostic. Require the students to use detailed words. From this acrostic, high-school students will be required to write their personal autobiography. To change things up, students could write a classmate's biography using the acrostic as a starting point.

Living in the Now: Have students talk to each other about a specific idea or theory, then share their ideas with the class orally. When making an assignment in which students have to present before the class, allow them to choose a topic they are interested in, something they could easily get excited about. To create a new social role, have students role-play in small groups: for instance, a White House press conference or a meeting with the author of their favorite book.

Methods for Developing Creativity in Oral Language

Oral creativity is another pathway to develop creative thinking in all students in the regular classroom. Socialization is very important to all students, including the gifted ones, and oral language plays a large role in socialization success. Often times, gifted students do not have an opportunity to express themselves and feel isolated from their peers (Clark, 2003). The following methods assist students to overcome fears of orally communicating and are also adapted to meet the needs of various student-learning strengths (Israel & Block, under review). Before long, through repeated use of the methods described next, all students, especially gifted readers, can overcome the fear of speaking before groups and realize how important their reasoned opinion and general thoughts are to their classmates and others.

Method 1: Complete the Sentence

Method 1 is used during classroom read-aloud time. While reading aloud, a teacher of gifted students identifies and teaches the ways that the main characters use language to express themselves effectively. To do so, the teacher pauses to perform a think-aloud after six different incidents in which a main character chose specific words, listened carefully, and crafted an effective response in the book. She then performs a think-aloud for each strategy the character used to develop good purposeful speaking. This activity proceeds by asking students to complete sentences orally so that they can begin to mimic expressions and phrases from the book. The format for these constructed sentences is as follows:

I wonder why (story character) did _____.

I wish I had known _____ about _____.

I wish I knew why _____ (story character) did _____.

I wish I knew why _____ (story character) did _____ because I _____.

The story took place at _____, which is like _____ that I know.

The most important part for me was _____.

I thought about _____, which was not in the book.

Only one sentence is used for several weeks in a K–2 classroom until it has become automatic. For example, before a teacher finishes each book for a two-week period, he or she would say, "I wonder why the story character did . . ." and ask the students to use that sentence following her answer. In a grade 3–6 classroom, a teacher can introduce two different sentences every six weeks. This allows students to choose which sentence they would like to say. In high school, a more complex sentence can be used so that students learn additional patterns for making effective oral statements. These patterns can be introduced singly or two at a time at the middle-school and high-school levels. Regardless of how many sentence starters are used, teachers should make a conscientious effort to use the Complete the Sentence method at least once a week until students become fluent oral communicators.

Method 2: Thoughts and Responses

This method provides an avenue for students to incorporate their own thoughts into the class discussion. In this method, the teacher asks the class open-ended questions for which there is no right or wrong answer. The following questions should be adapted to meet the classroom needs:

How does that make you feel?

What do you think about _____?

How would you interpret _____?

Could you summarize your classmate's comment?

Tell me about _____.

Can you give me an example?

Could you expand on your idea?

As a result of using this method, students' contributions will move beyond surface-level discussions and into an intricate and detailed dialogue. This method is effective because it demonstrates to students that their personal interpretations and ideas are vital to the learning process. "These language functions occur in direct correlation to the amount of time that teachers and students (a) cross-reference each others thinking, (b) engage in conversation by repeating the same phases spoken by others, and (c) hold authentic questions and answer periods as the heart of oral discussions in each content discipline" (Block, 2004a). In a K–2 classroom, focus on asking students about what they are feeling. (This question provides students with the opportunity to talk about how it makes them feel.) For grade 3–6 classrooms, have students write out their answers to three or four questions, then share them orally. In grades 7–12, divide students into groups of three and have them ask each other the questions from above. Talk to the students about the differences and similarities in the answers from their group.

Method 3: Write and Share

To begin this lesson, ask students to write down an interpretation that evolved about a character, theory, or conflict while reading the book being discussed. Students will be required to provide colorful details and to fully develop their thoughts. Each student will then share his or her idea with the class. In grades K–2, rather than writing down their interpretations, students can draw a picture that represents a question they have about the book. The teacher will then field questions that students may have about a character, theory, or conflict. In grades 3–6, have students write down their ideas in detail and compare with their neighbor. For grades 7–12, the students will write down their interpretations, but will also share their ideas with the class. After sharing they can act out a conflict or theory, or students can act out a character and have the class guess which character the student is playing.

Method 4: Groups, Goals, and Accomplishments

Divide students into small reading groups. Ask every group member to record three goals they wish their group could accomplish. Each student then shares his or her ideas with the group. Next, have the group decide collectively on one goal they wish to accomplish after they have finished reading the text. After this lesson, everyone is to assess the progress of the group's work in relation to the specific goal at hand. With grades K–2, read to the students the first chapter of a thrilling book, then ask them to talk about what they think will happen next. For grades 3–6, ask students to suggest goals they wish to accomplish as a class after reading the text, then read the text as a class and assess whether or not the goals were met. For grades 7–12, ask students to write down three goals they want their group to accomplish, then divide them into groups and have them share their goals with the group. Last, as a group, have them collectively choose one goal. This method works because students are able to decide the level of importance that setting goals and achieving those goals has.

In review, the four most successful methods of assisting gifted readers and their classmates to overcome communication apprehension are "Complete the Sentence," "Thoughts and Responses," Write and Share," and "Groups, Goals, and Accomplishments." As these methods are used, teachers will respect individual differences and provide ample opportunities for students to successfully develop their voices. It is important for teachers to be consistent with gifted learners. If given the opportunity, students affected by communication apprehension can succeed (Block & Mangieri, 1996). A steady pattern of incorporating oral language into the classroom will result in an enriched experience for both the teacher and the students.

TEACHERS PUTTING IDEAS INTO ACTION

1. What did you learn about your abilities to teach gifted students?

2. Which methods will be easiest for you to adapt into your classroom?

3. Which methods will be most difficult for you to incorporate into your classroom?

4. What strategies will you use to reach students with communication apprehension?

5. What did you learn about assessment methods?

SUMMARY

In this chapter, we described two methods teachers can use to help students develop aspects of creativity: "Who I Am" and "Living in the Now." We also

Figure 9.1   Literary Collection: Learning About Our Place in the World

Assessing Creativity of Oral Language

It is important for students to know that you hold them accountable for increases in their creativity and oral speaking ability. Many informal assessments can assist you in assessing students' growth and weaknesses. In this section, we describe three oral language informal assessment measures: one example of how to build students' higher level creative problem-solving abilities, one example of assessing students' oral needs, and one example of a test of creative thinking.

Assessment 1: Problem-Solving Assessment

Be yourself in the following situation and write about all that you would think and do. A friend comes to you with a problem. Your friend is consistently failing his or her math homework. Your friend does not know how to solve the problem. You do not know how to solve the problem either. Describe in essay form what the problem is and what you and your friend can do together to try and solve the problem.

Assessment 2: Oral-Language Needs Monitor

In the blank before each number, write today's date if you think you do that item well. If you know a way you want to improve on an item, leave the blank before the item empty and describe what you want to improve on the line after that item. Later in the year, when you have improved that ability, write the date in the blank when you achieve this goal (Block & Mangieri, 2003).

_____ 1. Pronounce words well: Recognize and correct substitutions ("w" for "v"), omissions ("member" for "remember"), insertions, and distortions.

_____ 2. Use good pitch and tone of speaking _____

_____ 3. Give reasoned judgments, support my opinions, and speak concisely and effectively.

_____ 4. Use appropriate speed. _____

_____ 5. Use adequate volume. _____

_____ 6. Check for accuracy of spoken statements. _____

_____ 7. Ask questions for clarification. _____

_____ 8. State novel but probable points. _____

_____ 9. Give solutions or compromises for conflicting data. _____

_____10. Do not let dialect interfere with meaning. _____

Assessment 3: Associative Word Test of Creative Thinking

Read the three words in each line and think of a fourth that when added gives new meaning or is related to each of the words: e.g., river, note, blood, _____. The fourth word may come before or after the given words.

This "associative" word answer is "bank." Now think of a word that fits with the three others in each row.

1. sunflower	butter	fever	_____
2. first	band	financial	_____
3. sun	reading	plastic	_____
4. class	stage	soccer	_____
5. file	head	toe	_____

*Answers to the Associative Word Test:

1. yellow
2. aid
3. glasses
4. coach
5. nail

discussed four methods for developing increased oral language communication: "Complete the Sentence," "Thoughts and Responses," "Write and Share," and "Groups, Goals, and Accomplishments." We also presented three tests and assessment instruments—Problem-Solving Assessment, Oral-Language Needs Monitor, and Associative Word Test of Creative Thinking—that can assist you to evaluate your students' strengths and weaknesses in each of these areas. The strategies discussed in this chapter will allow teachers to better provide for gifted learners. Teachers should be able to offer a more balanced experience while developing creativity. It was our desire to supply teachers with the necessary tools to enhance the literary success of gifted students. Also, it was our goal to eliminate communication apprehension in the minds of gifted learners.

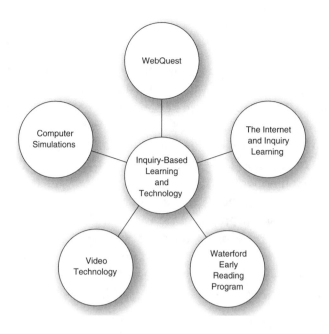

10

Building Efficiency in Using Information Through Inquiry-Based Learning and Technology

Dorothy A. Sisk

Jasmine, a four-year-old, quickly slipped into her seat in the Waterford Laboratory, shyly noticing the other five-years-olds who were already busily engaged in the daily lesson. The teacher showed her how to turn the computer on and how to move the mouse, and together they started the activity. Very quickly, she said, "I can do it." And she did—the program introduced her to the use of the mouse and how to be comfortable in responding to the cues given by the program in a self-directed manner.

Each day she generated a story on the computer to take home to share with her mother and grandmother. Jasmine progressed as well as the other students, mastering all of the reading standards for a kindergarten student. Her grandmother said the Waterford Early Reading Program stimulated her interest in reading, and Jasmine shared that she looked forward to spending time in the lab "working with my computer." She drew pictures of herself and her computer in her daily journal.

COLLABORATIVE LITERACY AT WORK

This chapter examines the use of technology to promote inquiry-based learning, ways to build efficiency in using information, and the importance of developing self-regulation in students like Jasmine. We explore the many possibilities for the use of technology, particularly its use in developing higher order thinking, which is a focus for many gifted education programs. We discuss subject matter acceleration through the use of distance learning as a viable means to meet the needs of secondary gifted and advanced students and include them as standards for all students in reading and content subject areas, and we provide examples of ways technology can be integrated within the regular classroom for all students through collaborative literacy activities. We discuss the research base for a number of program adaptations, followed by Ideas into Action, focusing on program adaptations in technology, including WebQuest, that build efficiency in using information and the Internet as a resource for inquiry. We also discuss the importance of transforming information acquired through inquiry into meaningful products.

We discuss the Waterford Early Reading Program and the use of CD-ROM storybooks for young children. We cover the use of computer software and technology tools including interactive software, software to develop higher order thinking skills, video technology, graphic organizers, and computer simulation as viable methods of meeting the needs of gifted students and advanced readers.

We provide a case study as an example of a classroom teacher using collaborative literacy in WebQuests, followed by Teachers Putting Ideas into Action to extend the content of the chapter.

The chapter goals are to:

- Build an understanding of the importance of technology in assisting gifted students and advanced readers in gaining and using information.
- Build an understanding of the importance of all students developing the ability to use the Internet and e-mail for gaining information and building good communication skills.
- Build an understanding of the importance of distance learning as a means to accelerate education for gifted students and advanced readers.

- Develop an understanding of how technology can assist inquiry-based learning and problem-based learning through WebQuests.
- Develop an understanding of the use of computer software and technology tools for all students and interactive software and video technology to extend information in collaborative literacy activities.
- Develop an understanding of how graphic organizers can develop and strengthen higher order thinking.

USE OF TECHNOLOGY TO PROMOTE INQUIRY-BASED LEARNING

There are limitless possibilities for the use of technology to promote inquiry-based learning for advanced readers and gifted students, and in many schools, students interact with computers in almost all phases of learning. The development of integrated software and powerful hardware and the expansion of the Internet have placed computer technology in the middle of what many educators call an information revolution, and the potential for the use of technology is far greater than currently realized in today's classrooms. Barr and Tagg (1999) stressed that intuitive learning, or learning through nonrational or nonlogical means, can be enhanced through the use of high-resolution graphics programs that encourage students to explore through visual representations and build intuitive understanding that is not possible in two-dimensional print pages. There are a number of ways teachers can use computers in the areas of word processing, technology, or electronic texts, including publishing the work of students, integrating the Internet into the curriculum, researching information on-line, using databases and spreadsheets for studying topics, and identifying and using various sites for a variety of instructional and management materials (Anderson & Speck, 2001).

Two technology tools that all students need to master are the Internet and e-mail. Computers can also be used with all students in computer-assisted instruction (CAI), including tutorials, games, and simulations, which can be highly motivating for struggling students. Computers help students to develop and refine their thinking skills and can serve as tools to facilitate independent and collaborative group inquiry-based learning through word processing and authoring systems.

Subject matter acceleration for gifted students and advanced readers can be implemented via distance learning courses, which can provide access to highly qualified instructors and advanced subject matter that small and rural school districts may not be able to access. At the high-school level, Advanced Placement (AP) courses are on-line to provide students opportunities to earn university credit, and many gifted students graduate from high school with 12–24 hours of college credit (Sisk, 2005a).

RESEARCH BASE

The research base for using information through inquiry-based learning and technology is quite positive for subject matter acceleration, as indicated by students who successfully master material in short periods of time.

Gilbert-Macmillan (2000) reported that a group of 18 eighth-grade students mastered one and one-half years in five months of instruction using the Stanford University Educational Program for Gifted Youth (EPGY). The current program used by EPGY is based on the work of Suppes (1980) with highly gifted students, ages 10–15 with IQs of 165, who were provided opportunities to complete CAI courses at their own pace from home through terminal access to the mainframe computer at Stanford University (Pyryt, 2003).

Longitudinal research studies conducted by the Johns Hopkins University support the effectiveness of AP courses (Brody, Assouline, & Stanley, 1990). In a study of early entrants at the Johns Hopkins University, it was found that the number of AP credits was the only statistically significant predictor of GPA, semesters on the Dean's list, and graduation honors. AP courses have been computerized through EPGY (Ravaglia, de Barros, & Suppes, 1995).

Bowman (1998) studied the effectiveness of the computer as a tool in the teaching learning process while working with low-achieving urban third-grade students in a three-month after-school program. Tutors used *PrintShop* software to support the teaching of word identification and phonic generalizations. The program provided practice with commercial electronic reading programs with feedback, continuous progress reports, and a World Wide Web–based project that paired students with other students in a nearby state to work on-line collaboratively in writing projects. The findings indicated that the reading performance of the students improved by one grade level in the three-month program, with additional improvement in computer skills.

Pinkard (1999) conducted an investigation with African American children in which culturally responsive software, including *Rappin' Reader* and *Say, Say, Oh Playmate*, was used. Small groups of beginning readers made substantial gains in basic sight vocabulary, and Pinkard reported that the software programs were very effective because the students could relate to the music that capitalized on their language and interests.

Chu (1995) studied interactive computer books with three first-grade boys, using literature-based hypertext software developed by Discis Knowledge Research. The computer books Chu included were *The Tale of Peter Rabbit* by Beatrix Potter, *Scary Poems for Rotten Kids* by Sean O'Huigin, *The Paper Bag Princess* by Robert Munsch, *Cinderella* by Charles Perrault, and *Benjamin Bunny* by Beatrix Potter. Chu made the following concluding comments about the study:

> The three readers benefited from their hands-on experience with computer books. They talked, moved about, and made contrasts and comparisons between story events, characters, and real life experiences. They were active learners, not passive recipients of information. (p. 364)

The Dallas Independent School District in Texas studied the effectiveness of the Waterford Early Reading Program for Levels 1 and 2, involving a total of 527 students, including 272 kindergartners and 255 first graders as participants. Students were tested in spring 1996 (kindergarten only), in 1997, and in 1998 on the ITBS. The ITBS subtest scores for vocabulary and word analysis (kindergarten) and reading comprehension (first grade) were used to determine outcomes, and district scores were used as a comparison. Robert Elementary, with a limited English proficiency kindergarten population of 80 percent and low-income population of 93 percent, made the most significant gains over the course of two years. By year two, the students demonstrated a gain of 37 on vocabulary and 17.9 on word analysis (Education Commission of the States, 2005).

Newark, New Jersey, initiated a Waterford Level program in eight classes and matched these classes with seven control classes for a total of 265 participating students. Students in the experimental and control classes were pretested in September and October and posttested in June, using the Waterford Reading Inventory (WRI), the Test of Early Reading Ability-2 (TERA-2), and the Lindamood Auditory Conceptualization Test. The results indicated that students in the experimental classes outperformed students in the control classes on all three of the assessment measures used, at the .001 level of significance (Education Commission of the States, 2005).

IDEAS INTO ACTION

WebQuests to Build Efficiency in Using Information Through Inquiry

Many people used to think that learning was all about gaining information and memorizing facts; however, today, with the information explosion, the best method of gaining information, particularly for those who teach advanced readers or gifted students, is the use of WebQuests.

> WebQuests are inquiry-oriented activities in which some or all the information that students interact with comes from resources on the Internet.

There are two levels of WebQuests. One is short-term to gather information and to integrate that information with the student's prior knowledge of the topic, enabling the refinement and extension of past knowledge. This integration is important for gifted students who may possess considerable background information on a topic prior to beginning an inquiry, yet they may still need to extend that knowledge or to refine it with up-to-date information.

The second level of a WebQuest is a long-term effort in which students are involved in analyzing a body of knowledge in depth and applying this newfound information in a creative way, perhaps creating something that other students can use in collaborative literacy activities, either on-line or off. Long-term WebQuests meet all of the requirements that Renzulli (1978) suggested for gifted students in his Triad Enrichment model for Level III of independent study. A long-term WebQuest may take from a week to a month depending on the nature of the inquiry, and a short-term WebQuest may take as little time as one class period. Short-term WebQuests can be used in small-group collaborative literacy study with the entire class working on an activity that can serve as an introductory lesson.

WebQuests are linked to the development and use of higher level thinking skills, one of the requirements in both state and national standards for gifted education as noted in the standards of the Council for Exceptional Children (CEC), the International Reading Association (IRA), and the National Council for Teacher Education (NCTE). Higher order thinking skills include inferring, predicting, summarizing, and analyzing, which are included in standards for all students in content subject areas. WebQuests provide opportunities for students to compare, identify, and discuss similarities and differences between the information they locate and the prior knowledge they bring to the inquiry. As students examine their information, there are opportunities to classify and group findings in categories and to infer generalizations from the gathered information. In addition, students can be involved in deductive reasoning in which they infer unstated consequences and conditions from generalizations located in their WebQuest. Last, there is ample opportunity for students to become involved in abstract thinking and in identifying and discussing themes or patterns that they note in their new-found information.

Surfing the net without a specific task is rarely productive for any student, and in most school settings connect time on computers may be limited. WebQuests are made up of several components, including setting the stage or an introduction, identifying inquiry questions, engaging the students in a search, and producing an end product such as a document, presentation, debate, or collaborative literacy activity that can extend the WebQuest to an entire classroom of students. If students are working in collaborative literacy groups, they can discuss the questions that are suggested as guides for their inquiry; students may select a question to address and then share their ideas in a group session. Gifted students and advanced readers may want to work independently on answering their questions.

Figure 10.1   Locating and Using Information

- What information do I need? How do I find it?
- Where is the information located? How is the information obtained?
- How reliable is the information?
- How can I share what I learned from this information?

Figure 10.1 shows a list of questions that students can use as guidelines to locate and use information in their WebQuest.

The Internet as a Resource for Inquiry

There are many valuable source of experts in many forms and disciplines on the Internet, and students can access and ask them questions that they've identified for their inquiry. Figure 10.2 lists a number of sources.

Figure 10.2 Ask the Expert

- Ask an Entomologist

  (http://www.ent.iastate.edu/mailinglist/bugnet/question.html)

- Ask an Ecologist

  (http://www.nceas.ucsb.edu/nceas-web/kids/ecology/index.htm)

- Ask a Biologist (http://askabiologist.asu.edu)

- Ask a Historian or an Archeologist:

  (http://www.cr.nps.gov/history/askhist.htm)

- Ask a Linguist (http://www.linguist.emich.edu/~ask~ling.htm)

- Ask a NASA Scientist

  (http://imagine.gsfc.nasa.gov/docs/askastro/ask_an_astronomer.html)

Transforming Information Acquired Through Inquiry on the Internet

When gifted students and advanced readers engage in inquiry, the type of product that they generate needs to reflect the depth and complexity suggested in the Layered Curriculum of Kaplan (2005). The product of their investigation or inquiry needs to represent more than just the acquisition of knowledge. A goal for gifted students and advanced learners would be to transform the knowledge into an application that involves synthesis and analysis. Maker and Nielson (1996) have listed seven steps that students need to address in inquiry:

1. Information filtration
2. Idea generalization
3. Centralization
4. Reflection
5. Manipulation
6. Execution
7. Communication

When students are engaged in information filtration, they process, interpret, refine, and extrapolate knowledge and ideas that they gain from their research. In idea generalization, they examine the information and emphasize and analyze selected elements, concepts, and ideas that are of high interest to them. In centralization, the students select, decide, and focus on a specific idea or element of information. In reflection, the students find time to consider, ponder, and then evaluate or judge the selected idea. In manipulation, the students engage in testing or experimenting with the ideas and change or improve the data as necessary. In execution, the students decide, organize, prepare, and produce a product to share or display the idea. Last, in communication, the students share, perform, display, or disseminate the product to an authentic audience (Maker & Nielson, 1996). Teachers can use the seven steps in a collaborative literacy lesson by assigning the students to small groups to become involved in inquiry. It is important to assign leadership roles to students who are willing and capable of monitoring and guiding their group's progress. Gifted students and advanced readers could assume these roles and work collaboratively with students of all levels. Learning-disabled and struggling students will benefit considerably from the structure in the process.

Technology to Stimulate Early Reading

Waterford Early Reading Program

The primary goal of the Waterford Early Reading Program is to stimulate early reading and to assist all children, particularly struggling readers, in building the skills to become successful readers. The program also introduces students to the world of the computer: They learn to use the mouse and to follow prompts to respond in a self-directed manner. The program can be used in kindergarten and has been successfully used in one research study (see box on Project Success Express) with low-income prekindergarten students. The primary components of the program are:

- Daily individualized instruction with highly interactive software
- Best teaching practices
- Ongoing assessment
- Ongoing professional development
- School-to-home link
- Parent involvement

PROJECT SUCCESS EXPRESS–A WATERFORD PROJECT

Project Success Express was initiated in Beaumont, Texas, in 2000 as a collaborative project between Lamar University, Beaumont Independent School District's Head Start Program, and Exxon Mobil. The program works with 36 Head Start children, and integrates teacher training focusing on creative teaching strategies. In 2005, the program was held at Dunbar Elementary School with two lead teachers and four participating co-teachers working with 18 children in each of the two classes. The teachers developed curriculum for the children using the theme of Animals. One class was introduced to activities focusing on the farm, and the other class focused on the zoo. Each class engaged in collaborative literacy activities with read-alouds and reading centers to identify the characters, the problem, and the solution of stories introduced in the read-alouds.

Algebraic thinking was integrated with all of the activities, using the CTMM standards for kindergarten. Children lined up for lunch, changes in classes, and bathroom breaks in patterns: boy-girl-boy, sandals-tennis shoes-sandals, and colors. They made Venn diagrams with hula hoops and used T-charts to indicate their preferences for stories, snacks, and activities. Each day, the children spent 20 minutes in the Waterford Lab with 18 computers, so each child had access to a computer and a laser printer to print the stories they generated. These stories were taken home for their parents to share, and a literacy afternoon was held for parents to work side by side with their children.

The program ran for two weeks from 8:00 a.m. to 1:00 p.m. for the children, and until 3:00 p.m. for the teachers to debrief, observe the videos of daily lessons, discuss the activities that the children experienced, and plan the next day. Each child was assessed on a pretest measuring their skills in math and their emerging literacy based on the kindergarten standards in reading. At the end of the session in 2005, 85 percent of the children mastered the kindergarten standards in math and reading, and three children were recommended for the gifted program. One child was fluently reading at the end of the session on a first-grade level (Sisk, 2005b).

There are three levels in the Waterford program: Level One for pre–K or K, referred to as emergent literacy; Level Two, implemented in first grade, is called Beginning Reading; and Level Three is for second-grade fluent readers. The Waterford Early Reading professionals suggest that school districts wishing to install the program provide one to four multimedia computers networked to a high-speed laser printer in each classroom. This will provide every student classroom with access to use the program for 15–30 minutes of daily individualized instruction in literacy skills. Waterford strongly encourages schools to implement all three program levels to achieve the goal of fluent reading for all students by the end of second grade.

CD-ROM storybooks present literature for children with text and illustrations similar to a traditional text, but they also include elements designed to enhance the reading experience for beginning readers. Gifted students and advanced young readers who have developed the ability to focus and self-regulate will enjoy the "hot spots" on many pages of the stories, which they can activate to produce animated graphics, sound effects, and other features. After the students produce their animated graphics, many of which can be printed for them, the teacher can bring them together for a collaborative literacy experience to share what they have created, identify which sounds they liked, and retell the story in their own words.

Students can manipulate and individualize their reading environment by choosing to highlight a word or phrase, hear audio pronunciations, or click on a word to access its definition. Some CD-ROM storybooks present spelling analogies for the children when they click on a word within the text, and others read the entire story automatically, simulating a read-aloud experience for the child.

CD-ROM storybooks enhance reading comprehension for all students, and students are able to give richer story retelling after reading them (Doty, Popplewell, & Byers, 2003; Pearman, 2003). They enhance gifted students and advanced readers' love of reading and stimulate their willingness and interest in communicating with others. In collaborative literacy discussion groups, gifted students and advanced readers who have just experienced story reading via CD-ROM and are still excited about the activity can be further involved in buddy reading or can work with other students in collaborative reading circles.

Computer Software and Technology Tools

Computer technology offers access to a multitude of information resources, promotes interaction among students, and encourages them to manipulate images and information. CD-ROMs with large databases make information available to students in word-processing format that they can learn to organize, and videodiscs can be used to access and hold information that the students can manipulate and from which they can draw conclusions and make interpretations.

Interactive Software

Interactive software such as *Gertrude's Puzzles* encourages students to use inductive thinking in situations that cannot be modeled with concrete objects. *Gertrude's Puzzles* (The Learning Company, 1983) simulates using attribute blocks and Venn diagrams to illustrate characteristics of sets. Students are not provided information on the attributes of a variety of sets; they must use their inductive thinking to infer the characteristics of a set by observing whether their placement of the figures remains in the circle or falls out. Students who are adept in spatial skills will profit by working in collaborative literacy groups to explore the puzzles, and they can serve as leaders with less able students in building spatial skills. Parks (2005) said that the unique learning aspect in *Gertrude's Puzzles* is that concept attainment is superimposed on a classification task.

Software to Develop Higher Order Thinking Skills

The *Higher Order Thinking Skills* (*HOTS*) program is one example of computer software to develop higher order thinking and questioning skills. Gifted students enjoy using *HOTS* because they can easily perform the tasks, and low-performing students can increase their skill development in higher order thinking by working in collaborative literacy groups with gifted and advanced reading students who can model and share their thinking involved in using the software. By talking about their thinking, all of the students are able to experience metacognition, or thinking about their thinking. *HOTS* was designed for middle- and high-school students, but it can be used with gifted students and advanced readers in elementary school as well.

Another example of computer software to stimulate higher order thinking is *Mindlink* (Mauzy, 1991). This software introduces students to the Synectics process of creative thinking, which uses four analogies to form or develop novel ideas or approaches. Direct analogies are used as similes of the problems; personal analogies often involve students in role playing parts of a problem; symbolic analogies use symbols to describe the problem; and fantasy analogies ask students to express the idea in a mythical or magical approach (Gordon, 1961). *Mindlink* involves students in generating ideas similar to brainstorming activities. Students are asked to think of as many possibilities as they can to discover new perspectives, to engage in different speculations, and to generate more ideas in simulated interactive participation. The software provides different stimuli and takes students on a creative "bird walk." This part of the software at first may appear to be unrelated to the problem, but it provides, through the imagery process, opportunities for students to use analogical thinking, which most students would not use if they were just asked to focus on the problem (Parks, 2005).

Video Technology

Video technology can assist gifted students and advanced readers in developing problem-solving skills using real-world problems. A series of videodiscs developed by the Vanderbilt Learning Technology Center (1996) engages students in generating and solving subproblems in order to resolve larger issues or themes. This incremental approach also works well in collaborative groups, as the more spontaneous students will stimulate the steady thinkers to become more involved in problem solving.

Using Graphic Organizers to Aid Higher Order Thinking

Graphic organizers can help students depict their ideas quickly and easily, and computer software can be used to download their ideas into diagrams. Diagrams serve as visual aids to creative thinking, critical thinking, decision making, and planning. One example of graphic software is *Inspiration* (Inspiration Software, 1994), which is programmed to reproduce standard design elements of graphic organizers (flowchart symbols, arrows, boxes, ovals, icons, clip art, etc.). Parks (2005) describes the use of *Inspiration* as "doodling with a computer," and says that students can draw out their ideas as quickly on the computer as they can sketch them on paper:

> Helping students use computer drawing to depict their thinking and learning improves their motivation to show what they know and models the thinking with computer skills that are becoming increasingly common in the workplace. (p. 273)

Computer Simulations

Computer simulations provide students with opportunities to move beyond the classroom walls to visit the White House, observe the latest expedition of NASA, experience current exhibits at the Smithsonian, check the status of the stock market, and interact with other students in classrooms throughout the world (Lewis & Doorlag, 2003).

Reporter Project is a computer simulation that encourages students to function as writers, using a simulated newspaper format. This simulation can be used with middle-school gifted students, and in high-school English classes with all students. A student reporter is placed in a situation in which he or she must choose which sections of the paper should target a story. This decision influences the way in which the story will be written and what facts will need to be highlighted. For example, if a student reporter is covering a sports story for the Sports section, details about the game, the players, and the scores will be included. Yet, if the same game is to be placed in the People and Style section of the paper, the story would highlight the dignitaries attending and would include some fashion information.

Students who role-play a reporter search for pertinent facts and then write their stories. Later, the reporter may role-play a writer who submits the story to the editor (the computer), who checks key words in the story and then provides feedback on the logic of the facts. Real news footage is available on this computer simulation, courtesy of CBS News, which provides added motivation for the visual learner. Reporter project software also enables the students to print their stories, which are particularly helpful for collaborative sharing with other classes.

Case Study

The use of WebQuests as an inquiry-based strategy is illustrated in case study format as Ms. Reid works with her high-school students. The tenth-grade students in her class come in quickly and arrange themselves and their chairs in a discussion circle, since she had previously reminded them they would be working in a collaborative literacy activity with WebQuests. Ms. Reid shares with the students that the superintendent of their district wants them to serve as reporters and to write several articles on the growing problem of school and community violence. She says that the superintendent wants their articles by the end of the month, approximately three class periods from now, and one article will be selected to be presented at the local Board of Education meeting.

Reid asks the students to brainstorm a series of questions that they can use to address the problem of violence, and they begin to generate a list that one of the students writes on a class chart:

- Does watching TV cause people to be violent?
- Do school crimes happen in all schools, large ones and small ones?
- Are metal detectors helping to prevent problems of violence in schools?
- Is bullying a part of violence?
- How much of a problem do we have in our school and in our community?

Ms. Reid introduces the class to the WebQuest *Krool Zone* and reminds them that the Internet represents a great source of information, but it is important for them to read between the lines. Several students share how they read between the lines when their parents change family rules or activities without any apparent reason. One student says that he always reads between the lines while he reads novels and that he can figure out what is going to happen next. Another student adds that she reads between the lines while watching television.

Ms. Reid gently guides the students back to the WebQuest. She asks them to examine the questions listed in the evaluation rubric of *Krool Zone* and suggests they discuss these questions in collaborative groups of four. She says, "This will energize you for your inquiry." The class forms five groups of four students, and they enthusiastically begin to discuss the three questions:

1. What do school counselors need to do to help schools?

2. What accounts for 20 percent of all deaths in the 10–24 age groups?

3. What seems to be the best explanation for the decrease in guns in school?

After considerable lively discussion, Ms. Reid asks the students to work in dyads to explore the subject sampler on school safety issues focusing on school violence. She reminds them to reflect on the question "What does this subject have to do with me?" Ms. Reid asks the students to explore a number of links to Web sites including:

Colorado Shooting—A Photo Journal; School Shootings—Interactive Map; Comments on School Violence; Burn the Schools—Save the Children; Fighting Back at School; Alternatives in Education—links; and President George Bush on Education.

Each dyad chooses the link or links they want to examine and then uses the evaluation rubric provided by the WebQuest to explore the link. The evaluation rubric asks the students to skim the information, choose or select one aspect they find interesting, and then apply the information by giving examples of how the information could be used and what action they might take; then they reflect on their feelings and relate the information to themselves.

Ms. Reid writes a summary of the rubric on the flip chart:

Which points *seem* most important to you?

What would you do to improve the situation?

The students talk softly in their dyads and then move to their collaborative writing center to begin their stories. Ms. Reid walks among the students and stops by several to examine their work. The bell rings, and she reminds them that they can work on their stories at home. They reluctantly gather their materials for the next class, and some of them are grumbling. Ms. Reid says, "I know, I know, our time is too short."

The students write stories using the information they discover, and one story is selected by the Superintendent to be published in the school district newsletter. The students suggest that one family in a neighborhood block be identified as an individual family to be contacted if danger of any kind or violence is noticed in a community. The students also identify people they want to invite to their class as guest speakers, particularly student volunteers for a safe campus at a nearby university. Ms. Reid said that the use of WebQuests increased the students' self-esteem and definitely increased their motivation to learn. The students were particularly interested in what parents can do to help their children to avoid becoming troubled teens. They stressed the importance of parents talking with young children to shape their attitudes, knowledge, and behavior while they are still open to positive influences. Many of the students also shared that it was helpful when someone talked to them or asked them questions.

TEACHERS PUTTING IDEAS INTO ACTION

Design a WebQuest

The steps in designing a WebQuest include generating an opening statement that identifies guiding questions for the inquiry, a search for information, comparing and contrasting the information with the guiding inquiry questions, and a conclusion. Design a WebQuest for yourself that would enable you to identify gifted students and advanced readers.

Boy, Interrupted

The Jonathan Sarfan Foer (2005) novel *Boy, Interrupted* tells of a nine-year-old highly gifted boy named Oskar who is an inventor, a jewelry designer, a percussionist, an origamist, a pacifist, a Central Park archaeologist, a romantic, and a collector of rare coins and butterflies that have died natural deaths and of Beatles memorabilia. Oskar lost his father in the September 11 disaster and his grandfather to the silence that followed the World War II bombs. The mute grandfather has the words *yes* and *no* tattooed on the palms of his hands, and the grandmother writes her life story on a typewriter that has no ribbon. One of the themes of the book is the undying hope for human connection and the courage to imagine a world without war.

Find a copy of the book and, in a small group of teachers, read parts of it aloud to one another to note how Oskar, his grandmother, and his grandfather take turns telling their stories of grief and healing, of silence kept, and silence broken. Discuss Oskar's characteristics and compare them to the lists of characteristics of gifted students in Chapter 1. How are these characteristics demonstrated in Oskar, such as his continuous stream of imaginary inventions that include a teakettle that can recite Shakespeare and a birdseed shirt that humans could use until they get wings?

Learning With the Computer Versus Learning From the Computer

Labbo and Reinking (1999) supported the view that learning with the computer can stimulate thinking and result in changing the orientations of students toward learning. This is particularly important for advanced readers and gifted students. Discuss the differences that you see between learning *from* the computer, such as in drill and practice exercises, and learning *with* the computer. Address how learning with the computer can support the instructional goals of developing the ability of all students to become effective problem solvers, decision makers, communicators, and informed, responsible, contributing citizens.

Access the Experts

Select one of the experts listed as an Internet source in Figure 10.2 of this chapter and generate a series of questions that you can send to the experts that are related to a specific discipline. How helpful did you find the expert that you chose? Find at least 10 additional Ask an Expert Sources on the Internet that students could use in their inquiry.

Transforming Information

Discuss the importance of gifted students going beyond the stage of acquisition of knowledge, and how the transformation of content relates to higher order thinking, which is an essential focus in gifted programs. The format that Maker and Nielson (1996) suggested as a guide is very helpful for teachers and students who are trying to create a product that represents more than mere sharing of facts and knowledge. How realistic do you think it is for gifted students to turn new knowledge that they have acquired in their inquiry into something more meaningful? Maker and Nielson said that the ultimate goal of product development for gifted students is to transform student research into new thoughts, ideas, and perspectives. Is this feasible in the regular classroom? Provide examples of your students or students that you know who have accomplished this transformation.

SUMMARY

This chapter discussed the use of technology to promote inquiry-based learning and to build efficiency in using information. We offered examples of how teachers can use computers in the classroom, including computer-assisted instruction (CAI) and distance learning for Advanced Placement (AP) courses, to accelerate the learning for gifted students and advanced readers. We summarized the research base for these program adaptations, followed by Ideas into Action. We discussed the use of WebQuests to build efficiency in using information through inquiry, with special attention to locating and using information and the importance of gifted students and advanced readers transforming information acquired through the Internet into unique products.

We introduced the Waterford Early Reading Program, a program that stimulates early reading and assists all children in building the skills to become successful readers. We discussed the use of CD-ROM storybooks for early readers and introduced computer software and technology tools including interactive software such as *Gertrude's Puzzles*, the *Higher Order Thinking Skills* (HOTS) program, video technology, the use of graphic organizers to aid in the development of higher order thinking, and computer simulations. We shared a case study in which a secondary teacher uses a WebQuest (*Krool Zone*) to illustrate how a WebQuest can be used with tenth-grade students. In Ideas into Action, we offered a selection of activities that teachers can explore to extend the information in the chapter; it included an activity based on Foer's novel *Boy, Interrupted* (2005) about a gifted boy.

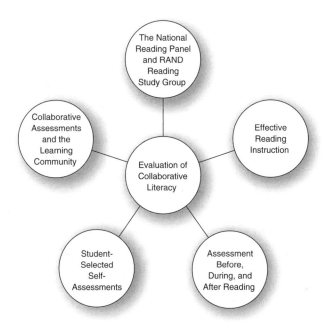

Evaluation of Collaborative Literacy in Every Classroom

Cathy Collins Block and Sheri R. Parris

PERSONAL REFLECTION

We would like to introduce you to Conrad, a gifted upper elementary school student. Because he answered every question on his Stanford Achievement Test correctly, we asked him to share his viewpoint on using the effective collaborative literacy assessments that this chapter describes. We interviewed Conrad because he blossomed as soon as Ms. Escamilla, his teacher, implemented the practices described in the previous chapters of this book. Conrad asked us to tell teachers the following:

> In my former classes, I made a deal with myself that I would answer only three questions in class all week, no matter how much the teacher

wanted someone in the class to give her a correct answer. I made this promise with myself for every year after first grade because the other kids in my class hated it when I raised my hand to answer. They would make fun of me and say 'sissy pants' before I could even answer. Now that I am in Ms. Escamilla's Literacy Class for my fifth grade, I no longer make that promise to myself. In her class, I take evaluations that enable my friends and I to learn and complete together. We help each other. I also take tests that show me where I can improve in both my areas of strengths and weakness. Because of this, I read what I want to. I do reports that are more thoughtful, I write more creatively, and I love working with my friends. It is so cool! I want to answer every question I can in class now and so does everyone else. Why aren't the other smart kids identified through tests like we use where everyone gets to shine?

Not only do students value the assessments in this chapter, but teachers also report that the new forms of testing described in this chapter increase their effectiveness. For example, a fourth-grade teacher, Mr. Nichols, stated,

I saw the results of my students' "Think Till the End Test," and talk about hidden talents! I never knew that my students thought so deeply when they read. I have four students that I did not think, prior to this test, were pushing themselves enough. They just didn't seem to want to do their best. Now that I've begun using Collaborative Literacy Assessments, I find that my students are working harder, have become more self-regulated learners, and are more motivated to participate in literacy discussions and creative writing. Also, I am able to allow them to select more books that they want to read because they enjoy reading harder books. The books they choose challenge them more than ever before. All educators must have new assessment tools that enable readers to reach self-regulated reading success, activities by which students can learn.

COLLABORATIVE LITERACY AT WORK

The purpose of this chapter is to demonstrate several evaluations that can assist teachers in identifying the unique needs and strengths of today's K–12 students in the diverse population that our schools serve. Each assessment in this chapter identifies specific cognitive strategies necessary for gifted students, potentially gifted students, and those who have yet to be instructed to their highest level of literacy capabilities.

The chapter's goals are to:

- Provide the research base that supports the use of new methods of evaluating literacy in every classroom.
- Provide instructions as to how collaborative literacy assessments can be used to advance all students' literacy.

- Describe the step-by-step procedures to insert such evaluation tools into a comprehensive evaluation program that includes No Child Left Behind, criterion-referenced assessments, standardized assessments, and other informal teacher tests.

RICH RESEARCH BASE

In this final chapter, in addition to the goals cited above, it is our desire to complete the circle of information that we began in Chapter 1. We want to answer the questions introduced in Chapter 1 about how assessments can proceed, inform, and follow collaborative literacy activities. We also want to provide concrete methods by which students' gifts can be identified as introduced in Chapters 3–9.

The National Reading Panel (1999) and the RAND Reading Study Group (Sweet & Snow, 2002) found that the elementary school years are the most critical years for educators to diagnose the depths of all students' collaborative thinking competencies. Unless such determinations are made by third grade, most children will develop defense mechanisms to camouflage their weaknesses. Their shame, guilt, and history of failure as readers diminish their desire to make meaning from text. The very precise and effective assessment instruments in this chapter will tap into students' thought processes while they are engaged in reading so teachers can assist them to disarm this arsenal of defenses. If these students' metacognitions are not developed early, their chances of ever experiencing pleasure from reading in their lives significantly decrease (Block, 2004).

Other studies are underway to examine the effects of staff development programs designed to enhance teachers' assessment abilities. These are entitled the Best Practices Consortium, sponsored by the Institute for Literacy Enhancement (Mangieri, 2004). These training programs are researching new assessment initiatives that enable teachers to "get inside" students' heads as they read silently. The work to date at this institute documents that teachers want new metacognitive assessment tools. They want tests that not only assess what they have taught but how much students are *actively* using high-level thinking to craft their own meaning (Block, 2004; Tierney, 1998). These metacognitive assessment principles, founded on the processes gifted readers use when they read, follow:

- Collaborative Literacy Assessments should lead from behind. Students and teachers should assess and deliver instruction to address individual needs after students' assessments have been completed. Assessment should extend beyond improving present tests to making new tests that are more conceptually valid, based on research about the reading processes expert readers use.
- Unfortunately, in the past, test developers tried to make tests culture free, which is impossible: "Cultural free assessments afford, at best, only a partial, perhaps distorted, understanding of a student's [meta]comprehension ability." (Tierney, 1998, p. 381)

- Future literacy tests must allow for different students to have differing amounts of encouragement and support to measure the degrees that they are interrelating several reading processes. Some students have the potential to reveal their inner thoughts accurately, others do not, and still others do not process meaning metacognitively as they read. Future tests must gauge this level of knowledge more directly.
- Some metacognitive skills worth assessing cannot be evaluated except through student self-assessment (e.g., self-questioning, self-reported engagement, and degrees of interpretation).
- The interaction between speed, factual recall, vocabulary development, inference accuracy, and comprehension must be assessed. Presently, few tests measure such interactions.

In addition to being developmentally appropriate, assessments should contain sustained silent reading rather than "dipstick approaches." Instead of measuring all abilities in one day, using only a few paragraphs or page-length passages, future literacy tests should continue for several days and be calculated through reading for longer than five minutes on a specific topic.

To implement the most recent changes in effective reading instruction, teachers are incorporating new methods of assessments to identify all students' literacy gifts. The authentic assessments described in this chapter allow teachers to measure the competencies exhibited in collaborative literacy activities, performances, processes, and situations as described in chapters 1–9. Included in these assessments are teacher observations, samples of student reflection, and student self-evaluations. Our goal is to provide evidence-based instructional tests that assist educators in the evaluation of metacognitive processes and advanced literacy processes in action. They do not test literacy skills.

Metacognition, simply put, is "thinking about thinking," before, during, or after a literacy activity. It is the evaluation of what is thought and why it is thought. There is a direct relationship between the ability to assess cognitive abilities and the emergence of greater metacognitive thinking during literacy performances (Block, 2004). As cognitive skills are increasingly engaged without conscious effort, more mental processing is available for directed metacognitive thinking. For instance, a student who masters the cognitive skills required to decode will have more mental "focus" available to comprehend what is read and how it relates to prior knowledge, and formulate questions raised during a reading that still need to be answered. The end result is an increase in reading power. Thus, through use of the assessment of metacognitive abilities, teachers are able to identify individual cognitive skills that need to be enhanced so all students can improve their own literacy.

To begin, it is important to note that most of the collaborative literacy assessments in this chapter can be administered before, during, and after reading. When they are administered before reading, they provide information about a student's understanding of the task at hand and how to proceed. Assessments during reading provide valuable information about comprehension of the material read, said or written, and information that students have self-selected to retain. Assessments after reading provide students the opportunity to spend time thinking about what they have learned, recognizing possible errors in thinking, and engage in self-correction. To clarify, we list below a few general suggestions for effective collaborative literacy assessment before, during, and after a literacy activity.

COLLABORATIVE TOOLS

Assessment Before Reading

Teachers can question students on their plan for completing the reading assignment. Indicators of students' successful prereading processing include the following:

- Reference to their prior knowledge or the knowledge they need to complete a task
- Recognition of the purposes for reading this selection
- Reasonable estimation of the amount of time needed to complete the task
- Description of a plan, or sequence of actions leading to task completion.

It is also important to note that indicators of successful prereading thinking for struggling readers are concerned with decoding strategies, automatic word identificaton, and fluency (Fletcher, Morris, & Lyon, 2003).

Assessment During Reading

Teachers can question students during reading about how they are maintaining their plan for reading. Indicators of students' successful during-reading processing include the following:

- Engages in self-evaluation of progress made in understanding material
- Self-monitors for errors in comprehension, vocabulary, decoding, and fluency
- Seeks appropriate help (i.e., dictionary, asks questions, etc.) about meanings of difficult words or passages
- Can describe (verbally or in writing) the thought processes used to create meaning from the text
- Indicators of unsuccessful during-reading processing are evidenced through mispronunciation of words, small number of pages read silently, difficulty in decoding, and nondescriptive responses to reading

Assessment After Reading

Teachers can ask students to evaluate their own reading through verbal or written reports, written tests that include open-ended questions, group/class projects or discussions, or performances. After-reading responses indicating the success of an effective collaborative literacy activity and students' literacy growth include the following:

- Ability to give a descriptive reflection of the cognitive processing that was engaged during reading
- Ability to explain errors and self-corrections in the course of thinking and reading as well as knowledge of how these affected understanding
- Ability to assess how tasks could have been completed more effectively
- Ability to connect and generalize new knowledge to other life situations
- Asking for further clarification or additional help in comprehension, decoding, vocabulary, or fluency

Responses indicating unsuccessful after-reading metacognition pertain to underdeveloped decoding strategies, an absence of using visual or context clues, and minimal oral or written responses about the content of the reading material (Garner, 1987).

Teachers or students can ask the following questions to increase each reader's literacy strengths and talents:

Before—When you are *developing* the plan of action, ask yourself[1]

- Why am I reading this selection?
- What in my prior knowledge will help me with this particular task?
- In what direction do I want my thinking to take me?
- How much time do I have to complete the task?
- What should I do first, second, and third?

During—When you are *maintaining/monitoring* the plan of action, ask yourself

- How am I doing?
- Am I on the right track?
- What information is important to remember?
- Should I move in a different direction?
- Should I adjust the pace depending on the difficulty?
- What do I need to do if I do not understand?
- Can I describe the thinking strategies that I am using during my reading?

After—When you are *evaluating* the plan of action, ask yourself

- Overall, how well did I do?
- Did my particular course of thinking produce more or less than I had expected?
- What thinking strategies will I use differently next time? Why?
- Which thinking strategies help me the most?
- How might I apply this line of thinking to other problems?
- Do I need to go back through the task to fill in any "blanks" in my understanding?

The tests in this chapter also determine whether readers can monitor, regulate, and direct their thoughts to obtain a complete comprehension of text (Block, 2004; Harris & Hodges, 1995). Gifted readers know how they comprehend and why, at times, they do not comprehend well. They activate relevant prior knowledge and easily use newly learned information in their lives (Pearson, Roehler, Dole, & Duffy, 1992; Pressley & Afflerbach, 1995). They rapidly identify and image the most important ideas in a text (Brown & Palincsar, 1985; Reznitskaya & Anderson, 2001). They ask questions, draw inferences (NICHD, 2000; NRP, 1999), and use a wide variety of fix-up strategies (Block, Gambrell, & Pressley, 2003; Garner, 1987; Block & Israel, 2004).

New Collaborative Literacy Tests and How to Use Them

Research has demonstrated that teachers can use the following assessments with success. Teachers report that these tests scaffold, support, and document students' self-initiated literacy processes better than previous forms of evaluation. They evaluate growth more effectively by pinpointing exactly when students become active and self-initiated learners. These research-based tools are prototypes, and as such can be modified to address the complexity of individual student needs in single classrooms around the world.

"What Do We Need to Fill In?" Test

Based on the research of Cummins, Stewart, and Block (2005) and Oakhill and Yuill (1999), one of the most effective literacy assessments is a "What Do We Need to Fill In?" test. It allows students to recognize and use their metacognition to resolve inconsistencies that occur in a text. In this test, children describe what needs to be "fixed" in a particular passage so that the information makes sense. Next, they add thoughts to link adjacent sentences seamlessly. Children who lack sophistication in perceiving inferences and connecting them with literal comprehension will not perform well on this test. The results will indicate which types of information (inferential or literal) are not being processed by individual students.

In kindergarten through grade three, this test begins with a blank sheet of paper turned landscape style. It is divided into eight (or fewer) numbered boxes of equal size. Next, a page is read orally from a text, with one connecting sentence omitted. In each box, students write a sentence or draw a picture that could be used to complete the idea that was read. In the first box, students are to write (or draw) the information that they have deduced is missing from the first page. The second box, progressing horizontally across the page, is used to record their prediction of the next logical step on the second page (which was not read orally). The teacher can instruct students to fold their paper into the same number of boxes (1, 2, 4, 6, or 8) as he or she has such metacognitive challenges to give.

For example, if the text selection described how a mother and daughter were baking cookies to take to an elderly bedridden neighbor, the test would begin with the teacher reading all the following sentences from the page except for the one that has strikethrough on it:

> The mother and daughter mixed the dough for the chocolate chip cookies. They rolled the dough out and used a round cookie cutter to form the shape of each cookie. They placed the unbaked cookies on a cookie sheet that had been sprayed with Pam so these chocolate chip treats wouldn't stick to the sheet. ~~Then they placed the cookies in the oven to cook.~~ Then the cookies were taken out of the oven to cool.

Students are to determine what is missing in the sequence of events (in order for all of the sentences to fit together) and then record this information in the first box. The second box, progressing horizontally across the page, corresponds to the information that they predict must occur on the second page, although it was not read orally. This test allows children to tell what needs to be "fixed" in a particular passage so that a text is complete.

For older students, this test becomes a silent reading test. They read a text selection with numbered sticky notes over a sentence that communicates vital literal information. Students are to stop at each covered portion of text and record the literal sentence that should appear at this spot to make the text coherent. They may record their sentences on a sheet of notebook paper marked with the corresponding number on each sticky note.

This test can also be administered orally. When used in this way, the following steps are taken.

After a student has read a section, he or she recounts what was read in a retelling. Next, the tester asks: "What should we add to make this story more complete or easier for others to read?" When children read and tell what needs to be added to make the text easier for others to comprehend, they reveal what they need to comprehend better. As students answer this question, the testers write down as many of their comments as possible in the first column of the "What Do We Need to Fill In?" test. This entry is dated, and a separate boxed test is used for each child. This assessment is administered four times during the year. As each student returns to his or her seat, and before the next pupil comes to read the same passage, the tester determines the type of instruction needed and writes the child's name in the appropriate column of the "What Do We Need to Fill In?" instructional planner shown in Figure 11.1. During the next week, the teacher places children into groups based on the types of literal and inferential processes that need to be taught.

This boxed-test format can be modified in many ways, as shown in the first- and second-grade classrooms in our study. For instance, Ms. Painter, a first-grade teacher, allows one full sheet of paper for a single box, in which students write and/or draw a picture of the comprehension processes they used to deduce a conclusion for the book. Students also draw what they think the last picture in the book will be. Ms. Zinke, a second-grade teacher, asks students to use only four boxes to describe what is needed at marked sections of the text to make it fit together. She then uses the bottom portion of the boxed test as a single unit. Students are to take the full bottom half of the page to write the moral that the author is communicating in the story.

Figure 11.1 "What Do We Need to Fill In?" Instructional Planner

	Group 1	Group 2	Group 3	Group 4
1. Did not recognize that they did not comprehend	Robert Lance Paige			
2. Did not make connections between paragraphs		Suzette Margueretta		
3. Did not find main ideas				Paige Josh
4. Could not recall the sequence				
5. Did not infer				
6. Could not summarize			Robert Megan	
7. Did not recognize cause & effect				
8. Did not determine author's writing pattern or till the text				
9. Could not draw a conclusion or summarize				

"Did You Till the Text?" Test

Tilling a text is defined as the ability to identify traits in an author's writing style that clue meaning. It includes recognizing a text's organizational format and methods used to place emphasis on key points, being able to deduce an author's inferred meanings, and being able to fall in line with the pace and depth of an author's train of thought. According to research, there is a significant correlation between students' abilities to till a text and their abilities to retain literal information (Block, 2004; Oakhill & Yuill, 1999). Less skilled comprehenders were more affected by the distance that existed between incongruent information than were skilled metacognitive readers.

The "Did You Till the Text?" test was created as an assessment to identify whether students tilled a text and noticed inconsistencies among several sentences. To conduct this test, a teacher can choose a passage and then insert a sentence on every other page that does not make sense. Then students are asked to read and decide where the passage does not make sense.

The statements individuals make will not only identify who can till a text, but also who can adapt to an author's writing pattern. The error rate on this test documents students' highest level of long-term memory and how much information can be retained. It is important to know that short-term memory stores and integrates information, whereas long-term memory processes this information to make inferences. Less adept readers are unable to monitor texts, detect anomalies, and make inferences if parts of a text are inconsistent. Integration is especially difficult for this population if unusually large portions of their mental energy must be allocated to decoding (Oakhill & Yuill, 1999; Perfetti & Lesco, 1979; Stanovich, 1986; Tergeson & Wagner, 1987).

For this reason, "Did You Till the Text?" tests can be conducted orally. When administered in this manner, students are asked what they noticed about a text feature (such as an author's subheading, character's dialogue, or descriptive passage) on a specific page. More advanced readers will use the same information that should ideally be highlighted to predict or make a connection within a text. This metacognitive test can also become a written self-assessment or a teacher-guided evaluation. In the written version, the teacher previews a text and lists the features of the writing style that should be attended to by a reader. These features are listed on a sheet of paper. If the written test is to become a self-assessment, students are to rank how often they paid attention to each of these features. An example of such a test appears in Figure 11.2. Alternatively, students can write what they were thinking as they came to each of these features.

If the test is teacher-guided, a student is asked to read a page silently or orally. The reader is asked to stop at a point and then asked what they were thinking as they read that authorial clue to meaning. If the student is "tilling the text" properly, the tester writes the answer given and continues reading. If the student is not processing the text metacognitively, the tester stops and performs a think-aloud that illuminates the thinking that should be engaged at this point in this text (and at similar points in future texts) to obtain a more complete meaning.

"Thinking to the End" Summary Test

This evaluation is administered after students have been taught to synthesize information at the end of paragraphs, stories, and pages. Students are to read a paragraph or page. Next, they are asked to describe their thinking when they inferred or imaged. When they describe what they did (whether they were putting single facts together, putting themselves in the text, or integrating new pieces of information into the ongoing story), their answers provide clues as to what children can do metacognitively when reading large bodies of information and what they can be taught to do to improve their self-initiated summarization/drawing conclusion processes.

Figure 11.3 is a prototype of the "Thinking to the End" summary test. In this assessment, students write their answers to each query in the space that follows it. When an answer is incorrect, the student is not self-initiating this step in the summary process. For younger students, instead of asking what they are thinking (which Pressley [1976] determined to be a very difficult task), teachers ask them to play school and teach someone else to read. Teachers also assess younger students' summative metacognitive processes by asking them to draw pictures to depict the end of a narrative or expository text that has not yet been read to them. As the children draw, teachers deduce what they are thinking and assess the quality of their independently generated summative thoughts.

"What Were You Unable to Think About in the Harder Book?" Test

For children ages 9 and older, this evaluation occurs by first giving students two books. One book is at their grade level, and the second one is on a different topic that is above their grade level. Both books should be selected by the child to

Figure 11.2 "Did You Till the Text?" Metacognitive Test

Name: _____ Grade: _____ Date: _____

Write the numbers to describe your most self-initiated metacognition during a recent reading in the boxes below.

GUIDE MYSELF THROUGH TEXT	Always Do Without Teacher Prompting 5	4	Sometimes 3	2	Can't Do at All Without Teacher Prompting 1
1. Set my purpose					
2. Make predictions					
3. Till the text					
4. Find summaries					
5. Draw inferences					
6. Ask myself					
7. Recognize important details					
8. Image					
9. Recall and apply information to life					

Figure 11.3 "Think to the End" Summary Test

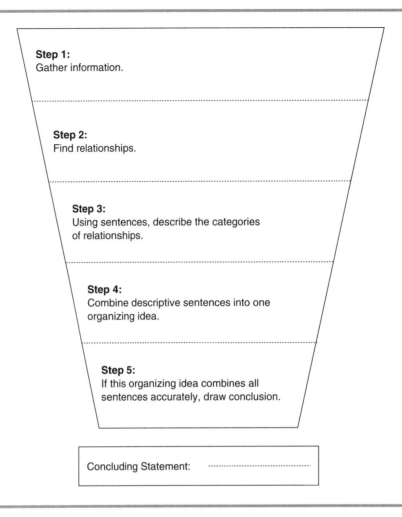

Step 1:
Gather information.

Step 2:
Find relationships.

Step 3:
Using sentences, describe the categories
of relationships.

Step 4:
Combine descriptive sentences into one
organizing idea.

Step 5:
If this organizing idea combines all
sentences accurately, draw conclusion.

Concluding Statement: ....

ensure that the affective domain is equally engaged in both testing situations. Next, students read two consecutive pages from each book. Third, the tester asks students what they thought about as they read the more difficult book. They are asked to compare the difference in their thinking patterns between the two books. Finally, they are asked to identify what they were unable to think about in the harder book and what they would like to learn to think more about so that comprehension will be easier when they read difficult books in the future.

The type of answers given could include: "I want to remember more of the details." "I want to think more about where the author's going." "I can't follow what's being said." "I want to learn how to find the big ideas." Or, "I want to summarize what I read better." This assessment is based on the principle that children can often determine (for themselves) where they need improvement.

Student-Selected Self-Assessments

Student-selected self-evaluations enable students to measure their own comprehension, vocabulary, decoding, or fluency abilities. Students can also select the self-assessment format they like best. Such forms include (1) a checklist in which they list the comprehension processes taught that week and give themselves a 5, 4, 3, 2, or 1 rating as to how well they learned each; (2) an essay test in which they describe what they want to learn next; or (3) work samples that they grade, stating the criteria they used to assess their own metacognitive ability based on their reading of a specific text. Such self-assessments as these have been demonstrated to increase students' motivation to think at higher levels as they read (Guthrie et al., 2000).

For self-assessments to be most effective, students should complete at least one every six weeks. Children should store these self-assessments in their portfolios or reading folders and share them with the teacher during one-on-one conferences.

Color-Coded Comprehension Process Portfolios

In this assessment, students choose the comprehension process for which they want to be evaluated. Students insert examples of text that demonstrate that they used a process correctly in a color-coded folder. For example, when students want to demonstrate how they let main ideas emerge as they read, they use a yellow highlighter to mark the top border of each paper that demonstrated their independent use of that literacy process. Or, when they are reading magazines or computer pages that can be printed and stored in folders, they mark a yellow strip across the top when they found the main idea independently. All papers with yellow highlights are stored together, or these papers can be placed in a yellow folder. When another process is taught, students highlight papers that demonstrate their independent practice with a different color. In like manner, when students independently initiate other metacognitive processes, such as imaging, inferring, or drawing conclusions, they can use a different colored highlighter to mark them.

When a teacher is ready to assess that student's independent ability to discern main ideas (or any other ability), the appropriate colored folder or highlighted sheets are referred to and students are asked how they deduced the main idea in one of the highlighted passages. The benefit of color-coded comprehension folders is that students learn processes fast because color serves as a mnemonic device. Also, this evaluation format enables students to be assessed using passages for which they know they have achieved a mastery of a specific process. In this way, their motivation, self-efficacy, and ability to choose books wisely increase (Block, 2004). Moreover, color-coded assessments enable students to set higher expectations than is possible through other forms of paper-and-pencil assessments, such as multiple-choice tests.

"Happy-and-sad face" assessments can be used for students in kindergarten through second grade. In this self-assessment format, students make a ☺ beside reading activities they enjoyed, on their individual papers, or on class charts. Happy and sad faces can also be used as an indicator of how well they feel they did on a retelling or writing.

"Tell What Literacy Process I'm Using" Test

This assessment is recommended for groups or individuals in kindergarten through second grade. During the instructional period, students are taught to move their hands to depict a specific comprehension strategy. These gestures allow younger students to grasp abstract mental processes such as "making connections" and "main idea" by connecting them to more concrete visual/kinesthetic representations (Block, Parris, & Whiteley, under review). For example, in the "Tell What Literacy Process I'm Using" test in Figure 11.4, students are taught how to make the Comprehension Process Motions (Block, Rodgers, and Johnson, 2004) that are displayed by the illustrations: Using Context Clues, Make Connections, Cause/Effect, Drawing Conclusions. After instruction, the teacher should distribute a copy of Figure 11.4 to each child.

To administer, the tester stops a student's reading at strategic points in a text when a particular process (depicted on the assessment) should be used. The tester says a number, for example, using "one" for the first time stopped, and asks students to write the number below the thinking process they are using at that point. If they are not using any of the processes depicted on the "Tell What Literacy Process I'm Using" test at that moment, students are instructed to write the number on one of the lines in the middle of the page. Next, students describe what they are thinking after marking the number on their paper. For this assessment, testers are asked to pause twice for kindergarten students, three times for first graders, and four times for second graders. After the written portion of the test is complete, the papers are graded individually and students are placed in groups for re-teaching using a form similar to Figure 11.1.

"Long-Term Memory" Test

To assess pupils' long-term memory, testers ask students to recall and list all the books that they have read (or all of the stories that have been taught within the past two weeks from the literature anthology). A review of this list will identify gaps in each student's long-term memory (e.g., the title of a story the child has read during the past two weeks that is not listed). Next, ask the child to tell you about that story, noting specific facts and gaps between information recalled during this prompted retelling assessment. In addition, the student is to tell (or write) about the most memorable book that she or he has read. When finished, the student tells the differences he or she discerns concerning how much was remembered from each reading experience. Finally, pupils deduce why those differences existed. These thoughts can be used to guide collaborative literacy instruction in coming weeks so that students' self-initiated thinking, without prompting, can be strengthened. A grid that can be used to make such records appears in Chapter 12.

Teaching Students to Assess Their Own Comprehension Processes During Book Selection

This test assists students in becoming more active participants in increasing their own literacy abilities. It also enables teachers to determine how well

Figure 11.4   "Tell What Literacy Process I'm Using" Test

Figure 11.4 (Continued)

Student self-assessment of tilling the processes

_____ 1. Tilled the text

_____ 2. Identified author's writing pattern as

      _____ a Main idea pattern

      _____ b. Problem-solution pattern

      _____ c. Similarity/difference pattern (telling both sides)

      _____ d. Sequence pattern (telling things in order)

_____ 3. Looked for the author's sequencing patterns with words such as first, then, or next

_____ 4. Determined whether the main idea was clear or reread if it was unclear

_____ 5. Looked for frequency of ideas and if the same idea was repeated in different ways

_____ 6. Noted the direction of the author's or characters' thinking

_____ 7. Compared what I read to similar events in my life

_____ 8. Organized the text in my mind as I read

students assume the responsibility of assessing their own abilities when they select a book.

Step 1: Gifted readers know that they can comprehend increasingly advanced books on topics of interest or on topics they have previously studied. Therefore, these students are taught and then assessed as to how effectively they choose a book on the basis of how much and what they want to learn for a particular reading experience. Do they want to learn, relax, review, or escape into another person's world? As students approach a set of books, their purposes for reading will also determine the thickness of the book that they select. For example, if they want to relax, they may choose a shorter book than if they wanted to learn very specific information about a topic.

Step 2: Gifted readers select books written by authors that they enjoy. Students are taught and then assessed as to how well they survey specific authorial writing styles. If a favorite author or captivating titles attract the attention of a highly skilled metacognitive reader, he or she examines that book, tills the text, and scans the authorial writing pattern before deciding to read it.

Step 3: Gifted students will thumb through a book to determine the density of the text and the amount of effort they will have to exert to enjoy this author's writing. Thumbing through a book entails selecting a single page near the middle of the book to read in order to determine whether they know the majority of those words. As they read that page, students can press one finger down on the opposite page for every word that they do not know. If the student presses down all five fingers on one hand before a single page has been read, this student should consider that this book may cause so much frustration in decoding that their comprehension and enjoyment of it may be compromised. In such cases, students are taught to metacognitively evaluate whether they should return to Step 1 to repeat the prior steps in this process.

Problems and Solutions

The assessments in this chapter are designed to identify whether a student is understanding and retaining necessary literacy strategies. In addition, we realize that teachers will be assessing students informally throughout collaborative literacy activities. When expectations are not met within the context of this type of learning environment, there are a few questions that should be considered.

First, does the student have the ability and desire to achieve the expected literacy goals in your classroom if additional time and support are provided? If the answer is yes, which of the learning activities described in this book would best utilize his or her learning strength(s)? How could you use these activities as a place to begin scaffolding the student toward tasks that are more varied and challenging?

Second, does this student have learning needs that cannot be addressed in the context of a collaborative literacy environment? If the answer is yes, how can you maintain a sense of group membership for all students while implementing a differentiated instructional experience for one member? One solution is to provide the student with a specific group role that will be challenging enough to promote his or her literacy growth, yet does not require continuous group attendance. This student's role should be designed in such a way that he or she can still make a contribution to the learning objectives for the group, as well as to the specific learning objectives for himself or herself.

Third, we propose that teachers schedule time to reflect on the collaborative literacy experiences that take place in their classrooms. Such self-assessment on the part of the teacher is one of the most valuable and significant factors in preventing, identifying, and effectively solving instructional challenges. As one component of this reflective process, we suggest that teachers briefly write down concerns as they arise during group activities. This will ensure that problems or potential problems will not be inadvertently overlooked later. Addressing concerns with positive actions will lead to increasingly effective group experiences, for both students and teachers.

TEACHERS PUTTING IDEAS INTO ACTION

1. Please rank order the assessments that were described in this chapter. Tell why the order you selected is best for assisting all the students in your care to understand their own literacy strengths and weaknesses.

2. Select the one test in this chapter that would best capture the new elements of collaborative literacy that you have created in your classroom. Be prepared to defend why this test is your best.

3. Administer one of the assessments in this chapter to students in your classroom. Write a note to parents to describe this assessment and its results. Send this assessment home after students have completed it. Ask parents to write back to you about what this assessment enabled them to ascertain about their student's reading, writing, or speaking abilities.

4. Identify an aspect of building a literacy collaborative that you have read in chapters 1–9. Describe an assessment that you would create to evaluate that aspect of your collaborative literacy environment.

5. Invite parents to use one of the collaborative literacy assessments in this chapter with their children or adolescents at home. After they have administered the test, ask them to tell you what they learned about their child.

SUMMARY

It is important that our profession expand its capacity to document gifted and all students' self-initiated literacy processing before, during, and after reading, listening, speaking, and writing. The assessments in this chapter have demonstrated important ways to do so. This chapter was designed to describe several of the newly developed collaborative literacy assessment instruments. Each is intended to demonstrate processes in action. Many are performance based, such as "What Do We Need to Fill In?" tests and "Did You Till the Text?" tests. Others assess students' abilities to reflect on their own literacy abilities, such as the 'Thinking to the End" summary test, the "What Were You Unable to Think about in the Harder Book?" test, the "Tell Me What Literacy Processes I'm Using" test, and the "Long-Term Memory" test. Many involve students' self-assessment or participation through written forms, folders, and multiple work samples (e.g., self-assessment systems, color-coded comprehension portfolios, and the book selection test). By using these evaluations, educators can provide valuable instructional and evaluative experiences for students. Through them, students and teachers can come closer than ever before in identifying specific meaning-making problems that have limited the pleasure and profitability of past reading experiences for gifted (and all) readers.

NOTE

1. Exerpted from *Strategic Teaching and Reading Project Guidebook* (1995, NCREL, rev. ed.).

PART IV

Final Reflections: Congratulations on Making Personal Connections and Building Collaborative Literacy

The Mind of
the Teacher:
A Meta-Reflection

Tools to Help Build Collaborative Literacy

Susan E. Israel

As a classroom teacher, I always spent so much time preparing for my lessons by researching and gathering materials and books that I could integrate in my classroom. Having a summary of resources that I could use for all my students in the regular classroom, including gifted students, would have been helpful. In addition, it would have saved me a lot of time, allowing me more time to spend with my students.

—Susan E. Israel, Former Fourth-Grade Teacher

COLLABORATIVE LITERACY AT WORK

Following is a list of support materials and professional resources that classroom teachers, reading specialists, parents, and those who teach in gifted reading programs can use to build collaborative literacy classrooms, as well as extend their knowledge base in the area of literacy and gifted education. All of the resources have been found to be particularly useful in the area of building collaborative literacy with gifted students in the regular classroom and have publication dates within the past five years. The goal of this section is to provide teachers with a list of gifted and literacy resources that will support professional development, enrichment resources for parents, and students. The resources have been organized as follows:

- Professional books
- Newsletters and periodicals
- Internet resources
- Professional organizations
- Theme-based literature selections

Professional Books Related to Literacy

The following resources can be used by teachers and parents to assist them in building collaborative literacy classrooms. The books can be used by teachers and school communities during inservice training sessions, as well as professional book study selections.

Aydelott, J., & Dianna, S. B. (2003). *Building literature circles.* Marion, IL: Pieces of Learning.

This comprehensive book provides general information on literature circles, as well as projects that are appropriate for gifted students and all students in the regular classroom. A list of literature circle book selections is also included.

Block, C. C., & Israel, S. E. (2005). *Reading first and beyond.* Thousand Oaks, CA: Corwin Press.

This is a valuable resource for all educators including literacy teachers of gifted students. Chapters focus on reading-first legislation such as phonics, phonemic awareness, fluency, vocabulary, and comprehension. In addition, this book discusses strategies on how to create instruction that emphasizes metacognition and writing. Parents can also find this book to be a valuable resource.

Chapman, C., & King, R. (2003). *Differentiated instructional strategies for writing in the content areas.* Thousand Oaks, CA: Corwin Press.

This concise guide helps teachers work with every student's unique skills and needs so that the student learns to apply information, demonstrate content mastery, and think critically and creatively when writing. Strategies are presented to also help students develop self-confidence in writing.

Delisle, J. (2004). *Look at gifted education from the inside out.* Pacific Grove, CA: Wadsworth/Thompson Learning.

The field of gifted education is presented in a unique way by highlighting stories and experiences of educators and researchers who have devoted their time and energy to gifted children.

Halsted, J. W. (2004). *Some of my best friends are books: Guiding gifted readers from preschool to high school.* Scottsdale, AZ: Great Potential Press.

This book helps gifted students use books as bibliotherapy to provide support, guidance, and intellectual and emotional growth. It is appropriate for all grades and can be used by teachers and parents.

Israel, S. E., Block, C. C., Bauserman, K., & K. Kinnucan-Welsch. (2005). *Metacognition and literacy learning: Theory, assessment, instruction, and professional development.* Manwah, NJ: Erlbaum.

This comprehensive volume summarizes all the research on metacognition. Educators who are interested in research-based strategies related to developing metacognition, self-regulation, and higher level thinking skills will find this book to be a real jewel. Each chapter discusses methods for classroom teachers to integrate metacognition with instruction.

Johnson, D. W., & Johnson, R. T. (2005). *Assessing students in groups: Promoting responsibility and individual accountability.* Thousand Oaks, CA: Corwin Press.

This practical guide can be used in any classroom with gifted students and all students to help teachers form productive groups and assess individual student performance in group work. It is a wonderful resource for teachers who enjoy building collaborative literacy environments yet want to encourage individual growth and assessment.

McEwan, E. K. (2004). *Seven strategies of highly effective readers: Using cognitive research to boost K-8 achievement.* Thousand Oaks, CA: Corwin Press.

This book emphasizes cognitive strategy instruction of exceptional readers. Research-based activities help teachers plan lessons in reading. It also presents strategy adaptations to help all readers in the classroom.

Piirto, J. (2004). *Understanding creativity.* Scottsdale, AZ: Great Potential Press.

This book offers advice on how to value creativity in literacy tasks. It discusses factors that influence creativity, such as environment and motivation. Readers will learn how to spot talent through a child's behaviors and how to encourage practice.

Polette, N. (2004). *Improvisation and theatre games with children's literature.* Marion, IL: Pieces of Learning.

Literature discussions are made fun by this valuable resource, which helps kids play improv and pretend. Creative and critical thinking skills are integrated with creative and inviting activities.

Newsletters, Journals, and Periodicals

Creative Kids

This magazine, published by Prufrock Press, is written for children and includes stories, activities, and research topics to inspire creativity.

Gifted Child Quarterly

This journal is the official publication of the National Association for Gifted Children. Articles of interest to educators and those with interest in gifted education highlight current research.

Gifted Child Today

This easy-to-read journal provides creative ideas and practical instructional strategies that focus on current issues in gifted literacy. This journal is published monthly by Prufrock Press and is a must-have for anyone working in gifted education. The special issue *English and Language Arts for Gifted Students* (Volume 25, No. 2, Spring 2002) is devoted to topics in gifted education and literacy. Suggestions for instructional programs, literature selections, and professional resources are discussed.

Parenting for High Potential

Parents and educators can use this journal to learn about current issues in education related to special features, advice columns, and resource reviews on how parents can help gifted and talented children. This journal is published quarterly by the National Association for Gifted Children.

Imagine

This exciting periodical for middle- and high-school students is published by the Johns Hopkins University's Center for Talented Youth. *Imagine* provides information, insights, and solid research topics of interest to young motivated readers. www.jhu.edu/gifted/imagine

The Reading Teacher

This monthly peer-reviewed journal, published by the International Reading Association, focuses on articles, essays, and research reports on reading and literacy development. Teachers in the regular classroom can easily adapt the strategies and ideas for all learners in the regular classroom.

The Question Mark

This newsletter, written for educators, is published by Reading for Gifted and Creative Children Special Interest Group, which is supported by the International Reading Association. It provides a wealth of information on topics related to gifted and literacy development. Membership can be obtained for $10.00 by submitting an application to Missy Allen, 28005, D. Meadow Park Drive, Bedford, Texas 76021.

Thinking Classroom

This bimonthly journal, published by the International Reading Association, focuses on encouraging professional development, reflection, and research. It includes articles written on inquiry-based learning, critical and higher level thinking strategies, and student-centered learning approaches.

Voices From the Middle

This journal, devoted to helping middle-school teachers, offers a range of articles from strategy instruction to ideas on how to help gifted kids in the content areas. One article by R. Olenchak (2001) titled, "When gifted readers hunt for books" focuses on helping teachers understand what gifted middle-school students look for when selecting books. This article can assist teachers in finding types of books they can include in classroom libraries and when doing literature circles.

Internet Resources to Support Gifted and Advanced Readers in Literacy

By: Beth Earley, University of Dayton

Center for Gifted Education
http://cfge.wm.edu

- Focuses on needs of gifted and talented individuals
- Publishes language arts units for gifted readers
- Curriculum resources in reading for gifted and talented children

ERIC Clearinghouse on Disabilities and Gifted Education
http://www.ericec.org

- A resource for parents on a wide variety of topics related to gifted children

Gifted Children Monthly
http://www.gifted-children.com

- A newsletter for parents of gifted children

National Association for Gifted Children
http://www.nagc.org

- Parent resources, book lists, summer enrichment programs, and resources
- Publishes magazine *Parenting* for high potential
- Sponsors a Virtual Exhibit Hall to search for literacy products and resources

National Research Center on the Gifted and Talented
http://gifted.uconn.edu

- Current research on gifted education and talent development
- Parent resources for special gifted populations

Insite Distance Learning
http://www.bsu.edu/eft

- Insite Electronic Field Trips are a dynamic combination of live, interactive broadcasts and on-line curriculum opportunities for teachers and students in K–12
- The learning experiences span the disciplines of science, mathematics, and literature
- Students are involved and excited during the electronic field trips

Odyssey of the Mind
http://www.odysseyofthemind.com

- A helpful Web site for those teachers interested in having their students participate in Odyssey of the Mind
- A competitive and creative experience that provides problem-solving opportunities for students
- Students are encouraged to analyze a situation, imagine all the possible outcomes, then synthesize the material

The Gifted Child Society
http://www.gifted.org

- A parent forum to address concerns about parenting gifted children

The Great Books Foundation
http://www.greatbooks.org

- Junior Great Books help students develop the capacity to gain a deeper understanding of what they read, so that ultimately they become better thinkers
- Great Books improves reading comprehension and helps students see that reading is thinking, asking questions, and working together
- Emphasis is placed on literary analysis by recognizing author's tone, purpose, and style as well as helping students connect texts to personal experiences and gain insight

The National Foundation for Gifted and Creative Children
http://www.nfgcc.org

- Pamphlets, free resources, recommended reading lists, parent's guide, and information on raising a gifted child

The International Reading Association
http://www.readwritethink.org

- Provides teachers with lesson plans for gifted children and advanced readers. The peer-reviewed lesson plans also provide information on how to adapt lessons for all students in the regular classroom.

Smart Kid at Home
   http://www.smartkidathome.com

   - A site for home-school parents

World Council for Gifted and Talented Children
   http://www.worldgifted.org

   - An international organization for gifted children and support for parents

International Resources

The U.S. Department of Education helps to represent the U.S. Government in international organizations that have an interest in education and gifted children and can be contacted to locate specific information regarding laws in various countries.

Some international organizations that might be useful are:

The Australian Association for the Education of the Gifted and Talented
   http://www.nexus.edu.au

Centre for Gifted Education (University of Calgary)
   http://ucalgary.ca/~gifteduc/

Internet Resources Related to Building Collaborative Literacy in Content Areas

Following is a list of helpful Web sites specifically with activities to help teachers differentiate instruction in the regular classroom or in content areas.

Multiple Intelligence Activities for Math
   http://www.kodak.com/global/en/consumer/education/lessonPlans/lessonPlan151.shtml
   http://www.igs.net/~cmorris/gr_7_math_lesson_plan.html
   http://www.eduref.org/Virtual/Lessons/Mathematics/Geometry/GEO0005.html
   http://www.eduref.org/Virtual/Lessons/Mathematics/Patterns/PAT0198.html

Multiple Intelligence Activities for Science
   http://teachersnetwork.org/booktour/hannonplan.htm
   http://www.montana.edu/4teachers/instcomp/multipleintel/electronics/electric.html

Multiple Intelligence Activities for Social Studies
   http://www.eduref.org/Virtual/Lessons/Social_Studies/History/HIS0009.html
   http://www.eduref.org/Virtual/Lessons/Social_Studies/History/HIS0015.html

http://www.kodak.com/global/en/consumer/education/lessonPlans/lessonPlan025.shtml

Multiple Intelligence Activities for Language Arts

http://www.kodak.com/global/en/consumer/education/lessonPlans/lessonPlan111.shtml

http://www.kodak.com/global/en/consumer/education/lessonPlans/lessonPlan143.shtml

List of Resources for Trade Books by Subject

http://www.mcps.k12.md.us/curriculum/socialstd/MBD/Books_Begin.html

http://www.neiu.edu/~neiulib/guides/young_adult.html

http://www.powells.com

Multiple Intelligence Activities

http://www.brewerteach.net/milesson.htm

http://teacher.scholastic.com/professional/assessment/100flowers.htm

http://www.todaysteacher.com/MILearningActivities.htm

Literacy in Subject Areas

http://www.eduref.org/Virtual/Lessons/Language_Arts/Reading/RDG0023.html

http://www.eduref.org/Virtual/Lessons/Social_Studies/History/HIS0010.html

http://www.eduref.org/Virtual/Lessons/Social_Studies/Geography/GGR0029.html

http://www.eduref.org/Virtual/Lessons/Language_Arts/Reading/RDG0017.html

http://www.eduref.org/Virtual/Lessons/Language_Arts/Writing/WCP0024.html

Vocabulary Activities

http://www.montana.edu/4teachers/instcomp/multipleintel/whales/whalpage.html

Gender Teaching Ideas

http://www.schools.nsw.edu.au/learning/yrk12focusareas/gendered/boyslitk6.php

http://www.woodrow.org/teachers/math/gender/11strategies.html

http://www.educ.sfu.ca/narstsite/publications/research/gender.htm

Differentiated Activities

http://www.lessonplanspage.com/printables/PMDLAArtSSMathCIOctoberHalloweenUnit4.htm

http://www.lessonplanspage.com/printables/PMDSSArtLACIDifferentiatedLearningEgyptProjects68.htm

http://www.makeworksheets.com/activityofweek/html/lessonplan.htm

List of Resources for Motivating Readers
http://www.bookadventure.com
http://www.bookitprogram.com
http://www.readingrockets.org
http://www.planetesme.com
http://www.educationworld.com/a_lesson/lesson/lesson035.shtml
http://www.eagerreaders.com/encourage.html

Ideas for Improving Self-Efficacy and Self-Esteem as It Relates to Reading
http://www.readingonline.org/articles/art_index.asp?HREF=/articles/handbook/guthrie/index.html
http://www.readingonline.org/critical/coles.html
http://www.baylite.ca/mentor/mrecent.html
http://www.thecoo.edu/~tanders/reading_ms.htm
http://liberty.k12.ca.us/reading%20aloud%20by%20rosemary%20spencer.pdf

HOW DO I INTEGRATE RESOURCES IN READING AND CONTENT AREAS?

Following is a summary of ways that teachers in reading and content areas can effectively integrate literacy materials. The lists are arranged by thematic topics, and uses the following format:

- Mission statement
- Thematic topic
- Summary of literary collection

Mission statement: by Linda Ashley, Megan Cox, Colleen Murphy, and Janelle Sculley, University of Dayton

The mission of our classroom is to promote an environment conducive to learning by opening up our students' eyes to the outside world through literature.

Books That Incorporate the Theme of Learning

Summary of books in literary collection:

Ackerman, Karen. (1994). *The night crossing.* New York: Alfred A. Knopf.
A Jewish family in Austria must leave their home with only what they can carry and travel across the country. This story teaches students lessons on humanity.

Curtis, Jamie Lee. (2002). *I'm gonna like me: Letting off a little self-esteem.* New York: Joanna Cotler Books.
A book dedicated to building self-esteem and loving yourself despite imperfections, because imperfections are what make a person unique.

Fritz, Jean. (1995). *You want women to vote, Lizzie Stanton?* New York: Putnam.
A biography of Elizabeth Cady Stanton, who believed in equality for all. This book teaches lessons on discrimination, equality, women's rights, and humanity.

George, Jean Craighead. (1959). *My side of the mountain.* New York: E.P. Dutton & Company.
A boy lives alone in the mountains, where he learns to adapt to new situations and environments and is taught an important lesson on survival.

Goldenbock, Peter. (1990). *Teammates.* New York: Gulliver Books.
True story of Jackie Robinson, the first black baseball player in Major League Baseball. Describes his struggle against prejudice and his friendship with Pee Wee Reese.

Hopkins, Lee Bennet. (1992). *Through our eyes.* New York: Little Brown.
A collection of children's poetry and pictures that show children and the society of the 1990s. The poems are about their thoughts, hopes, observations, and dreams; this book opens children's eyes to a different perspective of life.

Lorbucki, Marybeth. (1998). *Sister Anne's hands.* New York: Dial Books for Young Readers.
A new teacher comes to Anna's school, but she is not like any teacher the children have seen before. This book deals with the issue of racism and is meant for elementary grades.

Rockwell, Anne. (2000). *Only passing through: The story of Sojourner Truth.* New York: Alfred A. Knopf.
The story is about a young woman who struggles as a child but grows to become brave and strong and one of the most influential leaders of the abolitionist movement. This book teaches students about equality and different perspectives.

Speare, Elizabeth George. (1958). *The witch of Blackbird pond.* New York: Houghton Mifflin.
This book, about a young girl who is forced to move from the Caribbean to a Connecticut colony, is about adapting to new environments. It also emphasizes multiculturalism in a religious sense.

Steptoe, John. (1987). *Mufaro's beautiful daughters.* New York: Lee & Shepard Books.
Mufaro was very happy. He had two beautiful daughters: one was kind and sweet, the other bad tempered. This book shows familial relationships and demonstrates multiculturalism.

Books That Incorporate the Theme of Living and Learning

By: Stacey Hamer, Melissa Nies, Sarah Luckhaupt, and Jessica Norgaard, University of Dayton

Mission statement: Our mission is to take full advantage of teachable moments and help students see the underlying lesson in all books.

Fleischman, Sid. (1986). *The whipping boy.* New York: Greenwillow Books.
The book teaches Prince Brat to be responsible for his own actions and to become empathetic towards others.

Lowry, Lois. (1989). *Number the stars.* New York: Bantam Books.
This book teaches students how young adolescents like themselves can find strength and courage in trying situations.

Montgomery, Sy. (2001). *The snake scientist.* New York: Houghton Mifflin.
This book teaches students about animals and how scientists work in the field to gain a better understanding of animals and their habitat.

Uchida, Yoshiko. (1993). *The bracelet.* New York: Philomel Books.
This book teaches students what it is like to be "different" in the world, and also teaches them that you never forget those you love; they are always in your heart.

Steptoe, John. (1987). *Mufaro's beautiful daughters.* New York: Lee & Shepard Books.
This book helps students learn that being selfish and rude will not help them move forward in life or accomplish the goals they have for themselves.

DeFelice, Cynthia. (1996). *The apprenticeship of Lucas Whitaker.* New York: Farrar Straus & Giroux.
This book teaches kids about scientific discovery and how we have progressed in the medical field.

Pattou, Edith. (2001). *Mrs. Spitzer's garden.* New York: Harcourt.
This book teaches children that they are just like plants and with love and nurturing they will grow to bloom like beautiful flowers.

Greene, Bette. (1973). *Summer of my German soldier.* New York: Puffin Books.
This book demonstrates to students that two young people who are supposed to be enemies can instead put their differences aside and develop compassion and trust for one another.

Le Guin, Ursula K. (1968). *A wizard of Earthsea.* Berkeley, CA: Parnassus Press.
This book teaches students patience and coming of age.

Books on Learning

By: Ashlee M Hill, Brandon Godzik, and Hillary Barter, University of Dayton

Mission statement: We are committed to engaging our students in literature that promotes learning, leadership, and service.

Bridges, Ruby. (1999). *Through my eyes.* New York: Scholastic.
Ruby recounts the story of her involvement as a six-year-old in the integration of her school in New Orleans, Louisiana, in 1960.

Haley, Alex. (1994). *Roots.* New York: Vintage.

Alex Haley does an extraordinary job of tracing his family tree back six generations, discovering 16-year-old Kunta Kinte. The book depicts the life of Kunta, including all joys, hardships, deaths, and births.

Musgrove, Margaret. (1976). *Ashanti to Zulu: African traditions.* New York: Dial.
This book explains the traditions and customs of 26 African tribes, one tribe for each letter of the alphabet.

McNaughton, Colin. (1996). *Oops!* London: Anderson Press.
Students can learn to integrate multiple stories to make a new interesting story, just like this one does with "Little Red Riding Hood" and "The Three Little Pigs."

Gavin, Jamila, & Troughton, Joanna. (1986). *Stories from the Hindu world.* Morristown, NJ: Silver Burdett Press.
Teaches children 12 Hindu myths about the creation of the world and the gods and goddesses.

Landau, Elaine. (2001). *Columbus Day: Celebrating a famous explorer.* Berkeley Heights, NJ: Enslow Publishers.
Students can learn about the myths and assumptions about Columbus and how he treated the Native Americans.

Accorsi, William. (1992). *My name is Pocahontas.* New York: Holiday House.
Students learn about the Native American princess, how she met John Smith and the other English colonists, and how she was able to travel to England with them.

Walker, Niki. (1997). *Sharks.* New York: Crabtree Publishing.
Students learn all about sharks, their physiology, reproduction, habitats, diet, and endangerment.

Gower, Teri. (1999). *What I believe: A young person's guide to the religions of the world.* Minneapolis, MN: Millbrook Press.
Teaches children about Judaism, Christianity, Islam, Hinduism, Buddhism, Sikhism, Shintoism, and Taoism.

Books on Leadership

By: Elizabeth Dickson, Jessica Hayes, Kevin Prudhoe, and Camille Yancey, University of Dayton.

Mission statement: To promote leadership through the discovery of various literature activities and active participation. A greater understanding of leadership qualities will be attained through the literature opportunities so that the students will apply leadership to their everyday life experiences.

Blue, Rose, & Naden, Corinne J.. (1994). *People of peace.* Minneapolis, MN: Millbrook Press.
This book exemplifies individuals who have devoted their lives to the search for peace. These are short stories about influential individuals who have affected the world.

Davis. Todd. (2001). *The new big book of US presidents.* Philadelphia: Courage Books.
Contains small biographies of each U.S. president and how they ran the country during their years in office.

St. George, Judith. (2000). *So you want to be president?* New York: Philomel Books.
Presents an assortment of facts about the qualifications and characteristics of U.S. presidents from George Washington to Bill Clinton.

Giuliani, Rudolph. (2002). *Leadership.* New York: Miramax Books.
A personal account of how Mayor Rudolph Giuliani kept New York City under control during the attack of September 11 and what leadership techniques he used to do so.

Longfellow, Henry Wadsworth. (1983). *Hiawatha.* New York: Scholastic.
Legendary Native American leader named Hiawatha and his journey throughout boyhood into his responsibility into manhood.

Lowry, Lois. (2002). *The giver.* New York: Laurel Leaf.
Jonas struggles with his newfound knowledge of the world and his place in society.

Polacco, Patricia. (2000). *The butterfly.* New York: Philomel Books.
A young girl and her family living in a French village during the Nazi takeover aid a young Jewish girl in escaping from the Nazis.

Schraff, Anne. (1994). *Women of peace.* Hillside, NJ: Enslow.
Women who won the Nobel Peace Prize are presented in this informational chapter book.

Weigel, George. (2004). *Witness to hope: The biography of Pope John Paul II.* New York: Perennial.
A biography of Pope John Paul II, mainly about how he spread hope throughout the world through his leadership and strong devotion to the Roman Catholic Church.

Books Related to Lessons and Teachable Moments

By: Kristy Gattshall, Cassandra Heath, Amanda Johnson, Carli Nielson, and Kristin Leightner, University of Dayton.

Mission statement: The mission of our classroom is to embrace diversity as we become lifelong learners who embrace literature as a means to encourage service and leadership in education.

Wood, Douglas. (2003). *Old turtle and the broken truth.* New York: Scholastic.
The story begins with the truth falling from the sky, but as it falls, it breaks. Nature spends many years admiring a piece of it, until a human comes and takes it. This man shares it with his people, who become too proud to share his truth with others. This causes tension and destruction throughout humanity for years

to come. One day, a little girl recognizes that humanity needs her help so she seeks out the origin of the people's truth in order to learn how to save them.

Munsch, Robert, & Martchenko, Michael. (1980). *The paper bag princess.* Toronto: Annick Press.

The story is about a beautiful princess who is very wealthy. In her pursuit to find a captured prince, a dragon burns her clothes off. She replaces her clothes with a paper bag and continues on her journey to find a prince. When Princess Elizabeth finds Prince Ronald, he does not think that she looks like a princess. They do not live happily ever after together because Princess Elizabeth decides she does not need him anyway—looks are only skin deep.

Potter, Beatrix. (1999). *Tales of Peter Rabbit and his friends.* Lanham, MD: Derrydale Books.

The book includes 13 different stories about various animals' adventures. Every story includes a whimsical tale about some animal learning a simple life lesson through an adventure.

Leodhas, Sorche Nic, & Hegrogian, Nonny. (1965). *Always room for one more.* Toronto: Holt, Rinehart, and Winston of Canada.

Lachie MacLachlan lives with his wife and 10 children. He invites every traveler inside who passes on a stormy night. He assures that "there's always room for one more." Lachie's kindness is eventually repaid in the end.

Silverstein, Shel. (1999). *The giving tree.* New York: Harper Collins.

An apple tree and a boy have an interconnected relationship that lasts throughout the boy's life. The tree shows compassion for the boy by always doing what the boy asks of him. Through the book, readers are exposed to the idea of self-sacrifice.

Seuss, Dr. (1990). *Oh, the places you'll go.* New York: Random House Books for Young Readers.

Through rhyming lyrics, this inspirational story gives readers courage to pursue their dreams in the future.

Additional Resources by Thematic Topic: Leadership and Literacy

By: Susan E. Israel, University of Dayton

Rhodes, C. (2003). Lives of purpose: Preparing gifted girls for leadership. Paper presented at the National Association for gifted children, 50th Annual Convention, Indianapolis, IN.

Based on five females who participated in a leadership study, this report summarizes common characteristics of leaders such as commitment to self, seeks risks and challenges, sets high expectations, and has a need for balance.

Mandela, Nelson (Ed.). (2002). *Nelson Mandela's favorite African folktales.* New York: W.W. Norton.

Oral tradition is preserved by one of the great leaders of our time. Each folk-tale is introduced with information about its region or culture of origin, when and by whom it was translated, and a brief explanation of its message and connection to other stories.

Shaw, Maura. (2002). *Ten amazing people and how they changed the world.* Woodstock, VT: Skylight Paths Publishing.

This book introduces children to people who used their intelligence and creativity to change the world. Some of the past century's most famous leaders, including Gandhi, Mother Teresa, and Albert Schweitzer, are featured. The text can be used to understand how world leaders had to overcome issues related to world peace, cultural diversity, and racial equality.

Frasier, M. M. (2003). A master and mentor in the field of gifted education. *Roeper Review, 25*(4), 158–162.

This article summarizes an interview with Dr. Mary M. Frasier. She describes mentoring techniques based on a philosophy she describes as nurturing scholars who are independent, creative, and critical thinkers, not just extensions of her own work.

Women in Science, http://www.societyofwomenengineers.com

A Web site that overviews several women of past and present who are involved in science. It was created to promote science careers with gifted females. The women of past and present serve can serve as mentors and role models.

Wisdom in Literature

Reader's Digest Association. (2003). *The Reader's Digest children's atlas of the world* (3rd Ed.). Pleasantville, NY: Reader's Digest Children's Books.

Created by an international team of scholars, this visually stimulating thematic-based resource explains important geographical concepts, ranging from the structure of the Earth to the world's environmental problems. This book can be used in any service-learning unit to help students understand the world and their role as it relates to service.

The Rudiments of Wisdom Encyclopedia, http://www.rudimentsofwisdom.com

This Web site is both extensive and entertaining. Odd facts and obscure information are depicted using a cartoon format. This book can be used as a starting point for any discussion on the concept of wisdom.

Stapleton, E. J. (1991). *The calico buffalo.* New Bedford, MA: BOSC Publishing.

This book, written in the tradition of Aesop's fables, can help teach valuable lessons that can encourage wise thinking in students. The illustrations depict an American southwest style of art. The book can be used in teaching students to accept the good in other people.

Word Masters Challenge, http://www.wordmasterschallenge.com

A national competition for students in grades 3–8 that encourages higher level word comprehension and logical abilities that help students think both analytically and metaphorically.

Teacher Idea Organizer: *How Do I Use Putting Ideas in Action in the Context of Literacy Workshops?*

Teachers: Use the following organizer to record the new ideas learned and how you can implement them.

Location	My New Strategy Idea	How I Will Implement
Chapter 1:		
Chapter 2:		
Chapter 3:		
Chapter 4:		
Chapter 5:		
Chapter 6:		

Chapter 7:	
Chapter 8:	
Chapter 9:	
Chapter 10:	
Chapter 11:	
Chapter 12:	

Summary of Goals

At the beginning of this book, you were introduced to the concept of building collaborative literacy in the regular classroom. This book provided the reader with a unique window into understanding how to build collaborative literacy by responding to the statement, Why not use gifted and higher level thinking strategies for all students in the regular classroom? With that in mind, you established several personal goals for reading this book. In addition, after each chapter you had an opportunity to record your new ideas to help you realize your goals. Now you can return to your list of goals and evaluate what you have learned and how you will apply this new information gained in the classroom.

- How to create collaborative literacy classrooms in which all students have access to new and enriching knowledge.

_____

_____

_____

_____

_____

- How to integrate gifted education and higher level thinking strategies in the regular classroom in literacy instruction and content areas.

_____

_____

_____

_____

_____

- How to use collaborative literacy tools to enrich the learning environment for all students.

_____

_____

_____

_____

_____

Object Mysteries: Using critical thinking questioning to identify thingamajigs, doohickeys, and gadgets. Pacific Grove, CA: Critical Thinking Books and Software.

Through thought-provoking questions about interesting objects, students can engage in learning about vocabulary using this meaningful and stimulating resource.

Red Hot Root Words. San Luis Obispo, CA: Dandy Lion.

The study of root words as a catalyst for building vocabulary is the primary focus of this creative book, which can be used in grades 3–5 as a way of exploring Greek and Latin prefixes, root words, and suffixes.

AN INVITATION TO SHARE
YOUR READING SUCCESS STORIES

Congratulations! You are in the process of incorporating new research-based strategies and activities. You have explored questions that will help you extend the contents of this book in order to effectively begin to build collaborative literacy in your classroom and with the larger school community. We would like to conclude by reflecting on the major themes offered in this book and suggest to all teachers in K–12 education additional actions that will provide an invitation to continue enhancing professional development in the area of building collaborative literacy with all students, and generate questions for further reflection or discussion.

Teachers of Reading and Writing

Document literacy success stories related to how students were motivated by collaborative literacy engagements over the course of a year and submit your reflections to a literacy journal. How can you use reading success stories to help you focus on the needs of individual learners? What can you do to help provide more effective instruction for readers who were not so successful?

Reading Specialists and Literacy Coaches

Collaborate with other reading specialists and literacy coaches in other schools and discuss effective training methods to help classroom teachers easily integrate collaborative literacy in the curriculum. What training methods were particularly helpful in guiding teachers to effectively learn how to integrate collaborative literacy in the classroom? What actions can further be enhanced by teachers to work more closely with reading specialist and literacy coaches?

Teachers of the Gifted

Consider evaluating classroom materials that you are currently using and make decisions based on the research presented in this book and additional resources that will help you with gifted and advanced readers become more engaged. What types of resources do your students enjoy the most? What materials can you consider eliminating in order to focus on building more collaborative literacy environments?

Parents

The ideas presented in this book can help parents form collaborative literacy parent discussions where parents of the gifted and advanced readers can share ideas on what they are doing at home to help their child. How can parents use community resources to provide richer literacy experiences for their child? Share parenting ideas with your local newspaper so that parents who are not involved or might not have an opportunity to collaborate with other parents can discover new ideas.

Individuals Teaching in Education

Throughout this book, many research-based topics were discussed. Invite your students to select a topic of interest and write a model of a collaborative literacy conceptual framework on how this topic looks when integrated in the classroom for students of their age group. What research questions do you have related to your topic of interest?

Small Study Groups

Small study groups can select one chapter per meeting and elaborate on that topic. What does collaborative literacy look like in my classroom when I am thinking about this topic? How can I use the insight of others to reflect on instruction that will improve collaborative literacy engagements in my classroom?

Accomplished Teachers

The proven research presented is important because it provides the scientific evidence needed to support your instruction. Using your knowledge as an accomplished teacher, what are three research-based teacher ideas that have compelled you to make a change in your classroom? What were the three research-based ideas and how can you share your thoughts with novice teachers? Why did these new ideas compel you to make a change?

We wish you success as you develop opportunities to put new ideas into action, to show how gifted and advanced readers can be engaged through collaborative literacy, and to show how these same engagements can be used as a tool to motivate and enhance literacy learning for all students. You have acquired new capacities to provide opportunities for engaged learners, gifted students, and advanced readers to increase, extend, modify, and evaluate their literacy development through collaborative literacy.

Susan E. Israel
University of Dayton
Department of Teacher Education
6475 Salem Drive
Fishers, IN 46038

References

CHAPTER 1

Beers, K. (1998). Choosing not to read: Understanding why some kids just say no. In K. Beers & R. G. Samuels (Eds.), *Into focus: Understanding and creating middle school readers* (pp. 37–63). Norwood, MA: Christopher Gordon.

Butcher, K. R., & Kintsch, W. (2003). Text comprehension and discourse processing. In A. F. Healy & R. W. Proctor (Eds.), *Handbook of psychology, Vol. 4, experimental psychology* (pp. 575–595). New York: Wiley.

Creech, S. (2000). *The Wanderer.* New York: Scholastic.

Dewey, J., & Bentley, A. F. (1949). *Knowing and the known.* Boston: Beacon.

Follett, M. P. (1924). *Creative experience.* Longmans, Green and Co. (Reprint 1951). New York: Peter Smith.

Frasier, M., Garcia, J., & Passow, H. (1995). A review of assessment issues in gifted minority students. Research Monograph 95204. Storrs, CT: National Research Center on Gifted and Talented.

Harris, T. L., & Hoges, R. E. (1995) *The literacy dictionary: The vocabulary of reading and writing.* Newark, DE: International Reading Association.

Jensen, D. (2004). *Walking on water: Reading, writing & revolution.* White River Junction, VT: Chelsea Green.

Klinger, J., & Vaughn, S. (1999). Promoting reading comprehension, content learning, and English acquisition through collaborative strategic reading (CSR). *The Reading Teacher, 52,* 738–747.

Leppien, J., (2003, November). *The parallel curriculum.* Paper presented at the Texas Association for Gifted and Talented, Houston, Texas.

Leu, D., & Kinzer, C. (2003). *Effective literacy instruction.* Upper Saddle River, NJ: Merrill Prentice Hall.

Macy, L. (2004). A novel study through drama. *The Reading Teacher, 58*(3), 240–247.

McKenna, & Kear, D. (1990). Measuring attitude toward reading: A new tool for teachers. *The Reading Teacher, 43*(9), 626–639.

Muth, J. (2005). *Zen shorts.* New York: Scholastic.

Paulsen, G. (1987). *Hatchet.* New York: Aladdin.

Paulus, T. (1972). *Hope for the flowers.* Mahwah, NJ: Paulist Press.

Reis, S. (2004). *Talented readers.* Paper presented at the Javits Program meeting in Washington, DC.

Renzulli, J. S. (1978a). *The enrichment triad model: A guide for developing defensible program for the gifted and talented.* Mansfield Center, CT: Creative Learning Press.

Renzulli, J. (1978b). What makes giftedness? Re-examining a definition. *Phi Delta Kappan, 60*(3), 180–184.

Roeper, A. M. (1995). How to help the underachieving gifted child. *Selected writings and speeches.* Minneapolis, MN: Free Spirit.

Rogers, M. T. (1986). *A comparative study of developmental traits of gifted and average children.* Unpublished doctoral dissertation, University of Denver, Denver, CO.

Rosenblatt, L. (1978). *The reader, the text, the poem: The transactional theory of literary work.* Carbondale: Southern Illinois University Press.

Rosenblatt, L. (1994).The transactional theory of reading and writing. In R. B. Ruddell, M.R. Ruddell, & M. Singer (Eds.), *Theoretical models and processes of reading* (pp. 1057–1092). Newark, DE: International Reading Association.

Ryan, M. (2003). *Ask the teacher: Practitioner's guide to teaching and learning in the diverse classroom.* Boston: Allyn & Bacon.

Schallert, D. L., & Martin, D. B. (2003). A psychological analysis of what teachers and students do in the language arts classroom. In J. Flood, D. Lapp, J. R. Squire, & J. M. Jensen (Eds.), *Handbook of research on teaching the English language arts* (pp. 31–45). Mahwah, NJ: Erlbaum.

Silverman, L. (2003). *Characteristics of giftedness scale.* Unpublished paper, Denver, CO: Gifted Development Center.

Slavin, R., et al. (1992). Group learning and cooperative learning, *Education Research.*

Tarrant, J. (2004). *Bring me the rhinoceros.* New York: Harmony.

Tomlinson, C., Kaplan, S., Renzulli, J., Purcell, J., Leppien, J., & Burns, D. (2002). *The parallel curriculum: A design to develop high potential and challenge high ability learners.* Thousand Oaks, CA: Corwin Press.

Tracey, D. H. (2000). Enhancing literacy growth through home-school connections. In D. S. Strickland & L.M. Morrow (Eds.), *Beginning reading and writing* (pp. 46–57). New York: Teachers College Press.

VanTassel-Baska, J., & Brown E. (2005). An analysis of gifted education curricula models. In F. Karnes & S. Bean (Eds.), *Methods and materials for teaching the gifted.* Waco, TX: Prufrock Press.

Vygotsky, L. (1978). *Mind in society.* Cambridge, MA: Harvard University Press.

Vygotsky, L. (1986). *Thought and language.* Cambridge: MIT Press.

CHAPTER 2

Assouline, S. (2003). Psychological and educational assessment of gifted children. In N. Colangelo & G. Davis (Eds.), *Handbook of gifted education.* New York: Allyn & Bacon.

Assouline, S., & I Doellinger, H. (2000). Elementary students who can do junior high school mathematics: Policy of pedagogy. In N. Colangelo & S. Assouline (Eds.), *Talent Development IV: Proceeding from the 1998 Henry B. and Jocelyn Wallace National Research Symposium on Talent Development.* Scottsdale, AZ: Great Potential Press.

Benbow, C., Lubinski, D., Shea, D., & Eftekhari-Sanjani, H. (2000). Sex differences in mathematical reasoning ability: Their status 20 years later. *Psychological Science, 11,* 474–480.

Bonne, R. (1985). *Identifying multi-ethnic disadvantaged gifted.* Brooklyn, NY: Community School #19.

Chi, M., Glaser, R., & Farr, M. (1998). *The nature of expertise.* Hillsdale, NJ: Erlbaum.

Colangelo, N., & Davis, G. (2003). Introduction and overview. In N. Colangelo & G. Davis (Eds.), *Handbook of gifted education* (3rd. ed.). Boston, MA: Allyn & Bacon.

Gallagher, J. (2000). Unthinkable thoughts: Education of gifted students. *Gifted Child Quarterly, 44,* 5–12.

Gallagher, J. (2004). On being a survivor. *Roeper Review, 1,* 17–18.

Gardner, H. (1983). *Frames of mind: The theory of multiple intelligences.* New York: Basic Books.

Guilford, J. P. (1967). *The nature of human intelligence.* New York: McGraw Hill.

Hengen, T. (1983). Identification and enhancement in Canadian Indians. Paper presented at the annual conference of the National Association for Gifted Children, New Orleans, LA.

Kaplan, S. (1994). *Final report on California Javits project.* Unpublished and submitted to the U.S. Department of Education.

Kaplan, S. (2005). Layering differentiated curricula for the gifted and talented. In F. Karnes & S. Bean (Eds.), *Methods and materials for teaching the gifted.* Waco, TX: Prutfock Press.

Latham, A. (1997). Quantifying MI's gains. *Educational Leadership, 55*(1), 84–85.

Lubinski, D., Webb, R., Morelock, M., & Benbow, C. (2001). Top 1 in 10,000: A 10 year follow-up of the profoundly gifted. *Journal of Applied Psychology, 86,* 718–729.

Meeker, M. (1969). *The structure of intellect: Its interpretation and uses.* Columbus, OH: Merrill.

Meeker, M. (1976). *A paradigm for special education diagnostics: The cognitive area* (Report # EC082519). Paper presented at the Annual Meeting of the American Educational Research Association, San Francisco, CA.

Reis, S., & Small, M. (2003). Characteristics of diverse gifted and talented learners. In F. Karnes & S. Bean (Eds.), *Methods and materials for teaching the gifted.* Waco, TX: Prufrock Press.

Renzulli, J. (1978). *The enrichment triad model: A guide for developing defensible programs for the gifted and talented.* Mansfield Center, CT: Creative Learning Press.

Renzulli, J., & Reis, S. (1985). *The schoolwide enrichment model: A comprehensive plan for educational excellence.* Mansfield, CT: Creative Learning Press.

Richert, S. (2003). Excellence with justice in identification and programming. In N. Colangelo, & G. Davis (Eds.). *Handbook of gifted education,* (3rd ed.). Boston: Allyn & Bacon.

Ross, P. O. (1993). The future of education for the nation's most talented students. In *National excellence: A case study for developing America's talent* (pp. 25–30). Washington, DC: U.S. Government Printing Office.

Sisk, D. (1994). *Final evaluation report of the SOI project in Paris, TX.* Unpublished report submitted to Paris Independent School District.

Smith, W., Odhiambo, E., & El Khateeb, H. (2000). The topologies of successful and unsuccessful students in core subjects of language, arts, mathematics, science, and social studies using the Theory of Multiple Intelligences in a high school environment in Tennessee. Paper presented at the Annual Meeting of the Mid-South Educational Research Association, Bowling Green, KY.

State of Washington. (2005). *Annual Javits Report.* Washington, DC.

Sternberg. (2000). Patterns of giftedness: A triarchic analysis. *Roeper Review, 22,* 231–240

Strahan, D., Summey, H. & Banks, N. (1996). Teaching to diversity through multiple intelligences: Student and teacher responses to instructional improvement. *Research in Middle Level Quarterly, 19* (2), 43–65.

Tannenbaum, A. (1979). Pre-Sputnik to post-Watergate concern about the gifted. In A. H. Passow (Ed.), *The gifted and the talented* (pp. 5–27). Chicago: National Society for the Study of Education.

U.S. Department of Education, National Commission of Excellence in Education. (1983). *A nation at risk: The imperative for education reform.* Washington, DC: U.S. Department of Education.

U.S. Department of Education, Office of Educational Research and Improvement (1993). *National excellence: A case for developing America's talent.* Washington, DC: U.S. Department of Education.

U.S. Department of Health, Education, and Welfare (1972). *Education of the gifted and talented.* Washington DC: U.S. Government Printing Office.

Wasserman, S. (2001). Quantum theory, the uncertainty principle, and the alchemy of standardized testing. *Phi Delta Kappan, 83* (1).

Wiggins, G., & McTighe, J. (1998). *Understanding by design.* Alexandria, VA: ASCD.

CHAPTER 3

Albert, L. (1976). *But I'm Ready to Go.* Scarsdale, NY: Bradbury Press.

Baum, S., Owen, S., & Dixon, J. (1991). *To be gifted and learning disabled: From definitions to practical intervention strategies.* Mansfield Center, CT: Creative Learning Press.

Baum, S., Renzulli, J., & Hébert, T. (1995). Reversing underachievement: Creative productivity as a systematic intervention: *Gifted Child Quarterly, 39,* 224–235.

Baum, S., Renzulli, J., & Hébert (1995). *The prism metaphor: A new paradigm for reversing underachievement.* Storrs, CT: National Center on Gifted and Talented.

Bender, W. M., & Wall, M. E. (1999). Social emotional development of students with learning disabilities. *Learning Disabilities Quarterly, 17,* 223–241.

Carnegie Corporation of New York. (1996). *Years of promise: A comprehensive learning strategy for America's children. Executive Summary.* New York: Carnegie Task Force of Learning.

Colangelo, N., & Assouline, S. G. (2000). Counseling gifted students. In K. A. Heller, F. J. Monks, R. J. Sternberg, & R F. Subotnik (Eds.), *International handbook of giftedness and talent* (2nd ed., pp. 595–607). Amsterdam: Elsevier.

Colangelo, N., & Davis, G. (Eds.) (2003). *Handbook of gifted education* (3rd ed.). Boston: Allyn & Bacon.

Cramond, B. (2005). Developing creative thinking. In F. Karnes & S. Bean (Eds.), *Methods and materials for gifted students.* Waco, TX: Prufrock.

Cross, T. (1997). Psychological and sociological aspects of educating gifted students. *Peabody Journal of Education, 72,* 180–200.

D'Alessandro, M. (1990). Accommodating emotionally handicapped children through a literature-based reading program. *Reading Teacher, 44*(4), 288–293.

Davis, G. (2003). Creativity, thinking skills, and eminence. In F. Karnes & S. Bean (Eds.), *Methods and materials for teaching the gifted.* Waco TX: Prufrock.

Fine, L. (2001). Diamonds in the rough. *Education Week, 21*(8), 38–40.

Fleith, D. (2000). Teachers and students perceptions of creativity in the classroom. *Roeper Review, 22,* 148–157.

Gibson, J. (1980). *Do Bannanas Chew Gum?* NY: Lathrop.

Hansford, S, (1987). *Intellectually gifted learning-disabled students: A special study.* Washington, DC: U.S. Department of Education.

Hunter, E. (1969). *Sue Ellen.* New York: Houghton Mifflin.

Kaufmann, F. A., & Castellanos, F. X. (2000). Attention-deficit hyperactivity disorder in gifted students. In K. A. Heller, F. J. Monks, R. J. Sternberg, & R. F. Subotnik (Eds.), *International handbook of giftedness and talent.* (2nd ed., pp. 621–632). Amsterdam: Elsevier.

Lasker, J. (1974). *He's My Brother.* Chicago: Albert Whitman.

Law, K. (2005). *Strengthening instruction for gifted students.* Bellevue, WA: Bureau of Education & Research.

Leu, D., & Kinzer, C. (2003). *Effective literacy instruction.* Upper Saddle River, NJ: Merrill Prentice Hall.

McCoach, D. B., Kehle, T. J., Bray, M. A., Siegle, D. (2001). Best practices in the identification of gifted students with learning disabilities. *Psychology in the Schools, 38*(5), 403–411.

National Commission on Excellence in Education (1983). *A nation at risk. The imperative for educational reform.* Washington, DC: U.S. Government Printing Office.

Nelson, C. M. (1993). Students with behavioral disorders. In A. E. Blackhurst & W. H. Berdine (Eds.), *An introduction to special education* (pp. 528–561). New York: HarperCollins.

Olenchak, F. R. (2001). When gifted readers hunt for books. *The National Council of Teachers of English, 9*(2).

Olenchak, R., & Reis, S. (2002). Gifted students with learning disabilities. In M. Neihart, et al. (Eds.), *The social and emotional development of the gifted children.* Waco, TX: Prufrock Press.

Paulus, T. (1972). *Hope for the flowers.* Mahwah, NJ: Paulist Press.

Reis, S. (2004). Self-regulated learning and academically talented students. *Parenting for High Potential,* December, 5–9.

Reis, S., & McCoach (2000). What do we know and where do we go? *Gifted Child Quarterly, 44,* 152–70.

Reis, S., McGuire, J., & Neu, T. (2000). Compensation strategies used by high-ability students with learning disabilities who succeed in college. *Gifted Child Quarterly, 44*(2), 123–134.

Reis, S., Neu, T., & McGuire, J. (1995). *Talents in two places: Case studies of high ability students with learning disabilities who have achieved.* Storrs, CT: National Research Center on the Gifted and Talented.

Rejskind, G. (2000). TAG teachers: Only the creative need apply. *Roeper Review, 22,* 153–157.

Russ, S., Robins, A., & Christano, B. (1999). Imaginative youngsters become creative problem solvers. *Creativity Research Journal, 12,* 129–139.

Silverman, L. (1998). Through the lens of giftedness. *Roeper Review, 20,* 204–210.

Smith, D.B. (1975). *Kelly's Creek.* New York: Crowell.

Sisk, D. (1989). *Gifted children with learning disabilities.* Final report to Hillsborough County Board of Instruction, Tampa, FL.

Strop, J., & Goldman, D. (2002). Emotional issues of twice-exceptional students. *Understanding Our Gifted, 14* (2), 28–29.

Sugai, G., & Lewis, T. J. (1996). Preferred and promising practices for social skills instruction. *Focus on Exceptional Children, 29*(4), 1–16.

Taylor, C. W. (1963). Clues to creative teaching: The creative process. *Instructor, 73,* 4–5.

Torrance, E. P. (2002). Future needs for creativity research, training, and programs. In A. G. Aleinikov (Ed.), *The future of creativity.* Bensenville, IL: Scholastic Testing Service.

Torrance, E. P., & Sisk, D. (1997). *Gifted children in the regular classroom.* Buffalo, NY: Creative Education Foundation Press.

Torrance, E. P., & Sisk, D. (2000). *Spiritual intelligence: Developing higher consciousness.* Buffalo, NY: Creative Education Foundation Press.

Willard-Holt, C. (2002). Hunting buried treasure: The twice-exceptional student. *Understanding Our Gifted, 14*(2), 20–22.

Winebrenner, S. (2001). *Teaching gifted kids in the regular classroom.* Minneapolis, MN: Free Spirit.

Zentall, S. S., Moon, S. M., Hall, A. M., & Grskovic, J. A. (2001). Learning and motivational characteristics of boys with AD/HD and/or giftedness. *Exceptional Children, 67,* 499–519.

CHAPTER 4

Alvermann, D. E., Moon, J. S., & Hagood, M. C. (1999). Popular culture in the classroom: Teaching and researching critical media literacy. Paper presented at the International Reading Association, Newark, DE, and the National Reading Conference, Chicago.

Baskin, B. H., & Harris, K. H. (1980). *Books for the gifted child*. New York: R. R. Bowker.

Bates, G. (1984). Developing reading strategies for the gifted: A research based approach. *Journal of Reading, 27*, 590–593.

Baum, S. (1985). How to use picture books to challenge the gifted. *Early Years*, 48–50.

Bloom, B. S., Engelhart, M. D., Furst, E. J., Hill, W. H., & Krathwohl, D. R., Eds., (1956). *Taxonomy of educational objectives, Handbook 1: Cognitive domain*. New York: David McKay.

Clark, B. (2004). *Growing up gifted: Developing the potential of children at home and at school* (5th ed.). Columbus, OH: Merrill.

Cohen, E. (1986). *Designing groupwork: Strategies for the heterogeneous classroom*. New York: Teachers College Press.

Daniels, H. (1994). *Literature circles: Voice and choice in the student-centered classroom*. York, ME: Stenhouse.

Davis, S. J., & Johns, J. (1989). *Students as authors: Helping gifted students get published. Gifted Child Today, 12*, 20–22.

Dean, G. (1998). *Challenging the more able language user*. London: David Fulton.

Deizmann, C. M., & Watters, J. J. (1995). Off with the fairies or gifted? The problems of the exceptionally gifted child. Paper presented at the Annual Conference of the Australian Science Teachers Association, Brisbane, Queensland, Australia, September. 24–29, 1995.

Dooley, C. (1993). The challenge: Meeting the needs of gifted readers. *The Reading Teacher, 46*(7), 546–551.

Durkin, D. (1990). Matching classroom instruction with reading abilities: An unmet need. *Remedial and Special Education, 11*(3), 23.

Ee, J., Moore, P. J., & Atputhasamy, L. (2003). High-achieving students: Their motivational goals, self-regulation and achievement and relationships to their teachers' goals and strategy-based instruction. *High Ability Studies, 14*(1).

Encarta World English Dictionary. (1999). Redmond, WA: Microsoft.

Feldhusen, H. J. (1986). *Individualized teaching of gifted children in regular classrooms*. East Aurora, NY: DOK.

Fluellen, J. E., Jr. (2003). Teaching for understanding: Harvard comes to Pennell Elementary. A Teacher Research Report. ED 480 234.

Gerber, M. E. (1995). *The E Myth revisited: Why most small businesses don't work*. New York: HarperCollins.

Guthrie, J. T., & Wigfield, A. (2000). Engagement and motivation in reading. In M. L. Kamil, P. B. Mosenthal, P. D. Pearson, & R. Barr (Eds.), *Handbook of reading research* (vol. III, pp. 403–422). Mahwah, NJ: Erlbaum.

Halsted, J. W. (1994). *Some of my best friends are books: Guiding gifted readers from pre-school to high school*. Dayton, OH: Ohio Psychology Press.

Hauser, P., & Nelson, G. A. (1988). *Books for the gifted child*. New York: R. R. Bowker.

Johnson, R. (2003). Teaching artistically able students with exceptionalities. ERIC Digest. Bloomington, IN: ERIC Clearinghouse for Social Studies/Social Science Education. ED477906.

Kaplan, S. (2003). Is there a gifted-child pedagogy? *Roeper Review, 25*(4), 165.

Kauchak, D. P., & Eggen, P. D. (2003). *Learning and teaching: Research-based methods*. Boston: Allyn & Bacon.

Kulik, J. A., & Kulik, C. L. (1991). Ability grouping and gifted students. In N. Colangelo & G. A. Davis (Eds.), *Handbook of gifted education* (pp. 178–206). Boston: Allyn & Bacon.

Langer, E. (1997). *The power of mindful learning.* Reading, MA: Addison-Wesley.

Leu, D. J. (2000). Our children's future: Changing the focus of literacy and literacy instruction. *Reading Teacher, 53,* 424–429.

Leu, D. J. (2001). Internet project: Preparing students for new literacies in a global village. *Reading Teacher, 54,* 568–572.

Levande, D. (1993). Identifying and serving the gifted reader. *Reading Improvement, 30,* 147–150.

Mangieri, J. N., & Madigan, F. (1984). Reading for gifted students: What schools are doing. *Roeper Review, 7,* 68–70.

McCormick, S., & Swassing, R. H. (1982). Reading instruction for the gifted: A survey of programs. *Journal for the Education of the Gifted, 1*(5), 34–43.

McPhail, J. C., Pierson, J. M., Freeman, J. G., Goodman, J., & Ayappa, A. (2000). The role of interest in fostering grade students' identities as competent learners. *Curriculum Inquiry, 30,* 43–69.

Metts, S. (2005). Suggestions for classroom discussion. Center for the Advancement of Teaching: Illinois State University. Retrieved April 3, 2005, from http://www.cat .ilstu.edu/teaching_tips/handouts/classdis.shtml

Parris, S. R., & Block, C. C. (2006, January). *How to create effective collaborative learning experiences.* Paper presented at America's Choice 2006 National Conference, Los Angeles, CA.

Reis, S. M., Gubbins, E. J., Briggs, C., Schreiber, F. J., Richards, S., Jacobs, J., et al. (2003). Reading instruction for talented readers: Case studies documenting few opportunities for continuous progress. Storrs: National Research Center on the Gifted and Talented, University of Connecticut.

Reis, S. M., & Renzulli, J. S. (1989). Developing challenging programs for gifted readers. *The Reading Instruction Journal, 32,* 44–57.

Renzulli, J. S. (1977). *The enrichment triad mode: Guide for developing defensible programs for the gifted and talented.* Mansfield Center, CT: Creative Learning Press.

Renzulli, J. S., & Reis, S. M. (1997). *The schoolwide enrichment model: A how-to guide for educational excellence.* Mansfield Center, CT: Creative Learning Press.

Renzulli, J. S., Smith, L. H., & Reis, S. M. (1982). Curriculum compacting: An essential strategy for working with gifted students. *Elementary School Journal, 82*(3), 185–194.

Robinson, A. (1990). Cooperation or exploitation: The argument against cooperative learning for talented students. *Journal for the Education of the Gifted, 14*(1), 9–27.

Rogers, K. B. (1991). *The relationship of grouping practices to the education of the gifted and talented learner* (Research Monograph 9102). Storrs: The National Research Center on the Gifted and Talented, University of Connecticut.

Sandby-Thomas, M. (1983). The organization of reading and pupil attainment. *Journal of Research in Reading, 6*(1), 29–40.

Savage, J. (1983). Reading guides: Effective tools for teaching the gifted. *Roeper Review, 5,* 9–11.

Tinzmann, M. B., Jones, B. F., Fennimore, T. F., Bakker, J., Fine, C., & Pierce J. (1990). *What is the collaborative classroom?* North Central Regional Educational Laboratory, Oak Brook, IL. Retrieved April 3, 2005, from: http://www.ncrel.org/sdrs/areas/ rpl_esys/collab.htm

Treffinger, D. J., & Barton, B. L. (1988). Fostering independent learning. *Gifted Child Today, 11,* 28–30.

VanTassel-Baska, J. (1996). Effective curriculum and instructional models for talented students. *Gifted Child Quarterly, 30,* 164–69.

CHAPTER 5

Angelou, M. (1969). *I know why the caged bird sings.* New York: Bantam.

Anyon, J., & Wilson, W. J. (1997). *Ghetto schooling: A political economy for urban education reform.* New York: Teachers Press.

Au, K. (1993). *Literacy instruction in multicultural settings.* Fort Worth, TX: Harcourt Brace & Jovanovich.

Crawford, J. (1999). *Bilingual education: History, politics, theory and practice.* Los Angeles: Bilingual Education Services.

Delp, J. (1975) *Strategies for teaching gifted students.* Garden Grove, CA.

Delpit, L. (1988). The silenced dialogue: Power and pedagogy in educating other people's children. *Harvard Educational Review, 58,* 280–298.

Dewey, J. (1916). *Democracy and education.* New York: Macmillan.

Elbow, P. (1973). *Writing without teachers.* Oxford: Oxford University Press.

Esquivel, L. (1992). *Like water for chocolate.* New York: Doubleday.

Garcia, C. (1992). *Dreaming in Cuban.* New York: Ballantine.

Haberman, M. (1995). Selecting 'start' teachers for urban youth in poverty. *Phi Delta Kappan, 76,* 777–781.

Kingore, B. (2003). High achiever, gifted learner, creative thinker. *Understanding our Gifted,* 3–5.

McBrien, J. (2003). A second chance for refugee students. *Educational Leadership, 61*(2), 76–80.

Morrison, T. (1987). *Beloved.* New York: Signet.

Norton, D. (2002). *Through the eyes of a child: An introduction to children's literature.* Upper Saddle River, NJ: Prentice Hall.

Payne, R. (1998). *A framework for understanding poverty.* Baytown, TX: RFT.

Reutzel D., & Hollingsworth, R. M. (1991). Reading time in school: Effect on fourth graders' performance on a criterion-reference comprehension test. *Journal of Educational Research, 84*(3), 170–176.

Romo, J., Bradfield, D., & Serrano R. (2004). *Reclaiming democracy.* Upper Saddle River, NJ: Merrill Prentice Hall.

Ryan, M. (2003). *Ask the teacher: A practitioner's guide to teaching and learning in the diverse classroom.* Boston: Allyn & Bacon.

Schwartz, R., & Raphael, T. (1985). Concept of definition: A key to improving students' vocabulary. *The Reading Teacher, 39*(2), 198–205.

Sisk, D. (1985). *Creative teaching of the gifted.* New York: McGraw Hill.

Sisk, D. (1994) *Final report: Project Step-Up.* Washington, DC: R206A90520.

Slavin, R., & Cheung, A. (2004). How do English language learners learn to read? *Educational Leadership, 61*(6), 52–57.

Spies, P. (2004). The miseducation, reeducation, and transformation of a white male educator working for social justice. In J. Romo, P. Bradfield, & R. Serrano (Eds.), *Reclaiming democracy.* Upper Saddle River, NJ: Merrill Prentice Hall.

Stahl, S. (1999). *Vocabulary development.* Cambridge, MA: Brookline.

Stahl, S., Hare, V., Sinatra, R., & Gregory, J. (1991). Defining the role of prior knowledge and vocabulary in reading comprehension: The return of number 41. *Journal of Reading Behavior, 23,* 487–507.

Tan, A. (1991). *The kitchen god's wife.* New York: Putnam.

Taylor, C. W. (1984). The simultaneous double-curriculum for developing human resources. A research-based theory of education. *Journal for the Education of Gifted, 7.*

Taylor, M. (1981). *Let the circle be unbroken.* New York: Bantam.

Tolan, S. (2003). Self-knowledge, self-esteem and the gifted adult: Guiding the gifted child. Paper presented at the National Association for Gifted Children, Indianapolis, IN.

Wong, J. S. (1950). *The fifth Chinese daughter.* New York: Harper.

CHAPTER 6

Adams-Byers, J., Whitsell, S. S., & Moon, S. M. (2004). Gifted students' perceptions of the academic and social/emotional effects of homogeneous and heterogeneous grouping. *Gifted Child Quarterly, 48,* 7–20.

Bernal, E. (2003). To no longer educate the gifted: Programming for gifted students beyond the era of inclusionism. *Gifted Child Quarterly, 47,* 183–189.

Block, C. C. (2004) *Comprehension process approach.* Boston: Allyn & Bacon.

Block, C. C., & Israel, S. E. (2005). *Beyond reading first.* Thousand Oaks, CA: Corwin Press.

Cramond, B. (2004). Reading instruction for the gifted. *Illinois Reading Council Journal, 32,* 31–36.

Cross, T. (2002). *On the social and emotional lives of gifted children.* Waco, TX: Prufrock.

Feldhusen, J., & Feldhusen, H. (2004). The room meeting for G/T students in an inclusion classroom. *Gifted Child Today, 27,* 54–57.

Israel, S. E., Bauserman, K., & Block, C. C. (2005). Metacognitive assessment strategies. *Thinking Classroom/Peremena, 6*(2), 21.

Pierce, R. L., & Adams, C. M. (2004). Tiered lessons: One way to differentiate math lessons. *Gifted Child Today, 27*(2), 58–65.

Reis, S. M., Gubbins, J. E., Briggs, C. J., Schreiber, F. J., Richards, S., Jacobs, J. K., et al., (2004). Reading instruction for talented readers: Case studies documenting few opportunities for continuous progress. *Gifted Child Quarterly, 48,* 315–338.

Smith, K., & Weitz, M. (2003). Problem solving and gifted education: A differentiated fifth-grade fantasy unit. *Gifted Child Today, 26,* 56.

Stainthorp, R., & Hughes, D. (2004). An illustrative case study of precocious reading ability. *Gifted Child Quarterly, 48,* 107–120.

Stein, D., & Beed, P. L. (2004). Bridging the gap between fiction and nonfiction in the literature circle setting. *The Reading Teacher, 57*(6), 510–518.

Tomlinson, C. (1999). *The differentiated classroom: Responding to the needs of all learners.* Alexandria, VA: Association for Supervision and Curriculum Development.

VanTassel-Baska, J., & Sher, B. T. (2003). Accelerated learning experiences. In J. VanTassel-Baska & C. L. Little (Eds.), *Content-based curriculum for high-ability learners* (p. 33). Waco, TX: Prufrock.

VanTassel-Baska, J., Zuo, L., Avery, L. D., & Little, C. (2002). A curriculum study of gifted-student learning in the language arts. *Gifted Child Quarterly, 46,* 30–44.

CHAPTER 7

Block, C. C. (2003). *Literacy difficulties: Diagnosis and instruction for reading specialists and classroom teachers* (2nd Ed.). Boston: Allyn & Bacon.

Block, C. C., & Israel, S. E. (2005). *Beyond reading first.* Thousand Oaks, CA: Corwin Press.

Cramond, B. (2004). Reading instruction for the gifted. *Illinois Reading Council Journal, 32*(4), 31–36.

Henk, W. A., & Melnick, S. A. (1995). The reader self-perception scale (RSPS): A new tool for measuring how children feel about themselves as readers. *The Reading Teacher, 48,* 470–482.

Howley, C. B., & Howley, A, A, (2002). A personal record: Is acceleration worth the effort? *Roeper Review, 24*(3), 134–136.

International Reading Association. (2003). *Your gifted child and reading: How to identify and support advanced literacy development.* Newark, DE: International Reading Association.

Rash, P. K. (1998). Meeting parents' needs. *Gifted Child Today, 21*(5), 14–17.

Riley, T. L. (1999). Put on your dancing shoes! Choreographing positive partnerships with parents of gifted children. *Gifted Child Today, 22*(4), 50–53.

Robinson, A., & Moon, S. A. (2003). Advocating for talented youth. *Parenting for High Potential,* March, 8–13.

CHAPTER 8

Block, C. C. (2001). *Teaching language arts* (3rd ed.). Boston: Allyn & Bacon.

Block, C. C., & Israel, S. (2004). The ABC's of producing highly effective think alouds. *The Reading Teacher, 58*(2), 154–168.

Block, C. C., & Johnson, R. B. (2004). The thinking process approach to comprehension development. In C. C. Block, L. Gambrell, & M. Pressley (Eds.), *Rethinking comprehension research, theory and instruction* (pp. 54–80). San Francisco: Jossey-Bass.

Block, C. C., & Mangieri, J. (1996). *Reason to read (Vols. 1–3).* Palo Alto, CA: Addison-Wesley/Pearson.

Block, C. C., & Pressley, M., Eds. (2002). *Comprehension instruction: Research-based best practices.* New York: Guilford.

Gee, G. (2004, December). Discourse with a capital "D" and a lower case "d." Keynote address at the Annual Meeting of the National Reading Conference. Austin, TX.

Miller, H. (1997). *You be the jury.* New York: Scholastic.

Miller, H. (1998). *You be the jury II.* New York: Scholastic.

CHAPTER 9

Block, C. C. (2004a). *Teaching literacy difficulties: Diagnosis and instructions for reading specialists and classroom teachers* (2nd ed.). Boston: Allyn & Bacon.

Block, C. C. (2004b). *Teaching the language arts* (3rd ed.). Boston: Allyn & Bacon.

Block, C. C., & Mangieri, J. (1996). *Reason to read* (Vols. 1–3). Palo Alto, CA: Addison-Wesley.

Block, C. C., & Mangieri, J. (2003). *Exemplary literacy teachers.* New York: Guilford.

Clark, B. (2003). *Growing up gifted* (5th Ed.). Columbus, OH: Charles E. Merrill.

Israel, S. E., & Block, C. C. (under review). Scaffolding strategies to help children overcome communication apprehension during reading instruction.

CHAPTER 10

Anderson R., & Speck, B. (2001). Using technology in K-8 literacy classrooms. Upper Saddle River, NJ: Merrill Prentice Hall.

Barr, R. B., & Tagg, J. (1999). From teaching to learning: a new paradigm for undergraduate education. *Change, 27*(6), 12–25.

Bowman, J. (1998). Technology, tutoring, and improved reading. In *English update*. Albany, NY: University of Albany, SUNY.

Brody, L., Assouline, S., & Stanley, J. (1990). Five years of early entrants: Predicting achievements in college. *Gifted Child Quarterly, 34,* 138–142.

Chu, M. (1995). Reader response to interactive computer books: Examining literacy responses in a nontraditional reading setting. *Reading Research and Instruction, 34,* 352–356.

Doty, D., Popplewell, S., & Byers, G. (2003). Interactive CD-ROM storybooks and young readers' reading comprehension. *Journal of Research on Computing in Education, 33,* 374–84.

Education Commission of the States (2005). Programs and practices: Waterford Early Reading Program. Denver, CO: Education Commission of the States.

Foer, J. (2005). *Boy, interrupted.* Boston: Houghton Mifflin.

Gilbert-Macmillan, K. (2000). Computer-based distance learning for gifted students: The EPGY experience. *Understanding Our Gifted, 12,* 17–210.

Gordon, W. J. J. (1961). *Synectics: The development of creative capacity.* New York: Harper Brothers.

Inspiration Software. (1994). *Inspiration.* Portland, OR: Inspiration Software.

Kaplan, S. (2005). Layering differentiated curricula for the gifted and talented. In F. Karnes & S. Bean (Eds.), *Methods and material for teaching the gifted* (pp. 107–131). Waco, TX: Prufrock.

Labbo, L., & Reinking, D. (1999). Negotiating the multiple realities of technology in literacy research and instruction. *Reading Research Quarterly, 34,* 478–493.

The Learning Company. (1983). *Gertrude's puzzles.* Palo Alta, CA.

Lewis, R., & Doorlag, D. (2003). *Teaching special students in general education classrooms.* Columbus, OH: Merrill Prentice Hall.

Maker, J., & Nielson, A. (1996). *Curriculum development and teaching strategies for gifted learners.* Austin, TX: Pro-Ed.

Mauzy, J. (1991). *Mindlink internelis.* North Pomfret, VT: Mindlink.

Parks, S. (2005). Teaching analytical and critical thinking skills in gifted education. In F. Karnes & S. Bean (Eds), *Methods and materials for teaching the gifted.* Waco, TX: Prufrock.

Pearman, C. (2003). Effects of CD-ROM storybooks on the independent reading comprehension of second grade students. Unpublished doctoral dissertation, University of Arkansas.

Pinkard, N. (1999). Learning to read in culturally responsive computer environments. (CIERA Rep. No. 1–004). Ann Arbor: University of Michigan.

Pyryt, M. (2003). Technology and the gifted. In N. Colangelo & G. Davis (Eds.), *Handbook of gifted education.* Boston: Pearson.

Ravaglia, R., de Barros, J., & Suppes, P. (1995). Computer-based instruction brings advancement placement physics to gifted students. *Computers in Physics, 9,* 380–386.

Renzulli, J. (1978). *The enrichment triad model: A guide for developing defensible programs for the gifted and talented.* Mansfield Center, CT: Creative Learning Press.

Sisk, D. (2005a). *Scientists-in-schools.* Final Report to U.S. Department of Education. Javits Project # TX-R-20020624-001250.

Sisk, D. (2005b). *Success express.* Final Report to Exxon-Mobil. Beaumont Independent School District.

Suppes, P. (1980). The future of computers in education. In R. P. Taylor (Ed.), *The computer in school: Tutor and tutee.* New York: Teachers College Press.

Vanderbilt Learning Technology Center. (1996). *The adventures of Jasper Woodbury: Episode one* [Videodisc]. Nashville, TN: Vanderbilt University.

CHAPTER 11

Block, C. C. (2004). *Teaching comprehension: The comprehension process approach.* Boston: Allyn & Bacon.

Block, C. C., Gambrell, L., & Pressley, M. (2003). *Improving comprehension instruction: Rethinking research, theory, and practice.* San Francisco: Jossey-Bass.

Block, C. C., & Israel, S. (2004). The ABC's of effective think alouds. *The Reading Teacher, 47*(2), 117–130.

Block, C. C., Parris, S. R., & Whiteley, C. S. (under review). *Improving comprehension instruction through CPMS: Knowing what your students have or have not understood.*

Block, C. C., Rodgers, L. L., & Johnson, R. B. (2004). *Comprehension process instruction: Creating reading success in grades K-3.* New York: Guilford.

Brown, A. L., & Palinscar, A. S. (1985). Reciprocal teaching of comprehension strategies: A natural history of one program to enhance learning (Tech. Rep. No. 334). Urbana: University of Illinois, Center for the Study of Reading.

Cummins, C., Stewart, M. T., & Block, C. C. (2005). Teaching several metacognitive strategies together increases students' independent metacognition. In S. E. Israel, C. C. Block, K. L. Bauserman, & K. Kinnucan-Welsch (Eds.), *Metacognition in literacy learning* (pp. 277–296). Mahwah, NJ: Erlbaum.

Fletcher, J. M., Morris, R. D., & Lyon, G. R. (2003). Classification and definition of learning disabilities: An integrative perspective. In H. L. Swanson, K. R. Harris, & S. Graham (Eds.), *Handbook of Learning Disabilities* (pp. 30–56). New York: Guilford.

Garner, R. (1987). *Metacognition and reading comprehension.* Norwood, NJ: Ablex.

Guthrie, J. T., Cox, K. E., Knowles, K. T., Buehl, M., Mazzoni, S. A., & Fasulo, L. (2000). Building toward coherent instruction. In L. Baker, M. J. Breher, & J. T. Guthrie (Eds.), *Engaging your readers: Promoting achievement and motivation* (pp. 209–236). New York: Guilford.

Harris, T. L., & Hodges, R. E. (1995). *The literacy dictionary: The vocabulary of reading and writing.* Newark, DE: International Reading Association.

Mangieri, J. (2004). Best practices in comprehension. Report 312. Charlotte, NC: Institute for Literacy Enhancement.

National Institute of Child Health & Human Development (NICHD). (2000, April). Teaching children to read: An evidence-based assessment of the scientific research literature on reading: Report of the subgroup on vocabulary (NIH publication no. 00–4-4769, pp. 1–269). Washington, DC: NICHD.

National Reading Panel (NRP). (1999). National Reading Panel Progress Report to the NICHD. Washington, DC: NICHD.

Oakhill, J., & Yuill, N. (1999). Higher order factors in comprehension disability: Processes and remediation. In L. Cornoldi & J. Oakhill (Eds.), *Models of effective educational assessment* (pp. 111–135). Hillsdale, NJ: Erlbaum.

Pearson, P. D., Roehler, L. R., Dole, J. A., & Duffy, G. G. (1992). Developing expertise in reading comprehension. In J. Samuels & A. Farstrup (Eds.), *What research has to say about reading instruction* (pp. 145–199). Newark, DE: International Reading Association.

Perfetti, C. A., & Lesco, R. (1979). Sentences, individual differences, and multiple texts: Three issues in text comprehension. *Discourse Processes, 23,* 337–355.

Pressley, M. (1976). Mental imagery helps eight-year-olds remember what they read. *Journal of Educational Psychology, 68,* 355–359.

Pressley, M., & Afflerbach, P. (1995). *Verbal protocols of reading: The nature of constructively responsive reading.* Hillsdale, NJ: Erlbaum.

Reznitskaya, A., & Anderson, R. C. (2001). The argument schema and learning to reason. In C. C. Block & M. Pressley (Eds.), *Comprehension instruction: Research-based best practices* (pp.319–334). New York: Guilford.

Stanovich, K. E. (1986). The Matthew effects in reading: Some consequences for individual differences in the acquisition of literacy. *Reading Research Quarterly, 21,* 360–407.

Sweet, A., & Snow, C. (2002). The RAND Corporation: New perspectives on comprehension. In C. C. Block, L. Gambrell, & M. Pressley (Eds.), *Improving comprehension instruction: Rethinking research, theory, and practice* (pp. 7–23). San Francisco: Jossey-Bass.

Tergeson, J. K., & Wagner, J. (1987). What it means to learn to read. *Child Development, 56*(5), 1134–1144.

Tierney, R. (1998). A new look at reading assessment. *The Reading Teacher, 41*(3), 301–318.

Index

**CORWIN
PRESS**

The Corwin Press logo—a raven striding across an open book—represents the union of courage and learning. Corwin Press is committed to improving education for all learners by publishing books and other professional development resources for those serving the field of PreK–12 education. By providing practical, hands-on materials, Corwin Press continues to carry out the promise of its motto: **"Helping Educators Do Their Work Better."**